GW01003212

burnt barley

Previous books by Peta Mathias

Fête Accomplie
Don't Get Saucy With Me, Béarnaise
Salut!

burnt barley

peta mathias

VINTAGE

*To Tricia Mulhall,
with love.*

Thanks to Eily Kilgannon of Irish Distillers Limited Dublin
Thanks to Dave Quin, master distiller at Bushmills
Thanks to Phillip Doyle of Guinness NZ and Jean Doyle of Guinness Dublin
Thanks to Oliver Lee for help and information
Thanks to Irish Tourism for providing a rental car for a week.

Page 45 The Long Family, photograph from the *Evening News*, 16 August
1927, courtesy of the State Reference Library, State Library of
New South Wales, Australia.

'From Clare to Here', Ralph McTell, reproduced by kind permission of
David Platz Music (Australia) Pty. Ltd
'Raglan Road', Patrick Kavanagh*
'Song for Ireland', Phil Colclough, reproduced by kind permission of
David Platz Music (Australia) Pty. Ltd
'The Patriot Game', Dominic Behan* (copyright Clifford Music Co. Ltd)
'The Speed of the Sound of Loneliness', John Prine, reproduced by kind
permission of Bug Music/Festival Music
* every endeavour was made to contact the copyright holders of these
titles but without success.

A VINTAGE BOOK
published by
Random House New Zealand
18 Poland Road, Glenfield, Auckland, New Zealand

First published 2000
© 2000 Peta Mathias

The moral rights of the author have been asserted

ISBN 186941 427 6

Cover photograph: Garth Des Forges
Text design: Graeme Leather
Printed in Malaysia

contents

CHAPTER ONE

dublin 6

CHAPTER TWO

childhood 44

CHAPTER THREE

tipperary 68

CHAPTER FOUR

the wild west 106

CHAPTER FIVE

the south-west 146

CHAPTER SIX

the north 188

CHAPTER SEVEN

a fast walk in tipperary 218

LIST OF ILLUSTRATIONS 259

Chapter one
dublin

I was finally on my way to Ireland on my Irish passport to see what they eat and drink and sing about.

I had first applied for an Irish passport when working in France in the 1980s. Producing my birth certificate provided inordinate complication as does every bureaucratic transaction in France, because you couldn't have just any old birth certificate — you had to provide a *long birth certificate*, one that included the births, deaths and marriages of relatives back to the Inquisition. In the saga of trying to find the mother's birth certificate I discovered something I had often suspected — that the mother did not exist. I called the mayor's office in Tipperary where she was born.

'Hello, Madam,' I said politely, 'I'm looking for the birth certificate of my mother, Ann Long. She was born in your county sometime after 1920 and as a direct result of that I find myself being her daughter . . .'

'Glory be to God and you called all the way from Paris to tell me that. I'm sure you're a great credit to your mother,' said the voice on the phone.

'Yes, yes, but Mother doesn't have a birth certificate because her father didn't register her because the English said you had to so he refused as a matter of principle but I need some sort of a certificate to get a passport to work in France.'

'Well, that's a very interesting story but I'm afraid there is nothing we can do, pet. I can't invent a birth certificate for someone I have no record of and that's that.'

Stupidly I accepted this and went ahead and married a gorgeous Frenchman so I could stay in France. A few years later I noticed my brother Paul had an Irish passport which he had obtained by insisting on a replacement birth certificate for our mother. Within two weeks I was Irish.

The plane from London to Dublin left half an hour late, familiarising me early with 'Irish time'.

'Are you Peta Mathias?'

'No.'

'We saw your hair. I love your show.'

'It's not me. It's someone else.' Hailing a taxi.

'Goodbye, Peta. Have a great time in Ireland.'

The first thing you notice as you whiz into Dublin from the airport is all the street names in two languages. Besides English there is Irish, which is unpronounceable to any human other than a Celt. The girl's name Saoirse is pronounced Sear-she; the word for 'to your health', sláinte, is pronounced slaun-te. The second thing you notice is that it's gently raining. I knew they called it a soft Irish day so I decided to be very brave and positive about the softness. The Irish language has many words to describe rain — words for dew, kinds of drizzle, medium rain, wet weather, heavy rain, downpour, pelting rain and wet weather that may cause flooding.

The hotel was quite a nice one but in an insalubrious area on Lower Gardiner Street. The upside was that the desk clerk said 'Good night now and God bless' when he delivered my suitcase. The downside was that you had to rent your phone in lump sums of £5. It could suddenly run out in the middle of a conversation or email and you couldn't call the desk and pay more rent by phone. You had to actually go the 20km trek through a jungle of corridors, secret-coded elevators, expanses of dining room, dark-stained stairs and flamboyant decor to personally rent and pay for more time. All it required at the desk was the flick of a switch and an addition to my bill but no amount of intelligent persuasion on my part could change this mediaeval arrangement. I stayed there six days and when I asked for my bed linen to be changed halfway through, the request had to go through a supervisor.

Even on a soft day it's a long summer day in Ireland, the dawn twittering at 4am and the dusk obliterating all at 10.30pm. On my first night hunger drove me to the only food area I'd heard of, Temple Bar on the groovy side of the River Liffey. I crossed the river on the curved, ornate metal Ha'penny footbridge. This eighteenth-century cobblestoned part of the city is riddled with restaurants, pubs, alleyways and individuals below the age of 30 in equal quantities. It was as if there were a high school or university inauguration day going on. The smelly, drunken throng were falling out of pubs and restaurants, but so crowded were they that nowhere could you get a meal, a drink or a break. The best you would have obtained would have been beer down your frock, a grope and a view of the security cum doormen running around looking desperate and driven to distraction by the importance and stress of their jobs. They all had earphones which they kept touching as they squared their shoulders. My umbrella, my new J.P. Gaultier dress with Japanese dragons on it and I made a thorough, gut-rumbling tour of the place, hated it and decided to go home hungry. Without my supper I would look even better in that dress tomorrow.

On the way back across O'Connell bridge to the ungroovy side of town I was drawn to a sumptuous hotel entrance on the exquisitely named Bachelors Walk. The Arlington Hotel had a huge mediaeval decorated pub and dining hall done up in brocade, heavy beams, stags' heads, dark panelling and gloriously over-the-top decoration, Dublin style. The bars were lined with liquor bottles, books and footballs, a look guaranteed to confuse any outsider. I was to discover that Dublin specialises in voluptuous, outrageous, Rabelaisian decor in gigantic spaces. This place felt more civilised than Temple Bar so I sat down and ordered a pint and an Irish stew. Best to begin as you intend to continue. In Ireland when you order 'a pint' it means a Guinness. If you want something else you order it by name. To test if a glass of Guinness is ready to drink, you tap the side of the glass with a coin — there will be a dull sound initially and when it's ready the sound goes up a few notes to a clearer, ringing tone.

'Excuse me, are you Peta?'

'No.'

'Look, I'm from New Zealand and my friends bet I wouldn't come over and say hello. I'm sorry to do this. You must get so sick of it.'

'That's fine. I don't mind at all.' Shaking hands.

'My name's Lorraine. Anyway, we love your show and if you go to Belfast, this is the taxi you must call. George will take you on a tour of Belfast you'll never forget.' A large portion of stew arrived along with the band, who lurched into tourist favourites like 'Oh Danny Boy' and a dreadful sloppy thing about Irish unity, a topic big on the agenda in July 1999. At this very moment the peace accord talks were at a crucial negotiating point, with exhausted leaders from both sides being interviewed nonstop on television and radio. They also love interviewing terrorists and informers dressed in woollen hats and dark glasses with scarves around their faces saying things like: 'It doesn't matter what the politicians sign, there's still product [arms] on the ground.' Then they pull up their jumper and show the camera their battle scars. It was the topic on everyone's lips.

The stew wasn't much more real than the entertainment. It was served with slices of industrial white bread and butter and finding a bit of lamb among the spuds was like trying to find an honest lawyer at a fundraising banquet. This was my first night in Ireland. Were things going to get a bit more real or was this why their economy was so good? They've sold their souls to tourism maybe.

My hunt for real Irish music was on now. Next on the menu was a trio of Irish dancers, a man and two women. Unfortunately the intricate footwork was lost on the low stage but if you snuck to the front you got the full impact of the staccato tapping. The man, dressed in black, kept his hands on his hips in the traditional way but the women used their arms and hands a little in the new Riverdance style. They did some soft-shoe dances: so fine, so wistful, so unsuited to a pub.

When they asked for volunteers from the audience to join them, J.P. Gaultier and I slid off the stool into the soft, warm night.

Late at night, from around midnight onwards, good Samaritans, usually young women, are to be found crouching next to tramps who have settled into doorways for the night, offering them soup and the milk of human kindness from a flask.

Everywhere you go in Dublin you find Bewley's Cafés, or oriental cafés as they call themselves. These establishments are truly a Dublin institution. Some are tatty, some are upmarket but all are sumptuously splendid, huge, multi-levelled and somehow comfy. There's dark oriental wallpaper, mahogany fittings, big mirrors, open fires, bentwood chairs, marble-topped tables and stained-glass windows and ceilings. The bread and cake counters at the front sell the things they have become famous for: fruit buns; Mary Cakes made from sponge, covered in chocolate truffle mixture and topped with almond paste rounds; wheaten bread which is like a wholemeal soda bread; buttermilk scones; and porter cake (porter is the old name for stout). They also make barmbrack. Now this is a classic Irish sort of bread cake made with yeast and full of dried fruit, spice and peel. The word barm comes either from bairm (yeast) or from bairin (cake), and brack derives from breac, meaning spotted. And guess how you make Irish chocolate cake? Why, you just add mashed potatoes and Irish liqueur to your flour, sugar, eggs and chocolate — and I'm not making that up. They sell soda farls or griddle cakes, which are soda bread dough rolled thin, cut into four farls or quarters, and fried. The soda bread everywhere in Ireland is absolutely delicious and the secret, I found out, is the buttermilk. Before ovens, most bread was baked like this on a griddle, swung over the fire or set on a trivet, and it is very, very good eaten fresh off the heat, as is fadge or potato cake.

Which led me to the next section of Bewley's — the 'hot

kitchen', canteen style both in appearance and taste. It appears the Irish, in their wisdom, eat breakfast for breakfast, lunch and dinner — and anytime between. There are restaurants in Dublin serving nothing but. I bravely ordered an Irish breakfast and wavered in fascination over the bain-maries of black pudding, white pudding, baked beans, bacon, fadge, fried eggs, sausages, fried tomatoes and toast. Cup of tea comes with the deal. There is something unaccountably sad about being served up food by a thickset Irish girl in a hairnet — not a cute little cap of which there must be four gazillion in the universe, but an old lady's hairnet. This is how you subjugate a nation. Religion — puh! You put a perfectly fine human being in a hairnet in public and then ask yourself why the Irish lack self-confidence.

The black pudding was a delicious, large round of pig blood and I wolfed that down first. The Irish white pudding is not like the French boudin blanc — more like haggis in a sausage skin: grey, dense and intestinal, like piggy porridge. The lighting was just watery enough to depress you into writing a book like *Angela's Ashes* but too lucid to hide the white pudding and cold baked beans. And they love it. The various Bewley's are clattery, chattery, full to the gills, punters pouring in from 7 till 7 — country folks in good thick skirts, shoppers, American tourists, poets, politicians, rockers, students, lovers, bohemians and yuppies. In the old days there were all-male smoke rooms, table service from waitresses in black and white and stand up straight please, high society and no expense was spared. The Quaker Bewley family set up business in 1840, originally as tea merchants and chocolate makers. This was a good trade to go into in Ireland as tea is still part of the staple diet, along with breakfast and a pint. There are 23 Bewley's in Ireland, four in Britain and two in Japan. The thought of Japanese tucking into clotted blood and oatmeal in an Irish time-capsule is too desperate to contemplate.

Dublin is a small city so it's easy to wander around and I fell by chance upon one of the insider secrets of Dublin that probably only someone in the food business would even notice. I went back to Magill's deli at 14 Clarendon Street almost every day to dip into their beautiful produce. The old split-level shop, the size of a large postage stamp, has been there since 1922 and I shouldn't think much has changed in the decor department. The exterior was pure 1920s in black and gold, the tiny interior groaning with pungent, oriental-smelling whiskey and brandy salamis, sweet Dundalk ham, cured Spanish hams, wild Irish smoked salmon, well-finished Irish cheeses — goat, Cashel Blue and assorted cheddars — and smashing breads sourced from a dozen different bakeries.

At 7pm I found myself having a pint upstairs at the Duke on Duke Street. A famous literary pub, more black and gold on the outside, it gives succour to people (Americans) wishing to go on a literary pub crawl. You all meet at 7.30 and two actors take you on a tour, performing pieces from Irish literature all the while. Rosy-cheeked Jessica sweetly sang a drinking song called 'The Waxies Dargle', then we got a rendition from Samuel Beckett's *Waiting for Godot* from Derek and Jessica, followed by the dinner-party scene from Joyce's *Portrait of the Artist as a Young Man*. A waxie is a candle maker and this song is about their annual outing to the seaside town of Bray, 20km from Dublin.

Says my aul' one to your aul' one
Will ye come to the Waxies Dargle?
Says your aul' one to my aul' one
Sure I haven't got a farthin'.
I've just been down to Monto town
To see young Kill McArdle
But he wouldn't lend me half a crown
To go to the Waxies Dargle.

In the rain we traipsed to Trinity College and got Oscar Wilde's *The Importance of Being Earnest . . .* to lose one parent is unfortunate; to lose two is careless. Up with the umbrellas and off to M.J. O'Neill's pub in Suffolk Street, which has been on that site for 300 years. I sat and had a pint in the 'snug', a little room originally used by women drinkers who were separated from men in the pubs so as not to corrupt them. I corrupted nobody and moved on to the Irish Tourist Office, housed in the deconsecrated Anglican St Andrew's church, which became available due to spectacular lack of interest from the faithful. When the congregation got down to three they sold it.

We hung around outside the church while Jessica and Derek begged on the sidewalk from Joseph Plunkett's *The Risen People*. We listened to a fine rendition of the 'toucher' Hennessy singing 'Faith of Our Fathers', which tumbled me into a reverie and I caught myself singing along. 'It's a sad class of a day if a fine rendition of "Faith of Our Fathers" won't get you a few pennies.'

A toucher is an individual who begs enough money to buy the first pint, goes into the pub and sits next to his victim, the touchee as it were, agrees with everything the man says, then touches him up for a pint. In this way he drinks all day. In fact there used to be a 'holy hour' decreed by the Catholic Church. Between 2pm and 4pm the pubs had to close so men were forced to go home to their families for a while. What generally happened was they ended up staying home — otherwise they would have been in the pub all day and all night some of them. Holy hour was mainly in the cities and people I asked about it told me they missed it because if you owned a pub, it was the only break you got in the day.

The Americans and I ran through the rain to what is possibly the oldest public house in Ireland, the Old Stand. In 1659 Charles II renewed its licence but it is most famous for being the hangout of Michael Collins, the leader of the Irish

War of Independence. This pub I really liked for its smallness and the type of people drinking there. As in all pubs there was a wide age group all mixing together and a woman alone could sit at the bar or banquette and feel as comfortable as you would in a café. I ordered a pint and sat next to an otherwise fine specimen of red-headed manhood except for the fact that his eyes were unable to go in the same direction simultaneously. Through the cacophony and clinking we had a conversation. 'I've been here all day,' he said earnestly, as if telling the dentist of his symptoms. He was slumped on the banquette like someone who was about to fall out of a wheelchair in a nursing home — balanced but precarious.

'Why?' I asked.

'Ah, you know, love, sometimes it's the type of a day to be in the pub all day.'

'What is your work?' I inquired in my best Lady Windermere voice.

'I'm a bricklayer and you can't lay bricks in the rain. Who are you and where are you from anyway?'

'I'm from New Zealand and I'm writing about travelling around Ireland.'

He roared, as much as one can roar supine, with laughter. 'There's an original idea so. I think someone got there before you.'

I bristled, as one does. The bell rang and we stood outside in the drizzle to hear selected pieces from Mary Lanvin's *The Vocation*, which was only an excuse to move on to the final pub on the tour, Davy Byrne's on Duke Street. I sat at the bar, ordered my pint and waited.

'You're not the one on that TV show in New Zealand are you?'

'No.'

'I'm from Nelson,' said the barman. 'My friends have been on your show.'

'What are you doing here then, in Dublin?' I asked.

'My parents are Irish and I've come back to live. Came for a visit and couldn't get away.'

I wonder if that'll happen to me. The first time I went to France I went for the weekend and stayed for 10 years.

I decided to go on my shank's mare (legs) rather than take the bus to the Guinness brewery on the west side of the city, and was rewarded for this decision by meeting the fish lady, Theresa Kelly. Thomas Street, in the working-class area known as the Liberties, had a street market every day from what I could work out. There were the usual cheap bric-a-brac stalls along with fruit and vegetables, and everyone yelling their heads off. I bought a punnet of sweet Irish strawberries from a woman with a fag hanging out of her mouth and hair that looked like it had been through the trouser press in my room . . . and then I met Theresa. There she was at her little fish stall, an old woman with the most beautiful eyes and open smile, with a pink scarf tied under her chin, a pink cardie and a filthy smock. Her stall consisted of some cartons, a wooden table and a small tin fish table with sides on it, through which fish slime oozed like thick veils of snot onto the footpath. Not a slither of refrigeration defiled this Joycean scene. At her feet was rubbish, papers and bits of fish innards all mucking around in a slutty mess. When she smiled her pretty smile at me I loved her instantly.

'What are you after writing about me there?'

'Hello. I'm from New Zealand and I'm writing about Irish food. My name's Peta. What's yours?'

'Theresa Kelly, no Fox, no I believe it says Kelly on my licence.' I couldn't believe anyone would have a licence for this marine graveyard.

'What fish have you here, Theresa?'

'Oh, there's plaice and mackerel and that's cod over there. On Fridays I have smoked cod. I've lived in the Liberties all my life and had this stall for 50 years.'

People came and went and bought the fish, which she

filleted on the spot with a big kitchen knife. I have to say, in spite of the health hazard her fish smelt only of the sea and was clear eyed and red gilled.

'How do you eat fish when you're at home in your own kitchen?'

She looked querulously at her client.

'She means how do you cook it, Theresa. Do you boil or fry it?'

'Oh, boil it. Always boil it. You're a grand girl . . . where are you off to now?'

'Down the road to Guinness.'

'Look-it. Watch your basket and put that notebook away. If the buggers see that, they'll know you're not from here. Goodbye and God bless now.'

I wove my way past cake shops with windows full of brown and white soda bread till I reached the dark, hulking estate of Guinness, the largest brewer in the world. The brewery and its buildings and parks take up a whole neighbourhood of 25 hectares. Across the road is St Patrick's mental hospital, which treats alcoholics among others, and what's the first thing they see when they're released, all dried out? Guinness. They say St Patrick's has a revolving door. Only the Irish could claim that St Patrick brought porter to Ireland with him along with the faith. In the fifth century he arrived on these green shores with his brewer/priest called Mescan from one of the many monasteries that flourished in those times. The monasteries were basically the main outfits producing alcoholic drinks and a monk was allowed a gallon of ale daily. To this day the very paternal Guinness empire gives its employees two glasses of stout a day, plus many other benefits such as free doctor's visits and medical insurance, which of course can't cost them much because as everyone knows GUINNESS IS GOOD FOR YOU.

In the eighteenth century there was a corn market at Mother Redcaps opposite the brewery and they brewed a bad sort of ale from the corn, but in general beer was unknown in rural

Ireland, where whiskey, gin and poitín (home-made firewater) were the tipples of the day. Then in 1759 a man called Arthur Guinness took over a disused distillery at St James's Gate (one of the old outer gates to mediaeval Dublin), originally owned by one Charles Mee. For £100 he signed a 9000-year lease on it at an annual rent of £45 and took possession of one copper, one kieve, one mill, two malthouses, stables for 12 horses and a loft that could hold 200 tonnes of hay.

The new brewhouse has the capacity to produce four million pints of Guinness a day. The public relations person, a pleasant blue-eyed blonde called Jean Doyle, took me for a fine beef and Guinness stew and a pint at the hopshed. This stew had everything my introductory Irish stew lacked. Pretty and colourful with its carrots, celery and meat, it was tasty and rich with the gorgeous undertaste of yeasty stout. Shy they ain't and never have been at Guinness, advertising and promotion being a hefty part of the portfolio. James Joyce called Guinness the vin ordinaire of Ireland and they say here that doing business without advertising is like winking at a girl in the dark — you know what you are doing but nobody else does. Their most brilliant ad man was John Gilroy, who invented the famous slogan MY GOODNESS MY GUINNESS in the 1930s. It was he who introduced the wonderful animals to advertising, most memorably the pelican with seven pints of Guinness balanced on its beak. The slogan was:

A wonderful bird is the pelican
Its bill can hold more than its belly can
It can hold in its beak
Enough for a week
I simply don't know how he can.

This was altered by Dorothy Sayers, who changed the bird to a toucan and put fewer pints (they went down to two) on it to be less offensive:

If he can say as you can
Guinness is good for you
How grand to be a toucan
Just think what toucan do!

Stout gets its ruby black colour and caramelised flavour from roasted barley. According to urban mythology Arthur Guinness was making ales to start with, then one day there was a fire and the barley got burnt and that's how stout was created. In fact stout or porter came from London and was so called because of its popularity with the porters of Covent Garden.

To make Guinness, first you roast the finest Irish-grown barley and malt, then grind it and mix it with hot, pure water from the Wicklow mountains. The liquid is separated from the grain in a kieve or brewing vessel and transferred to the kettle, where hops are added and the mixture boiled. Once cooled, the brew is put into a fermentation vessel to which yeast is added to convert the sugar into alcohol. Next the yeast is removed and the stout is left to mature and condition, whence it is kegged.

They say the secret is in the original yeast strain introduced by Arthur Guinness and still in use. Draught Guinness is brewed in New Zealand to be as close to the international specifications as possible and is of exceptionally good quality. Irish-brewed canned draught is also sold. This stuff is interesting because supposedly it's exactly the same as the real thing — with the thick creamy head and all — and how they do it is with their In-Can-System. A plastic widget with a minute hole is placed at the bottom of the beer can, and once the can is sealed under pressure and the beer chilled, about 1 per cent of the beer is forced into this chamber. It is forced out of the chamber when the pressure is released by opening the can. The effect is to produce a series of small bubbles, which rise to the surface to form the creamy head of stout. It is exactly the same process that occurs when Guinness is served from a tap at a bar in Dublin. A new product on the market is Breo Guinness or white beer. Personally I wouldn't touch the stuff.

The taste of Guinness is complex and rich with a mellow, slightly burnt, bitter taste and a smooth creamy texture and I believe one is born to it just as one is born to be a good mother. Either you have a taste for it or you don't and every time I drink it I think of bedpans. It was as a starch-encased nurse in the geriatric and maternity wards of Auckland Hospital that I learned to appreciate the black velvet caramel. For every pint I doled out at six in the evening for the high iron content there was a swig for me. My classmates used to say it tasted like something a Catholic would drink to kill guilt.

As a young girl I had only ever wanted to be a nurse. A girl had more or less three choices in those days — you could be a teacher, a secretary or a nurse. If you were very bright you went to university but your father usually said, 'What's the point? You're only going to get married anyway.' My true talents — whatever they were — were not considered career options by me or anybody else. All through school I had been in charge of the first-aid kit and fed my missionary complex by always being the one to patch others up. I have always associated stout with superior dietary habits and being kind to people and consider it my moral duty to drink and encourage others to drink of much as the stuff as I can.

That evening I took a taxi to a cultural centre outside Dublin in well-to-do Monkstown with the unpronounceable name of Comhaltas Ceoltóirí Éireann. These culture clubs, started in 1951, are all over Ireland — and indeed the world — their stated mission being to promulgate native traditions and promote knowledge of Ireland, her status and aspirations. The driver was unstoppable as we drove past Dublin Bay, she of no more prawns. Together we covered accents, his son in New Zealand, expressions, the peace plan, traditional dancing and singing and the price of fish. In breaks in the conversation he sang. He told me that the expression 'Are you going for a jar?' comes from the time when workers would take their pint across the road where they were working and never bring the glasses back, so the proprietor started giving them their pints in jam jars. He also told me about the DART train that plies the coast.

'The train goes bot ways so. You can go nort or you can go sout.'

'Why don't you say your h's?'

'Dat's the way we talk. It's not dat we can't pronounce h, it's just dat we choose not to.'

The way the Irish speak English is a product of the particular historical circumstances that led the population in the nineteenth century to be forced to exchange Irish for English as their mother tongue, a psychologically disturbing form of internal linguistic dispossession that caused the people to undergo one of the major traumas of emigrating without actually leaving home. Ancient Irish language structures and vocabulary have affected the way they speak English today. However, it must be said that Elizabethan English was very beautiful (Shakespeare, Cranmer) and, when combined with the literal translations of Irish idioms, produced the dynamic speech of Irish-English. Today, even though everyday Irish speech has been eroded by the Americanisms of television, it is still very rich, sardonic and as many-chambered as a heart.

'Tell me why you don't move your arms or hands in traditional dancing,' I asked him. 'I have a theory but I want to hear yours.'

'Well, I tink it's a question of aestetics like. You don't do anyting that will detract from the beauty and complexity of what the feet are doing.'

'Mmm. I think it has to do with Catholic repression. Dancing could have been an occasion for sin, therefore you showed no pleasure on your face or movement above the rigid hips. All the sinful action went on downstairs where maybe no one would notice.' The car swerved to avoid contact with another. 'Jaesus gobshite, will you look at dat one hoggin' the road. I can make me own mistakes witout the likes of him teaching me some new ones.'

Incidentally, shameful behaviour such as living in S-I-N and fornication are no longer sins according to the Church of England. Fat chance for the Catholics — they have added a few new ones to keep everyone on their toes: corruption, tax evasion and pollution. 'Get down on your knees and ask the Blessed Virgin Mary to forgive your pollutin' ways.' The Vatican has also recently intimated that those who give up smoking stand a better chance of going to heaven — all those who 'mortify the flesh' by forgoing a pleasure or addiction such as smoking or drinking would be 'doing a partial penance that will help to prepare them for the afterlife'. In Ireland, as in France, smoking and drinking is practically obligatory and there isn't a lot of preparation for the afterlife going on.

I went down the steps of the beautiful mansion which houses Comhaltas and paid my £4, entitling me to as much dancing and fiddling as I liked and a cup of tea. There were many rooms in this house and in every corner groups of people playing music. The tea-room with scones was at one end so I went straight to the bar at the other for a jar and smiled sweet and sour at the barman for his remark that I was the best-looking All Black he had ever seen. The main hall was all decked out in Celtic symbols and there was a céilí (dance) in full swing, with the caller up on the stage and the band of two fiddlers, a pianist, a drummer and an accordionist. These were the reels and jigs of my childhood but all the dancers were American tourists. The most entertaining thing about it was watching the helpers in their hopeless task of teaching the dances to the young Americans. I watched for a while but wasn't tempted to step the dances of my forebears with a tourist. If I were to dance, it would be with an Irishman.

I found the room with the biggest session and sat down. Sessions are musical get-togethers to which anyone can turn up and play with the others. It's not a jam session; all the songs and tunes are known. In this room were a banjo, an accordion, a guitar, some tin whistles, a flute, some fiddles and several bodhráns (pronounced bow-rawn) — 45cm one-sided goatskin drums played with a tipper or short stick in one hand. The other hand presses the back of the skin to temper the sound. They told me if you wet the skin you get a different colour and intensity of sound. What makes traditional Irish music distinctive is that it does not use the same modal scales as European or western music of the last two centuries. In the modal system there are seven scales whereas Irish music uses only four of these, which makes the tonal character more interesting. It is essentially monophonic or single sound, so you don't harmonise but can greatly embellish and decorate. The players sat in a circle, starting and stopping as the inspiration took them. It didn't seem to be about anyone shining, there were no solos as such and there was no leader — leaders waned and waxed and came and went as new tunes were led into directly from the previous one.

The only drink I saw anywhere was the burnt barley going up to the weathered faces, the peaches and cream faces, the curly black hair and dark eyes, young hands, huge butchers' hands playing fine fiddles. The flautist sat bolt upright all night, her delicate fingers like feet dancing in a fire. Nobody talked to me all evening and still I sat there. Next to me a young American man asked the banjo player if he could play 'The Wild Rover', to which he disdainfully replied, 'Of course I can' and, ignoring him, went on playing. I found out later that this is common at these places: there is an elitism and an aloofness. They are there to play pure, traditional music and quietly disdain anyone who is not in the inner circle.

I went up to the bar and asked if I should order a taxi home in advance, as we were a way out. 'Ah sure, you can order it whenever you like — it'll still take three hours to get here. You'll never get a taxi at this hour of the night. This is Ireland, you know.' Five minutes before the taxi arrived I got into a conversation with a man named Tony who was also there listening to the music, so I had to tell the taxi to go away, which he did with grace and good humour. In New York I would have had my throat ripped out for that. I had a good talk with Tony and finally got up the courage to ask another session to sing for me, which they did with a rendition of 'Danny Boy' and 'Wild Mountain Heather'. An 80-year-old man sang 'The Bold Teddy Quill', a sporting song.

I found out that the national repertoire of songs as it is today is rooted in the popular music of the seventeenth and eighteenth centuries, but much more recent compositions are also sung. It was here I first heard the haunting, beautifully poetic song 'Raglan Road', written and scored by the much-loved poet Patrick Kavanagh who died in 1967. Raglan Road is in Dublin and the song is assumed to be autobiographical. Kavanagh, originally from County Monaghan, was a huge man, badly dressed, raw-boned and clumsy, which hid his highly developed and sophisticated intellect. One of his most famous poems, the long and bitter 'The Great Hunger' about his Irish rural life before he came to Dublin, was banned, to which he defiantly remarked, 'Just as well they banned it because if a policeman could read it, it was probably a lousy poem anyway.'

> *On Raglan Road of an autumn day, I saw her first and knew*
> *That her dark hair would weave a snare that I might one day rue.*
> *I saw the danger and I passed along the enchanted way,*
> *And I said 'Let grief be a fallen leaf at the dawning of the day.'*

*On Grafton Street in November, we tripped lightly along the
     ledge*
Of a deep ravine where can be seen the worth of passions play.
*The Queen of Hearts still making tarts and I not making
     hay.*
*Oh, I loved too much and by such, by such, is happiness thrown
     away.*

'Tony,' I asked, 'why are the arms kept rigidly by the sides in
Irish dancing?'

'I think it's a question of balance.' This didn't make sense
to me. I would have thought it would aid balance to use your
arms but he stuck to his theory.

'How can the Irish be so pleasant and easy going after all
they've been through in history?'

'My generation basically lack confidence but not the young
people. They have a completely different view of themselves
and the world; life is grand for them. I'm worried they will
lose their Irishness — the throttle-hold of the church is over,
the Troubles are a dead dog, prosperity reigns. Will Ireland
stay Ireland?'

Tony took me home and we agreed to dine together the
following evening. He said to be sure I didn't have lunch so
we could stuff ourselves. I starved myself all day, which did me
no harm whatsoever, and continued to starve myself all night
which was slightly less comfortable as Tony was never seen
again. Probably quietly at home sipping soup with a wife.
When I left New Zealand my publisher, Harriet, sent me a
postcard that said: 'Happy journeying. Beware the charmers
— see over for what they'll give you.' On the reverse side was
a painting of a woman's hands writing. Overlaid were the
words infidelity, deception, love, betrayal, lust, illusion. I
picked up the postcard propped on my desk and crossed off
deception (by means of hunger).

Next day I jumped on one of the double-decker bus tours

of Dublin, which once again was subtly geared to Americans. Dublin is, in fact, not a particularly pretty city but it's among the best-preserved eighteenth-century cities in Europe because it was never bombed in the war, Ireland being neutral. The severe Georgian architecture in the huge, plain brick buildings feels rather oppressive and overweening. It is saved by the stunning doors. Georgian doors are very big and they're all different colours. This is because when Queen Victoria died, England decreed that everyone in Ireland paint their doors black in mourning. So the Dubliners turned around and painted them bright subversive colours. However, it is true the squares are aristocratic and the mansions noble, evoking a world of elegant life and eccentric behaviour.

There are lots of bookshops and most of them have books by Irish writers past and present in the window displays. One of the numerous literary summer schools in Dublin is devoted to the Clontarf-born Bram (Abraham) Stoker, who wrote *Dracula*. Stoker never actually went to Transylvania and probably took his inspiration from his exposure to Catholicism and the stories his mother told him of banshees and people sucking blood from cattle during the famine. A Hungarian explorer apparently told him about Vlad the Impaler, the fifteenth-century tyrant, and Stoker grafted him onto the myth of the vampire. The word Dracula may have come from the Irish droch fhola, meaning bad blood.

I had read in various obscure publications about a restaurant called Muscat and was determined to try it. I found it around the corner from Magills at 64 South William Street. Muscat turned out to be a treasure of a place and like all treasures, its entrance was secretive and subterranean, down a few steps behind lace curtains. I pushed the door open and judged by the disorder that, this being a Monday, it was closed. A friendly man with a beard and glasses on his nose confirmed this and when my face crumpled he quickly invited me in to have a sustaining glass of wine to stop me fainting dead away from hunger and disappointment. We talked and talked the way you do with the Irish about wine, other restaurants, France, refill the wine glass, talk some more. Not only a lover of wine but also a lover of books, Brian dragged out his favourites for me. He had found an old copy of Shakespeare's historical plays signed on the cover page by Anew McMaster, the last of the great strolling players. Folded inside was a red and black leaflet to publicise the playing of *Richard III* produced and directed by Laurence Olivier: ONE MAN — TWISTED IN MIND AND BODY BROUGHT DEATH (in bright red) TO ALL WHO STOOD IN HIS WAY. I finally stumbled out into the softness with umbrella number three and ran into Cooke's restaurant across the road.

The next day I faithfully returned to Muscat and was treated like a member of the family by all the staff, especially the bearded one, owner Brian Cornish. It looked like an intimate Parisian bistro perhaps in the 2nd arrondissement around rue des Petits Croix with its two little rooms, a monstrously small kitchen, green tables and buttercup walls. There was very much the feeling of being at a friend's house for lunch, it being clear that all the customers knew Brian and his partner Bernie. They had only their Christian names on the business card and turned away 50 to 100 people on a good night.

This was a place that had one page of food on the menu and three pages of wines and other alcohol. For lunch you had a choice of four starters, four mains and two desserts, and for dinner slightly more. I like menus like this. I suspect that as far as Brian was concerned, the food was just something that accompanied his wine. First you chose your wine — or wines, because he regaled you with information about his favourites — then you figured out what dish would go with it. Although I said I only wanted a main, he insisted I taste the duck liver parfait with black pudding on toasted brioche. The dry Italian Muscat-Muscaté appealed to me but I wondered if it would go with the chicken I had ordered. I asked his advice (not mentioning my preference) and he chose the Italian Muscat. As Oscar Wilde said, 'I have nothing to declare but my genius.'

Now, making liver parfait is as simple as falling off a barstool but making it so fine and flavoursome that it tastes like foie gras is quite a hat trick. The dish was exactly what it said it was — a fresh, buttery slice of homemade toasted brioche bread, a layer of moist black pudding topped with a generous slice of duck liver parfait. No carry-on, no cacophony, no drama, just good fresh food in an interesting combination. I reluctantly let half the parfait go to make room for the chicken supreme on a parmesan mash with sherry vinegar dressing.

Muscat's chef, Janice Timothy, was a tall attractive woman with short dark hair, a stunning smile and an impressive culinary background. In the corner of the restaurant they called the kitchen she moved quietly around with the other chef, a large red-headed man and true 'grafter' (hard worker) according to Brian. This was what you call real food — or slow food — and unlike in most of the good restaurants in Dublin, the bill was not outrageous at all. I think I paid about £14 in all, but maybe I was being spoiled. But here's the thing — everyone spoiled me in Dublin. At Peacock Alley my dining partner and I were treated to a continuous line-up of little treats we hadn't ordered.

A branch of the Slow Food Movement has just been launched in Dublin. This movement started in Italy 10 years ago and now there are 400 convivia (groups) in 35 countries, rediscovering the flavours and savours of regional cooking and banishing the degrading effects of fast food. They have a cultural agenda and a passionate manifesto promoting a philosophy of pleasure, safeguarding traditional food and wine heritage and educating young people into a proper relationship with food. Slow Food has taken as its symbol the wise slowness of the snail because they believe, quite rightly, that we have been enslaved by speed and fast life and the only way to oppose this folly of mistaking frenzy for activity is to eat flavourful real food where the taste has been developed rather than demeaned. They also have a scientific research and documentation project called Ark, aimed at safeguarding and benefiting small-scale agricultural and food production. Thousands of different kinds of charcuterie, cheeses, animal breeds and plants are in danger of disappearing for ever — the ironing out of tastes, the excessive power of industrial companies, distribution difficulties and misinformation are the causes of a process that could lead to the loss of an irreplaceable heritage of traditional recipes, knowledge and tastes. Slow Food also has lots of get-togethers and a beautiful magazine called *Slow* available in many languages.

Johnny Cooke's restaurant across the road from Muscat has been a phenomenal success since it opened its fashionable doors in 1992. The cuisine is California/Italian sliding towards fusion/Pacific Rim (yes, they even do Pacific Rim in Dublin) and the wonderful trompe l'oeil red, gold and black decor, tiled floors and black marble tables reflected it. Head chef Harry McKeogh, who was about to open his own restaurant, started his culinary life as a pastry chef, trained at La Gavroche and worked in California. He got most of his fresh produce from Meath, north of Dublin, and the fish fresh from Cork, and told me one of the main reasons food has undergone a revolution in Dublin in the last 10 years is because the infrastructure is so improved — better roads mean faster and more reliable transport from the source. Since his fish was so fresh I ordered the bar (sea bass). It came in a sumptuous deep plate — lightly fried fish surrounded by a salsa and sparkling leafy salad on the side. It was very simple and very expensive at £18. Maybe you pay for freshness but I thought the price outrageous.

On the same street is a wonderful little French food shop called La Maison des Gourmets selling foie gras, Toulouse sausages, terrines, cured hams, French cheeses, olive oils, wine and takeaways. Sitting under the counter glass were little discs about the size of coasters called Provençale tarts. They were slim rounds of pastry topped with paper-thin concentric circles of aubergine, tomato and courgette, crowned in the centre with a nipple of pesto.

At the end of the street the George Street Market, a marvellous old Victorian covered market which sold only food in its heyday but now had only a couple of food stalls, the rest being filled up with clothes, books etc. Right at the front of the market was Guy Stewart Foods selling good bread and cheese and Mediterranean foods, and up a bit on the right-hand side was a dry-goods stall with fresh vegetables and grains. And of course there was the fabulous Sheridan's cheese shop on South Anne Street, overflowing with warm Irish cheeses in its cool controlled atmosphere.

In fact that whole area in there behind Grafton Street is the best part of Dublin, sort of like a mini St Germain des Pres, criss-crossed with little streets of designer clothing shops, upmarket bars and interesting restaurants. I ate at Mao on Chatham Row, an airy, two-storeyed open-kitchened restaurant with oriental/Irish food and no oriental chefs or staff. It was a hip, healthy mixture of Thai, Japanese, Chinese and Indo-nesian with really fresh ingredients and all cooked to order — tempura tofu with wasabi yoghurt, fresh crab spring rolls and dipping sauce with lettuce and coriander to wrap them in, green beef curry with coconut, nasi goreng with a poached egg on top. Sawyers Fishmongers, there since 1959, was on that street too. Sybaris on Balfe Street had beautiful shoes from Italy and Spain and Vivian Walshe on Stephen Street had ethereal handmade jewellery, unusual hats and designer shoes.

Being a whiskey drinker from my childhood days when my father gave me thimblefuls cut with water to teach me how to drink it, I made swift contact with Eily Kilgannon, international PR manager of Irish Distillers. This turned out to be one of the brightest ideas I had in Dublin because Eily was not only knowledgeable and passionate about Irish whiskey but very, very good company. She was the sort of woman whose open easy laughing manner belied her sharp intelligence and cultivated background. Blonde with red lips and extraordinary grey/blue eyes, she was comfortably rounded as you would expect of a person who lived well and loved all the good things in life — food, wine, travelling and France. Hailing from Sligo, Eily spoke Irish, good French in spite of never having lived in France, and Italian after a few Jamesons. Her two most common phrases were 'it's distilled three times, you know' and 'God, you're mad'.

We started our chauffeur-driven night out at a book launch for a restaurant guide held on a little barge on the canal across the road from Bord Fáilte, the Irish Tourist Board. I had written to Maeve Binchey who suggested I get in touch with Bill Morrison at the board, so I went directly from his office to champagne and black pudding amuse-gueules with the top restaurateurs of Dublin. Quoting that 'the Irish are a very fair race — they never say well of each other', they proceeded to rectify the situation by presenting one another with horrible pottery prizes for being so clever. One of the people who received a prize was Conrad Gallagher, the imposing, mahogany-haired owner and head chef of Peacock Alley, reputedly one of the best Michelin-starred restaurants in Ireland. He stood out, dressed all in black with suede shoes that matched the colour of his ponytail — a young, fleshy but good-looking face and a reputation for arrogance and tanties in the kitchen. Eily had reserved a table at Peacock Alley for later on so I was looking forward to seeing what he could do with his hands. But first we had to work.

Dan the chauffeur was ready for us as we slid off the barge and with Eily's help the car negotiated its way through the back streets of rush-hour traffic to Jameson's distillery in Smithfield. The old distillery is the original eighteenth-century building, until recently in very bad shape but now restored with the sympathetic ultra-modern addition of a glass and steel ceiling. Eily took me for a private tour of the showrooms where you can see how whiskey is made, which was only a hurdle to get me to the bar where I found out the meaning of 'it's distilled three times, you know'. She had all the whiskeys produced under the Irish Distillers umbrella laid out in plastic thimbles for me; I could smell the roast dinner that always followed my father's whiskey sippings (except he drank Scotch). Up until now my preferred whiskey had been Lagavulin but hey, I was open. Some time later we decided the ones I liked the best were Bushmills Three Wood 16-Year-Old Single Malt and Jameson 1780. I was complimented on my robust tastebuds. Bushmills is the oldest licensed distillery in the world, whiskey making at that site in County Antrim going back to 1276. The 16-year-old is matured in Spanish Oloroso sherry butts, whence to bourbon barrels, then finished in port pipes. You stick your nose in and you can immediately smell that it is well balanced and malty, then when you roll it around the mouth the sherry, honey, woody bits hit you. It remains only to say sláinte and let it go down to where it belongs in your little Irish veins.

I have always been one of those smart people who scorn ice or water with whiskey on the grounds that it takes them 16 years to get the water out — far be it from me to put it back in again. But the grand Eily taught me something: 40 per cent proof is bloody strong and you can't go on for very long at that power level. Also when you add exactly half the amount of water you can see the fumes lifting off, which opens the whiskey up, releasing the aromas. Try it. Taste it straight up first, then do the water test.

The Jameson 1780 is a 12-year-old with a mellow sweet nutty character, again coming from the sherry wood. As with all whiskeys that have been distilled three times, it is incredibly smooth on the palate. Whiskey was invented in Ireland because they didn't like drinking perfume. No. What really happened was that in the sixth century monks from the Middle East brought an apparatus to Ireland called an alembic to distil perfume. Strangely enough the Irish monks found something better to do with this thing they called a pot still, and named the liquid they produced 'water of life', in Irish uisce beatha (pronounced ishka baahaa), which was anglicised to 'whiskey'. Ireland is blessed with a temperate climate and lots of good pure water, not to mention acres and acres of the basically organic barley needed to make good uisce.

If you want to make Irish whiskey at home, first you malt your Irish barley, not by smoking it as the Scottish do, which is why their whisky tastes smoky, but by drying it in closed kilns to ensure you get the honeyed, clean taste of the malt. Then you mill together malted and unmalted barley (whence the expression grist for the mill) and mix it with hot Irish water in the mash tun, whereupon the starches are converted to a liquid called wort. This is separated from the residual grains and pumped into the wash-backs where you add the yeast, which ferments and bubbles and troubles, converting the sugars to low-strength alcohol or wash. Then IT'S DISTILLED THREE TIMES, you know. The result of the first distillation is called low wines, the second feints and the third spirit. Get your cooper in with his handmade casks, fill them with the spirit, hide them in a dark aromatic warehouse and go away for a few years while you both mellow out and mature. Blend it, bottle it and the rest is history. You are now a fully rounded human being.

Chaffeur Dan was at the gate waiting for us and off we went to dine at Peacock Alley overlooking the fashionable and famous St Stephen's Green. If I had read the publicity material I wouldn't have had the courage to go there because it clearly stated the rules of engagement: 'You do not visit Peacock Alley to be cosseted in old-style comfort. Here you get the new-style luxury and you share it with the fashionable crowd, film stars, designers, artists and business moguls.' Nowhere did it say writers, television starlets or PR executives. A mogul I ain't, and neither was anyone else there. They looked like rich Americans and suits to moi, but who's complaining? When you have Eily for a companion you don't have time to look around. The decor was slick and minimalist, which I liked, with pale aubergine chairs, stark paintings, skylights, restful deep blue and green walls and crisp white linen. Very nice. The wine list with over 200 bins was huge and I was pleased to see a preponderance of fish on the menu.

We were treated by the lovely French, Irish and Australian waiters to a teaser of cappuccino of pea soup with a long thin cheese stick and chives balanced on top that was warmth and lightness itself. I groaned. 'God, you're mad.' I groaned again when a surprise plate of little tastes arrived — foie gras, cured wild salmon, tiny duck rillette ravioli, crab and coriander salad. Now we were almost full but there was more to come. I had tortellini of langoustine with braised scallion, parmesan, confit tomato and fresh peas. Eily's was roasted scallops three ways — avocado and chilli pepper stew, panchetta and quail's egg, and stew of eggplant and coconut cream. It was sensational but very busy. This was followed by a bracing passionfruit sorbet topped with fromage blanc mousse. When we were completely exhausted the mains arrived on huge trays carried by staff who appeared to be genuinely delighted with the whole performance and our 'mad' reaction to it. While I was having gustatory orgasms all over the place, the straight-backed American face-lifts next door didn't have to shut their faces like books because they were already sewn shut. Heroically we raised our knives and forks to my roasted breast of duckling with caramelised orange and vanilla, artichokes, shiitake duxelles, pink peppercorns and béarnaise sauce, and Eily's loin of lamb wrapped in leeks with ratatouille, pesto couscous, zucchini, spinach, thyme and sweet peppers. See what I mean by busy? The really exciting bit was that the duck dish was ringed with a hairline of chocolate (very clever) and the downside was the breast was not pink in the middle.

'God, I love béarnaise sauce,' said Eily.

'You know, I wrote a book called *Don't Get Saucy with Me, Béarnaise*,' I replied.

'You didn't. God, you're mad.'

Its supporters say this sort of food is about assaulting your tastebuds from every angle: full of wacky combinations, constant inventiveness and utter confidence. They say that each dish is an exhilarating excursion through a torrent of flavours, an intense reworking of our expectations of what cooking is about. As soon as I tasted and saw the starters I knew it was the cuisine of a young man — show-offy somehow and with far too much going on. Conrad Gallagher is brilliant, it's true, but wonderful and colourful as it is, I believe, as an older woman, that his cuisine needs the third distilling.

As was his wont, there was Dan standing downstairs with the car door open, waiting for us to heave ourselves in for the last leg of our evening. This was my second association of cars with eating since I'd left New Zealand. It was during my first, when I was sitting on the side of the road in Islington with an ice-pack on my head, that I marvelled at how few accidents and misadventures I had had with the almost constant travel I subjected myself to. On that occasion I had been in a car with three other food-mad people rabbiting on to a woman possessed of the marvellous name of Ursula Feringo about cooking classes in Italy, when a red car made the mistake of driving into my personal space rather than along the main road. The driver had been 'beastly' as Ursula said, about us being in his way and made not one enquiry as to the state of the brain cells on the left side of my head. An hour later my friend Sarah and I were safely ensconced in the Sugar Club medicating ourselves with Tattinger and Irish scallops with sweet chilli sauce and crème fraîche. But now having Dan to manage the car side of things meant I could devote my remaining brain cells to the food.

'Eily,' I said, 'you don't have to continue on this route to destruction with me if you're tired. I'm quite happy to go on my own.'

'Are ye mad? What class of jiggery-pokery is that? There's no way you're leaving me behind.' She leaned over. 'Dan, could you take us to the Wishing Well in Blackwell, please. Peta says there's a session on there.'

There was an overwhelming but pleasant whiff of oysters and the sea in the Dublin air as we drove past the bay to our destination. We walked through the spacious modern pub right to the back, around a corner and into a room that bore no relation to the rest of the place, thank goodness. It was small, rustic, filled to the rafters with people and as usual in the corner were the musicians playing away, never seeming to need rest or toilet breaks. In the madness their drinks were passed to them over people's heads and this time there was a woman singing 'The Bold Fenian Men', a song about ancient battles.

> *Side by side for the cause have our forefathers battled*
> *When our hills never echoed the tread of a slave*
> *In many a field where the leaden hail rattled*
> *Through the red gap of glory they marched to the grave.*
> *And those who inherit their name and their spirit*
> *Will march 'neath the banners of Liberty then;*
> *All who have foreign law — Native or Sassanach*
> *Must out and make way for the bold Fenian men.*

There's all sorts of music in Dublin and when friends from New Zealand turned up they whisked me off to a Russian gypsy concert at Whelan's pub on South Great Georges Street. The little theatre was around the corner from the main pub and a marvel it was with its old-fashioned balcony, ornate iron railings and Celtic design painted all over the walls. What happened next was wild — music as theatre. Three men walked onto the stage dressed in black leather pants, knee boots and red satin shirts, and with their two violins and guitar proceeded to stun everyone with their passionate virtuosity. Their faces contorted with concentration as sometimes they plucked, sometimes seduced, sometimes caressed their instruments in a performance of haunting power and glorious harmonies. When they sang they moaned, gasped and harmonised fluidly like caramel running down the stage, with the instruments answering one another like voices, birds, trees rustling, rivers running, a train, horses galloping to a stop, a woman sighing and lamenting. All in the flamboyant Russian gypsy tradition with the audience going mad. That was Loyko and they live in Dublin when they're not travelling the world's music and cultural festivals.

As in New Zealand, cooking in Ireland is the fashionable profession of the 1990s and beyond. Until fairly recently 'Irish cuisine' was considered an oxymoron internationally, not because it didn't exist but because it was simple and unsophisticated. Now, black pudding, crubeens and champ are all over the trendy menus like new olives on an old tree. The changes were of course market-driven by the upturned economy, overseas travel and mass media. Now there are new cooking schools, gourmet shops and young chefs who enjoy the stardom formerly reserved for movie stars or — fil-um stars as they say here. Petronius, the Roman senator writing in the first century AD, said: 'When food is no longer simply a necessity for survival and becomes elevated to an art form, then society has become decadent.'

What's extraordinary about Ireland is that they have moved to this from a history of starvation and a gastronomic tradition based on poverty, and this has happened very quickly. Today Ireland's middle class live to eat rather than the other way around. The 'new foodies' are veritably drowning in a lake of extra virgin single-estate olive oil, organic everything and a chic holier-than-thou attitude that gets regurgitated every time the vitamin pills go down.

Yet that the famine struck 150 years ago was Ireland's greatest calamity and is deeply ingrained in the country's soul. A population of eight and a half million people was, through famine, emigration and disease, reduced to a staggering two and a half million in the space of 80 years. The population is now just over five million. The Irish people as a whole have a huge psychic hurt, which has been pushed way down to the subconscious. Also there was the guilt that survival of the famine imposed on those who made it through, akin to the phenomenon noted in survivors of Nazi concentration camps. Like the Jews, the Irish have a huge capacity for forgiveness and it's as if this has seeped over into their exuberant new ability to eat for pleasure rather than need.

Of course the freedom to choose what you eat is a luxury dependent upon economic success and prosperity. It is old news that Ireland in the past 20 years has leapt from relative poverty to almost blatant prosperity. The EU has been the fairy godmother since 1973, allowing Ireland to break away from economic subordination to Britain, but Ireland has done a lot to help itself. In 1969 the Industrial Development Authority was created to encourage foreign companies to settle in Ireland with the lure of generous grants and light taxation. By the mid-1990s some 40 per cent of Irish industry was foreign owned, predominantly by American, English and German companies which invested heavily. The well-educated, comparatively low-waged English-speaking Irish workforce are highly regarded and enjoy excellent labour relations with the employers.

Food has become a lifestyle accessory like a car, a beach house or designer clothes. The church has been shown to be corrupt, and nobody admires politics, so redefining your lifestyle by turning food into art is fast becoming the new religion in Ireland. The 'New Wave Celts' as they have been called spend most of their spare time and holidays eating, drinking and living the life of Reilly while throwing back previously unheard of delicacies like truffles, French and Irish cheeses, marinated olives and Udon noodles. The very successful Irish *Food and Wine Magazine* after 16 issues went recently from bi-monthly to monthly, and a new magazine has just been launched for conspicuous consumers with the unabashedly vulgar name of *Spend*. As with tourism, once the good-life ball is rolling, there ain't no going back. The old joke 'why do the Irish call their pound a punt? Because it rhymes with bank manager' hardly applies now.

While I was in Dublin everyone was talking about a new hotel that had opened on Lower Ormond Quay called the Morrison, with interior design by the well-known Hong Kong/Irish clothing designer John Rocha, so I paid it a visit, little realising I would want to move in, memorise the decor, win the lottery and build a house just like it. It was so different from the rest of Dublin, it was hard to believe you were not in Japan or Hong Kong. The requisite black-suited, ear-pieced doormen opened the portals with a stiff 'Good evening, madam' distinctly lacking in emotion. Every time I am confronted with these social amputees I have to fight the urge to laugh and say 'You're only a bloody doorman . . . sweetie . . . get over yourself.' There's something ghastly about stupid people taking themselves so seriously, a bit like a sow in a room full of silk purses.

Brown silk velvet curtains framed the entrance, their voluptuous quietness giving a taste of the world about to open to you — a world of interconnecting spaces with no doors, giving a sense of both openness and womb-like security. It was light and dark, ebony and ivory, utterly restrained and elegant, with a balance between stylish serenity and an exciting atmosphere. The walls and corridors were curved and the silk velvet followed through the entire hotel in the form of throws and cushions ranging in colour from flame orange to earthy brown to green to ivory to crimson. It was all very Zen, and faithful to the principles of feng shui, constructed from marble, wood, glass, cream limestone, grey granite and stone floors, with luxurious handmade carpets underfoot. There were two café bar areas and a stunning split-level dining room like a huge, high minimalist stage. The beautiful patrons were of course dressed in ebony and ivory to match.

The food at the restaurant Halo was not as Asian-influenced as I expected — more French/Italian/modern Celtic than anything else. I never expect exceptional food in a hotel, no matter how grand or thrilled with itself it is, so I wasn't disappointed that it wasn't perfect; also it was early days and it takes a chef months to settle into a new kitchen. I tore myself away from my favourite food — squab pigeon with duxelles, duck foie gras and rocket salad — and snipped into a risotto of duck aiguillette with girolles and truffle oil, which was very harmonious, creamy but al dente. I fell as I always do for a Sancerre to go with the Szechwan peppered rare tuna served with green asparagus, basil gnocchi and red pepper emulsion. I love these emulsions because they are very sophisticated and take the place of naughty sauces. The tuna was not rare, more of an insipid pink, and unfortunately the baby potatoes roasted with lime leaves had ideas of their own and as soon as I tried to spear one it skidded off the table onto the shoes of an Australian next door, which didn't count but nevertheless . . .

I then forced myself to bypass the crème brulée, the only sweet I ever permit myself, and took the waiter's punt on a raspberry tartlet with chibouste cream and raspberry caramel sauce. It was quite refined and built up like a little round cheese, and oddly enough the caramel went very well with the fresh raspberries. The waitpersons were dressed in aubergine shirts and floor-length black aprons which I rather liked and I had the best waiter in my whole stay in Ireland — funny, very smart without being over-familiar, and adorably doting.

Nothing screamed here and the service from everyone was very charming and efficient considering the place was so new.

In the morning I called my cousin Tricia Mulhall in County Tipperary and asked if I might come down for a visit. Her voice was deep and warm. We had never met before and her response to my question 'Can I stay a week?' was 'Sure, you can stay as long as ye like.'

'Would a lifetime be okay?'

'Course it would. We've got lots of room. I have to take some boy scouts away for a weekend in July but you are quite welcome to join us.'

'I don't think it's my thing,' I ventured.

She laughed. 'Ah, you never know now.'

It's true that maybe my eye falls on a younger man from time to time but I thought scouts were pushing it a bit.

'The train from Dublin doesn't stop at Cashel so I'll pick you up at Thurles.'

FIRE EXIT

Chapter two

childhood

The trip into my past and my family history took an hour on the train but 49 years by the map of the heart. My mother was Ann Long before she married New Zealander Harvey Mathias and her parents were James Long and Margaret Shanahan of County Tipperary. They left Ireland in 1927 and there is a newspaper photo of Ann's family arriving in Sydney on the ship from Ireland — the family of mother and nine children all lined up with my mother being one of the smallest — Sunday best, faces solemn.

Hearing my cousin's voice on the phone took me back to the voices of those who had educated me and to a large extent formed my life. I remember the primer classroom of the convent I went to in Auckland, a concrete and wooden school with dark classrooms and polished corridors. We and the nuns were the ones who kept that school clean and shining, on our hands and knees with wax and cloths. They made their own polish from turpentine and boiled oil mixed with methylated spirits and vinegar. There was tennis, rugby, basketball and endless line-ups outside classrooms where we were whipped into perfect, motionless rows by the loathed prefects. The convent school was a breeding ground for thwarted passion and unrequited love fertilised by the harsh, zealous repression of the saintly Sisters of Mercy.

The nun I loved most was Sister Mary Agnes, a small powerhouse of vitriol and sarcasm of whom everyone was terrified. I found her adorable. 'Oh, here comes that Peta Mathias or should I say the BBC. Miss Never-Knows-When-to-Stop. The boldest, brassiest creature God ever saw fit to squeeze through creation. Remove those wet shoes at once and why don't you talk louder and broadcast to the whole country?' Sister Agnes would pronounce, hands on hips, heavy rosary beads rattling. She always called you by your full name. She raged and ranted and spat her irritation at her disappointing life and I couldn't wait to get home and tell the mother all the details. The way home was strewn with

Protestant children (to be poked and insulted), honeysuckle (to be sniffed and sucked for the honey) and flowers in front gardens (to be picked for the mother). It was very easy to get distracted. Tramped in, threw school bag, hat and body onto floor. The mother was reading usually, while feeding a baby.

'Mum, you know what Sister Agnes said today?'

'What, dear?' Putting afghans with bits of cornflakes sticking out of them and milk in front of me.

'She said that Jesus had been nailed to the cross for the likes of me and that I had a great career ahead of me in radio. She made me take my wet shoes and socks off and threw all the boys' outdoor shoes out the window into the football field because they weren't lined up in rows.'

The mother laughed her head off from the kitchen where she seemed to spend her entire life boiling milk for babies' bottles. No sooner did one baby turn into a child and start getting in my way than another one would appear. Sister Agnes was my second role-model after my mother — even at five I admired her pitilessness and flamboyance and felt a great consanguinity with her.

Our wooden villa had four bedrooms all with big sash windows, a wide hallway and a large sitting room that no one ever went into. It was for special guests and full of valuable ornaments, polished brocade furniture, embossed wallpaper and flowery carpets. Out the back was a yard with tree huts, flowers, vegetables, chickens and fruit trees. All summer we picked passionfruit, peaches, apples, oranges, lemons and plums. I would lie next to the asparagus bed and eat the tender shoots as soon as they were long enough and always got into trouble for doing it but couldn't stop. The only incongruous element amid the otherwise resolutely fifties decor in our house was a shocking pink sliding door between the kitchen and the dining room. One day the mother had risen from her bed, said, 'I can't stand the sight of that boring door another minute' and painted it shocking pink. It was the talking point of the neighbourhood for about a year.

Every night after we had done the dinner dishes we all knelt on the dining-room floor and said the rosary together. The mother always said that the family that prays together stays together, and strangely enough, during this semi-pagan ritual of kneeling on the floor all chanting the same words was the only time we actually did feel part of a larger whole.

Primary school wasn't a bed of roses. Bullies made my life uncomfortable enough for me to understand that I didn't entirely measure up, either in personality or looks. Of all the humiliating memories I have, being made to sit on the boys' benches to eat my lunch alone is the one that stands out. The other children frequently put me there under the pohutukawa tree by the basketball court because I had an exotic and unfeminine name. The girls' seats were on the other side of the court (the nuns didn't have to keep us separated at that age — we did it naturally). This was not only a physical rejection of my girl appeal but a rejection of my very identity — my mad name.

The clouds boiled black over my head as I sat very straight, uncomprehending and hardening in the playground of my life. The children all liked Vanessa Pratt who was Grace Kelly in miniature, the most popular girl in the world. I knew how they felt — I too was charmed by Vanessa and carried her school bag for her until I finally got a life.

In the get-a-life department I didn't do well initially but caught up fast. Something had to be done about the fact that nobody liked me, that I felt like an alien and that I wasn't Vanessa Pratt. Sticks and stones will break your bones, said the mother, but names will never hurt you. This is a lie children are told to cut down on future psychiatry bills. Like all children I desperately wanted to be a fly on the wall — not even king of the flies, just a fly among others — but it was never going to happen with a stigmata like Peta. I have no idea where it came from, just a name my mother picked up in Australia. The names my schoolmates found for me cut deeper than any beating could have and they galvanised me into action. By the time I had sat on that bench a few more times and felt the full force of social exclusion, my ruthless mind had started seriously looking around for a new persona. I could see that I would never be as pretty, blonde, ladylike and indifferent as Vanessa. I decided instead to be smarter, funnier and more staunch and once I had achieved that they could all kiss my bum. It worked eventually. Could it be there was a God after all? Being funny worked wonders in fact — it made me slightly more popular, it took the edge off my unhappiness at not being blonde and pliant and it covered up the fact that I had an outlandish name, which was unforgivable in 1950s New Zealand.

I continued through primary school blissfully unaware of sex or the true meaning of a female's life. We girls all trudged from classroom to classroom in our heavy black shoes, thick black socks, black pleated serge uniform, yellow and black striped tie, black hat and black cardy. Tiny, innocent children all dressed in black to ward off the backsliding and heathenism waiting at every corner. Even at seven a girl had to be vigilant. With my freckled face, dark curly hair and small body terminating in particularly solid ankles, decked out in the black and white, I looked like an ambulant pedestrian crossing.

A strong character was neither to be admired nor encouraged at convent school (or anywhere else for that matter); in fact it was to be wrung out of a person by the Irish passion-killers, also dressed in black. A failure to examine my conscience rigorously enough and impure thoughts led to my first brush with the law. These latter were big on the agenda in confession and I had lots of them. It was only when I voiced them outside the confessional that the mother had to come down to school and sit on the team for the defence. The prosecution invariably consisted of the head nun and the witness or victim and the crime usually involved slander, impurity, insubordination or all three.

The revolutionary thing about the legal system of the Sisters of Mercy was that the judgement and punishment both took place before the trial. This thick brown strap of leather was used on the bare legs and hands of tender little girls and the buttocks of boys to strengthen their backbones or break their spirits, whichever came first. The boys used to put newspapers or exercise books down their pants until that protection was discovered and a stop was put to it smartly. The thing was, you couldn't cry or show any emotion because that was a criminal offence in itself. Sometimes the pain got the better of you, however, and sitting down or trying to pick up a pencil afterwards always proved a challenge in the tear department. The dramatic audience with the mother was a mere formality, a scene condemned to be oft repeated through the years. The prosecution made it clear that I was skating on thin ice, and being a brazen hussy was the least of it. The defence denied the accusations on principle no matter what they were, with flashing eyes and citations of impeccable family background. The prosecution then threatened the 'E' word. Being expelled was on a par with getting pregnant or having sex with wetas. The 'E' word was only whispered with the whites of the eyes showing. It always astounded me how vociferously the mother took my side against the nuns. Lucky she did. She was going to need the practice.

Most of my criminal, impure history was either a case of innocent inquiry (as in the incident of the lifting up of Sister Agnes's black habit to see what was underneath), or stating the obvious (as in the incident of saying that another young sister was far too pretty and snappy to be a nun and that being the case she should get out there and find herself a husband). This statement caused such an uproar that even I realised I had said something sacrilegious.

But nuns were a source of crucial and compelling mystery

to me and I was naturally determined to get to the bottom of their lifestyle and dress habits. Anyone who wore so many clothes in the heat of a New Zealand summer had to have something to hide. It stood to reason. The mediaeval outfit of black stockings, black shoes, long black habit, black veil and white headgear required explanation. But a smart mouth was the fast road to hell and instilling fear and guilt were the traditional Catholic methods of control, as laid down in the *How to Repress an Entire Nation Handbook.*

Music and singing unchained my heart and harmonised my little life. It was an ecstasy that I could tap into at will in the unhappiness and confusion of childhood. At eight I began piano lessons in the music room at the convent. This wonderful room was part of the house where the nuns lived rather than part of the school. It was polished, calm, full of flowers, had a shining piano and always seemed to have a summer, sea-perfumed breeze blowing in through the window. I was enchanted that, given that I had no redeeming qualities in any other department, fate had given me musical ability and a good ear.

Our family went to Mass every Sunday and the father went every day, a habit we all found faintly eccentric. Singing hymns in church along with the choir and the organ up above was the upside; the dreary downside was fainting from having fasted since midnight the night before. My sisters and I wore identical dresses with full skirts, hats and white gloves to Mass and kneeled together like Russian dolls, fighting nausea and boredom. The boys would be dressed in grey pants, white shirts and blazers. One of us would usually keel over. At one end was the current baby gurgling loudly at the priest and at the other end I scanned the church for anyone better dressed than us. Dad left Mass 10 minutes early to race home and bake the scones, which would be just coming out of the oven when we arrived, having exhausted all possibilities of socialising outside the church. Some were plain and some were with dates, all wrapped in a teatowel with butter and jam at the ready. He still makes the best scones I have ever eaten — light, moist and fragrant. When the fasting rule was gradually eased from midnight to three hours to one hour, the mother was horrified at the laxness of it. You had to suffer for the sake of godliness, just as you had to suffer for the sake of beauty.

Our Irish friends down the road lived in the same sort of villa that we did and they provided an instant, exciting social life. Caroline Reynolds was my best friend with whom I learned Irish dancing every Saturday morning, with whom I went to céilís and with whom I shared the secret crushes on boys. Her family were a completely different kettle of fish from ours in that they were recent immigrants rather than New Zealanders like us. Altogether two different kettles of Irish scnapper. My mother spoke with a tutored accent and Caroline's parents Sean and Lilly, Aunt Mamie and Uncle Charlie had a broad Irish brogue. In flagrant contrast to my ordered household, they talked at the tops of their voices and were spectacularly permissive, a state of affairs that did not escape my notice for one second. At home we were requested not to talk unless we had something intelligent to contribute, which rarely happened because my main topic of conversation was, 'Why do I have to eat with these hooligans?'

'They are your brothers and sisters,' the mother would say patiently. 'You must learn to live with other people.'

But at Caroline's house they had free-range dinner conversations: 'Caroline, will you have another spud?'

'No thanks. I'm full, Mam.'

'Eat another potato for God's sake or you'll starve to death — look at the size of you. You don't see Paetie refusing food that God has seen fit in his mercy to provide.'

'Where did you get these spuds anyway, Lilly?' Sean would ask.

'From the maternity hospital. Where do you think I got them?' Screams of laughter.

'Aren't you the trick with your sense of humour? If you're buying them from that grocer up the road there he'll be diddling you for sure. He's so mean, he wouldn't give you the steam off his piss. Pass the butter.'

They ate huge meals of potatoes boiled in their jackets, lamb stews and giant steaks. I had never seen a potato cooked in its skin and was fascinated that they would cook them then peel them, instead of the other way around. Hulking plates of sausages, black pudding, pork, turnips, liver and steamed puddings were par for the course. They drank tea and ate bread thick with salted butter with their meals, and had beer or stout at social occasions, customs unheard of in our house. A favourite meal for Sean was boiled chook with the cooking juices taken as a soup beforehand.

Every meal was accompanied by potatoes in one form or another. For breakfast Lilly cooked big yellow eggs and thick rashers of bacon cured by the butcher up the road in a centimetre of cooking fat. She spooned the hot fat over the eggs to cook them rather than turning them over. My mother would no more have lent herself to serving up a cooked breakfast (apart from porridge) than fly to the moon. Caroline's family talked loud and fast, burst into emotional song at the drop of a shamrock, and thought I was the cleverest, most refined thing they had ever set eyes on.

'Paetie, sure, will you look at the hands and feet on that child?' Lilly would exclaim. 'They're so small and dainty, sure I don't know how she does anything with them at all. Sean, have you seen these hands?' And everyone would have to look at my hands. To have such positive reinforcement from such a humble quarter was almost too exquisite to bear, especially seeing I was so disenamoured of my body.

One day I was sewing a skirt for Caroline (with my famous hands) on Lilly's sewing machine, an instrument Lilly had no idea how to use.

'Will you look at that,' she exclaimed. 'Sure, I have never

seen such a straight line in my whole life. Paetie, how is it that you can sew such a straight line? Caroline, get in there and sew a straight line like that for me now.'

Punishment at Caroline's house was handed out in an arbitrary, explosive way. You could be having a conversation at the dinner table when suddenly someone would get a clout over the ear, shriek, and then conversation would continue as if nothing had happened. The randomness surprised me, whose own home did not permit outbursts or unplanned discipline. But when sleeping over with Irish families I enjoyed much more freedom — I got to go to parties, dances and Mass at 10 in the morning instead of eight. Going at eight was sanctimonious according to the mother; going at 10 was indolent.

My friendship with Caroline and being a good Irish dancer (ankles were not an issue here) meant lots of knees-ups with other Irish families. I loved Irish dancing because of the flamboyant green and gold costumes and the plaintiveness of the fiddle music. My ordered side was attracted to the rigidness and intricacy of the style — no movement whatsoever above the hips, expressionless face, limp arms and not a pelvic movement in sight. Bit like being a nun but with a better outfit. We went off hand in hand every Saturday morning, taking with us our soft pumps, tap shoes and half crowns to pay for the lesson. I never had to be nagged to take dancing or music lessons and practised till my fingers and feet hurt.

Dances. If it hadn't been for the céilís at the Irish Society I would never have met Irish boys either. Donal and Patrick McCaffrey were the eldest sons of a family of eight, big families being nothing out of the ordinary for Catholics, even in New Zealand. The Martins had 11 children with the junior children being younger than their nieces, and the Malavoys had 10 who all looked like drowned rats. The mother was very tall with a hunch and the father pallid. My father, possessed of a dry Welsh wit, maintained that their relationship was a triumph of one hump over another. The mother laughed till the tears ran down her face. Donal's parents were famous for being the first in the parish to buy an electric blanket and have it catch fire. The children were jeering too much to put it out till they got a few backhanders. The fire brigade arrived and remarked that it gave a whole new meaning to the term hot sex, ha ha.

Irish boys were Catholics but they also had sex appeal somehow — they were confident and had a humour and cheek I was quite unused to in the children at school. Confidence and scrappiness seemed to be the qualities that attracted me most in a boy.

Socials were held at the Irish Club on Karangahape Road. The club consisted of a hall almost entirely bereft of decoration save for enlarged photos of Irish politicians, heroes and saints, green ribbons on the walls and a stage that had no shortage of performers. Choreographed along the same lines as New Zealand socials, the three important rules of Irish céilís were:

(1) Boys lined up against one wall, girls against the opposite wall.
(2) It was essential to undertake a complete geological and tactical survey of the dance hall situation including critique of dress, analysis of pimple situation and general testing of the atmosphere.
(3) You had to completely ignore any boy who showed a vestige of interest in you (unless it was Donal or Patrick).

It is a wonder the race has ever been able to reproduce itself. The fiddles would strike up a reel, and suddenly the posturing would cease and all hell would break loose. The boys came marching over to our side, grabbed the girls around the waist and led them blushing and twittering into one of the most charming set dances ever invented — the reel. Let's just say there was a lot of fancy footwork and partner changing involved in a reel, not the least of which was manipulating the situation and your friends to get the partner you wanted more often than your turn. The delicious part was the anticipation of waiting till the man of your dreams came back to you again. I loved the ritual of these old set dances, which in their way were very erotic. We stamped, reeled and tapped on the wooden dance floor to a live Irish band, usually composed of a few fiddles, an accordion, a piano, maybe a guitar and sometimes a double bass. The band, the priests and the parents all got roaring drunk and forgot to keep an eye on the children, which never happened with my parents who didn't drink more than socially. The boys would be out the back having conversations about the girls.

'Auch, no. She doesn't want to dance with you.'

'She does so. She's begging for it. I swear to God she'd let me kiss her or worse if I could only get her on her own.'

'She's not the type. She'd have you for breakfast before you even realised your tie was missing.'

'Jaesus, Mary and Joseph but envy's a terrible thing. Would you ever like to go and take a shit for yourself?'

In fact, the most licentious thing that went on was handholding and that was enough to satisfy me, who still didn't know what else was supposed to go on anyway. All I knew was that you never let a boy put his hand anywhere but on your waist. The Sisters of Mercy had said save it for marriage, so I saved it. We dressed in pleated skirts and twinsets and wore artificial shamrocks pinned to our cardigans.

There weren't only céilís, there were weekend trips away for dancing and music competitions, private parties, visits to country pubs (gasp), weddings and concerts. Caroline's family and extended family loved singing and taught me all the maudlin songs like 'The Black Velvet Band', 'I'll Take You Home Again, Kathleen' and 'If You Ever Go Across the Sea to Ireland'. The sadder the better. If I could get them all crying it was a sign of success. Sometimes I even wept myself. I stood up whenever I was asked to sing, and like a good girl performed to order, my long wavy dark hair tied up in a pony-tail with green ribbons, hazel eyes flashing. Irish days were happy days.

At 13 I exchanged the black uniform and brown strap of primary school for the blue uniform and black strap of secondary school. More Sisters of Mercy but the methods of humiliation were much more sophisticated and the strap was only ever used on your hands. This uniform had even more accessories to keep track of than its predecessor. There was a boater hat and blue tartan frock for summer, a royal blue serge pinafore and beret for winter, navy blue gloves, tie, lisle stockings, socks, cardigan for indoors, blazer for outdoors, indoor shoes, outdoor shoes, bloomers for gymnastics. The dresses were always too long because any dress your mother took up was too long full stop, and I perpetually misplaced or lost the accessories, usually on the bus. It was strictly against the rules to remove any article of clothing before you got home but I removed as much as I could on the bus and the rest in between the bus-stop and the house.

Underneath the uniforms were such titivations as suspender belts — white ones, as black ones were sinful. The boarders had their underwear controlled much more closely than the day girls like me. Bikini briefs, which had just come into fashion, were the height of depravity and until recently girls had been encouraged to undress and bathe in a light cotton robe so as not to be tempted by their bodies. After an outcry these requirements were eventually dropped but it remained mandatory to wear underpants to the waist. When the boarders were caught with bikini briefs in their drawers, so to speak, the offending items took a trip to the incinerator (hell) where they belonged, thank you very much. The tripe-coloured stockings were bulletproof and the bras designed to survive a nuclear holocaust. That any determined boy ever got past all this is one of the remaining unsolved scientific mysteries of our time.

The school itself was large and medium wealthy, with lots of new classrooms so only some rooms were dungeon-like, split levels of playgrounds, hockey fields, tennis courts, swimming pool and chapel. Once again the music school was the most beautiful part — in a separate house on the grounds that was a realm of culture, order and happiness. I loved being in there as somehow you became a human being, the nuns gave you tea and biscuits and you met extraordinary people and famous opera singers like Mina Foley, Malvina Major and Kiri Te Kanawa. Anyone in New Zealand with any talent had been taught by our Sister Mary Leo and they all came back in velvet dresses exuding Chanel No. 5 and minor constellation quality.

Unlike in the classroom, which held little interest for me, you actually learned something and made progress in the music house. Some people said that Sister Leo was a hard taskmaster but I couldn't think what they were talking about. I had been brought up by women who were strict and uncompromising so to me it wasn't behaviour out of the ordinary; in fact like the rampaging Sister Agnes, Sister Leo was just another fascinating character in my life. If any adult had asked my opinion on anything at all, I would have been shocked at the permissiveness of it. In those days you didn't have arguments with your elders — the answer was yes or no, it wasn't negotiable, they were in charge, we were afraid of them. It was like benign fascism — you weren't happy but you weren't necessarily unhappy either, and you were never in any doubt as to where you stood.

Terrible things happened, like our mothers still having children. As 14-year-olds we were dreadfully embarrassed by this depravity and evidence of our parents' sexuality. Only death could have released us from the shock of our mothers' late pregnancies — having a mother who was 'expecting' when you were 14 was worse than getting pregnant yourself.

It was like someone announcing that the house across the road was a whorehouse when you thought it was a bed and breakfast. It was as if our asking each other about sex had provoked this extreme reaction — you talked about it and suddenly someone got pregnant. As if that weren't enough to have to deal with, to add insult to injury, every so often the nuns would decide to add to the misinformation about boys and sex by passing around sexual manifestos and question-naires. The questionnaires asked extraordinary things like:

When you dance with a boy are the lights low?
Why is there such poor lighting in coffee bars?
What has black eye makeup got to do with the holy sacrament of marriage?

They seemed to be obsessed with darkness, seeing it as being the crux of the problem of loose behaviour. My friends and I and our mothers were paralytic over these absurd question-naires. Masturbation was never mentioned because everyone knew that it, like lesbianism, didn't exist. Friends lulled me into a false sense of security by saying it was absolute nonsense that it affected your eyesight. But then I found an article in the *New Zealand Herald* that said research had shown that in fact temporary blindness may result from haemorrhages caused by ruptures in the eye's blood vessels during sudden spikes in blood pressure associated with orgasms. (Had to have a long discussion to find out what an orgasm was.) Among the tragic case studies were a gentleman who had sudden blurred vision in his left eye 'while his partner was performing a variant of heterosexual intercourse on him' and a gentleman who lost right-eye vision 'while engaging in particularly rigorous autoerotic activity'.

I had been sent to this college because it had the best music school in New Zealand. Music and singing students were tolerated by the pupils and resented by the nuns for our preferential treatment in being allowed out of class to attend lessons. God forbid that you should stand out. Never mind tall poppies — anyone who was not as humble as ground-cover was a thorn in the side of Jesus.

Although I was a high achiever in this narrow area I was devoid of ambition, admiring it in other people but being unable to relate to it personally. Singing in harmony was one of the great joys and a few of us were the leads in Sister Leo's famous choir. For swept-up performances the entire choir wore cornflower-blue pleated frocks, creating a sea of shim-mering, polyester virgins.

Then the Beatles performed in Auckland, which caused a revolution. They played the sort of innocuous, melodic music that alienated no one and they seemed such nice boys. Even the parents were into this music, getting our live-in house-keeper (an unmarried mother) who was a super dancer to teach them how to shake, rattle and roll. The boarders were not permitted to go to the concert at the town hall, so a few day girls helped them tie sheets together during study time, and opened the windows of their bedrooms that night. At the concert was an ocean of hysterical, screaming, sobbing girls who fainted, burst blood vessels in their throats and ripped their hair out. My friends and I were faintly disparaging of the crowd behaviour as we considered ourselves too intelligent for such rabid displays of emotion. Up front on the stage was a bunch of blokes in naff suits that nobody could hear, laughing their heads off. Two of the boarders who had masterminded the great escape were expelled as the ringleaders and for once my name didn't come up.

School had never had anything to recommend it and secondary convent was no exception. The tedium of Latin, geography and algebra classes was relieved only by the polish-ing of such skills as teacher torturing, lying and inventing new hairdos. Hairdos could be tricky though because the nuns used them to great effect in public humiliation exercises. What other adults hadn't taught me in the art of emotional blackmail, the nuns willingly did.

I should have learned to type but it was considered socially and intellectually below par. So I learned really useful things like the gross national banana output of Outer Mongolia and how to conjugate verbs in Latin for future use in the sluice rooms of Greenlane Hospital. Needless to say, my thinking was way ahead of my time in ascertaining the futility of learning things you didn't want to know. I smilingly danced into traps set by the nuns, not even realising after the event what my crime had actually been.

One of these episodes revolved around an essay the fourth-formers were set to write entitled My Ideal Day — the title in itself was a provocation to any normal teenager. I wrote a treasonous composition about what a normal 14-year-old girl should be doing on a stiflingly hot summer's day instead of inappropriately wasting away in a classroom. It involved studying only what impassioned you — like music, French and English — and chucking the rest, and studying only at sane times of the day, for example first thing in the morning or last thing in the afternoon. The whole middle part of the day was to be given up to more suitable pursuits like horse riding, going to the beach and sleeping in a hammock. There happen to be whole cultures that exist and educate exactly like this, but I didn't know that and apparently neither did the nuns. I can't remember if the mother was summoned or not but there was some sort of drama about this essay and my dodgy political orientation.

And then there was rugby. I had learned the correct sideline behaviour expected at rugby games from the enthusiastic mother who was only one little woman but had the mouth of 10. She planted herself firmly on the sideline wrapped in woolly hat and scarf, yelling, exhorting, waving at her sons. For Pete's sake, Mum, they would say, snuffling into their filthy football shirts, imploding with embarrassment.

Opposing teams would tremble if they knew they were scheduled to play St Peter's College. Dad stood on the other side of the field smiling shyly and making jokes. Even at 15 I knew that people who play rugby are 2.5 chromosomes away from Neanderthal and have the table manners of warthogs. But rugby was associated with boys, so you pretended to be madly interested in the fact that spotty adolescents the size of articulated trucks were chasing a small innocent ball around a sea of mud cleverly disguised as a field. Of course it was not a small innocent ball. It was a slimy, vindictive bomb that had to be destroyed at any cost.

My friends and I didn't make fools of ourselves because we were far too cool, but we did follow the teams around in a frenzy of barely suppressed oestrogen overdrive. Our testosterone-poisoned objects of desire never acknowledged our presence, salivating over the ball as if it held the meaning of the universe. Which of course it did. These rugby jocks weren't very interesting but at 15 interesting was not a quality I looked for in boys. I wore things like powder-blue bell-bottoms, pink fluffy jumpers and pale pink lipstick, and did my hair in two long ponytails.

Every so often the nuns of my college and the brothers of St Paul's or Sacred Heart would put on a joint dance. The boys smoked outside and drank beer out of big DB bottles and acted macho. The girls hung around inside supervised by the nuns and their fathers picked them up at midnight. Naturally I forbade my father to come in, insisting he park the car in the next block and STAY THERE till I was ready to leave. Of course there was no alcohol allowed but a boy called Willy and his mates flouted the law in a way I knew I could never get away with. Everyone was riddled with hormones looking for a meaningful exchange, so people got as loose as they could under the circumstances. The Beatles and the Rolling Stones were played on a record player with speakers attached, and sometimes there was a live band. My friends and I shook, did the swim and stomped in our pink A-line frocks. I always forgot about the nuns after about an hour, which was about the time I ended up on Willy's knee, pashing. This unspeakable looseness was duly noted and reported. She's just highly strung, pleaded the mother, hands neatly folded in lap in hard chair in Mother Jerome's office the next day.

This was the age when you began climbing out the bedroom window to see boys and when I climbed back in many hours later the mother was waiting with a wooden spoon. I was supposed to faint with fright at the sight of this weapon but she had to give up her primitive form of discipline at this stage because my siblings and I could now hold her at arm's length. I wasn't a delinquent only because I was held in such tight rein and was far too terrified of pregnancy to actually sleep with boys. In 1964 to get pregnant was to have your life ruined. Shop-soiled, second-hand goods. Your entire extended family was brought into disrepute, you yourself would probably go to hell or worse, but far more serious than any of these, *You Could Kiss Goodbye to Ever Getting a Husband*.

I didn't wag school either. It would never have entered my head. I only got into trouble when I opened my mouth, my brain congenitally lacking the area concerned with diplomacy, tact and word games. I said exactly what I thought, considering tact a form of dishonesty.

Sister Cecilia the form mistress was a nasty piece of work who took pleasure in baiting and thwarting me. Her vitriolic tongue was not tempered by either personality or humour and she was a specialist in posing unanswerable questions then humiliating you because you couldn't answer them. On my reports she wrote 'Peta is inattentive and heedless at school', which loosely translated meant: Peta has not been brought to heel yet but if it's got anything to do with me, I will deliver her to you broken. One bright day I turned up in Sister Cecilia's class in a new hairdo that involved a lot of backcombing of my long, wavy hair and a frightening array of pins and clips. She stood me up in class so that she could explain to the hushed Form 4Ac2 students why I was a perfect example of a slattern on the road to you know where.

'Peta Mathias, I require an explanation for the growth sticking out of your head.'

'It's not a growth, Sister, it's a hairdo.'

'Is it being smart you are now, madam?'

'No, Sister.'

'What are you then, may I be so bold as to ask?'

'I don't know, Sister.'

'You don't know. So you're not only ridiculous with your growth but you're stupid. What are you, Peta Mathias?'

'Ridiculous and stupid, Sister.'

'What are you?'

'Ridiculous and stupid.'

The pinched face reddened against the starchy white wimple, the black arm pointed to the door, the viper tongue intoned, 'Peta Mathias, remove yourself from this room, then remove that lump and those foreign objects from your head.'

They will all be sorry, I promised myself, when they find out who I really am, and then they can burn.

Although the academic standards were high, every bit of creativity and individuality was beaten out of us girls by brain-washing techniques such as multiple-choice questionnaires, Christian doctrine classes and ballroom dancing. In multiple-choice questionnaires you were asked about things you had never heard of in your life and the answer was always 'the Great Lakes of Canada'. In Christian doctrine class you explored the intricacies of the Holy Trinity. I was the only one in the class who actually did well in this esoteric subject, having no trouble whatever in grasping the concept of a triple personality. I felt I'd been leading a double life since I was five and was fascinated by the idea of pulling off a triple one.

Still mesmerised by the church and its dramatic ostentation,

I always looked forward to the only worthwhile ritual Catholics ever invented — the retreat. Carmelite retreats saved the mother from committing mass murder and me from losing my mind. Every time the mother returned to the seven other members of her family after a retreat she said, 'From now on I'm going to be a perfect mother and I'll never rouse again.' We all smiled. After every retreat I was determined to be a better person and not be a trial to my parents. They smiled.

The Carmelite nuns were aesthetes and intellectuals, worlds apart from the Sisters of Mercy and their stressful lives. It took me a while to realise why the nuns I had grown up with were so acid and vindictive. Oh, there were the obvious things like long hours, no pay, no thanks, no freedom, no rights and little fun; but these poor women, some of whom were nothing but girls, had been removed from their families to the other side of the world, maybe never to see their loved ones again. My Uncle Pat said he remembered large groups of 16-year-old novices on the boat coming out to Australia, weeping and weeping inconsolably. They had to wear long heavy garments in nauseating heat, give up brilliant careers some of them and subject themselves to the control of priests who used them as free housekeepers and cooks (and God knows what else) while they themselves socialised, drank and went to all the dances.

Conversely the Carmelites, naively serene, calm and myst-erious, were never seen outside their beautiful convent, where they led lives of contemplation and prayer. They wore brown habits, cream capes and brown sandals, a uniform that hadn't changed in four centuries. The retreat house was palatial, the food great and the library engrossing. They made porridge exactly the way the father did — piping hot and covered in thick North Island cream and soft brown sugar. You ate the top layer of porridge then poured more cream and sugar on and finished it off. The smells from their kitchens blossomed with melting cheese, roast lamb and mint jelly, freshly shelled peas from their gardens and caramel sauce to go with apple roly-poly. In the afternoons we drank tea and ate melting moments stuck together with lemon icing and butterfly cakes stuffed with whipped cream. Before retiring there was hot chocolate.

The Carmelites turned me on to the Abbé Teilhard de Chardin and the 'terrific three': Socrates, Plato and Aristotle (in simplified form). Far from being accused of loose thinking and loose living I was encouraged to argue, to rationalise, to form ideas. Far from being punished for being outspoken, I found myself spending hours talking and walking in the ordered gardens with these admirable creatures. I had never read anything like this before, found it truly mind-blowing and decided to add it to my list of suitable subjects for young women to study at school — *thinking*. They also taught me to meditate — no mean feat for someone whose longest time sitting still without getting bedsores occurred at mealtimes.

I hated leaving to go back to the real world and this was when it entered my head that there was an alternative career for me aside from marriage — I would become a Carmelite nun. It turned out sainthood was not my vocation, however, and the debutante ball was coming up. I asked a boy I was keen on to escort me. I was five foot four and danced beautifully; he was six foot four with 30 left feet. My friends said 'Who cares about the height difference when you're lying down?' and we collapsed into a heap of giggles on the tennis court. The mother made me a white silk organza ball gown embossed with tiny daisies. She lined the dress with the palest pink satin to give it depth and made silk flowers studded with diamantes sewn all around the hem. I begged her to lower the modest neckline but she refused. My long hair was rolled into huge petals, silk flowers were stuck in it and the whole story was topped off with elbow-length white kid gloves and silver satin pumps.

The Catholic debutante ball's ostensible purpose was to

present young maidens to society. We were introduced to the market by the Archbishop of Auckland in the pomp and ceremony of the town hall. This wonderful old room of gilded angels, embossed rosettes, sweeping staircases and red carpet with fleurs-de-lys welcomed 80 girls all in white and 80 boys all in black with bow ties. We snow maidens were all led the length of the town hall on the arms of our adoring fathers. When I waltzed with my partner my eyes reached his chest and he had a Catholic sense of rhythm — it felt great but it didn't work.

Chapter three

tipperary

Come in the evenings
Come in the morning
Come when you're looked for
Or come without warning.
A thousand welcomes you'll find here before you
And the oftener you come
The more we'll adore you.

When I arrived at the Thurles (pronounced Tur-less) train station there were approximately zero people waiting to meet me so I hung around for a while, then headed for the phone booth. There was no reply at cousin Tricia's, which was good news. Idly I looked around as the phone rang in my ear and caught the eye of a young woman smiling at me from over the fence. She had her finger crooked and was beckoning me. Tricia and I had never asked each other what we looked like but in the confidence that belonging to the same family instils, I had assumed she would resemble my aunts or cousins. In my head I saw her as a straight but friendly middle-aged farmer in sensible shoes, which was why it was so improbable that this girl over the fence could belong to me.

'Are you Tricia?' I stared.

'Yes I am.' She smiled. 'You must be Peta — ye look like Margaret. Will ye look at the hair on ye.'

'Hi. You look like a combination of Margaret and Mary and I thought you had forgotten me.'

'Ah sure, I'm late for everything . . . 'tis a miracle I got here so early . . . I'm in the hay, you know. We have to rush back and turn the hay while the sun is still shining.'

The sun was certainly shining and continued to do so for the next two weeks, an extraordinary event the national newspapers and television called a heatwave. I started laughing the minute I arrived in Tipperary and didn't find reason to stop the whole of my stay there.

We smiled, hugged, lugged things into the boot of her pale

blue Mercedes covered in dust and mud. There she was — a little creature of about 34 in a black singlet, filthy tracksuit pants and flip-flops with waist-length brown hair loosely gathered into a scrunchie halfway down. The most striking feature about her pixie-like suntanned face was the large piercing green eyes, very intense and intelligent. She talked nonstop out of her little rosebud mouth all the way back to her farm, about which members of my family she had already met, the weather, the hay and Australia. It took her days to accept that I actually came from New Zealand and she never got a handle on my name. I became Pip or P, stayed that way, and as far as the rest of the county was concerned that was my name. And as they don't say their h's my surname became Matias.

We flew through the pretty market town of Thurles, flat rich farmland, green countryside and narrow country roads to the farm in Clogher, Clonoulty. The way was paved with stone walls, beech, elm, ash trees and hedges that seemed to be made up of anything that was growing — berry bushes, brambles, hedging. The car passed between two short pillars and swept up the drive to the house — a large 300-year-old two-storeyed stone building with little sash windows peeking out of the ivy and pink roses that covered it. A murderously large lawn with more rose bushes and big old apple trees encircled it front and left and off to the right were the farm buildings: hay barns, milking sheds with riding gear hanging everywhere and hen and pet lamb accommodation. One of the outhouses was an old kitchen where Tricia's grandmother used to cook for the farm workers because she wouldn't let them in the house.

As soon as she got out of the car Trish was mobbed by a wildly enthusiastic gaggle of admirers — the dogs Rufus and Scout, the lamb Bubba, the cat Charles and assorted chooks and ducks. She returned this welcome as if she hadn't seen them for three weeks, talking to them all as if they were people. Bubba was the most demonstrative and appeared the most able of all of them to communicate and express affection. He was like a little child, followed her everywhere, put his head through the window and licked my laptop as I wrote and always seemed to be talking and asking questions. Huge and strong at three months old, he had only ever known Tricia as his mother. Her giving him milk with a bottle and teat resembled a wrestling match and sounded like a drain being vacuum cleaned. Bubba had no idea he was a sheep, alternately trying to mount the dogs, grazing with the horses when he could get into their paddocks and wandering around the kitchen exploring. The dogs could make him do anything; if they said go out on the road and make a nuisance of yourself, he would do it, if they said Pip's lying on that blanket over there, he would come and lie almost on top of me in his desire for company.

Tricia cast an eye over my city getup and said, 'Do ye have any daecent work clothes on you, Pip? I'm off to the hay and you can come with me if you like.'

'Um, I have a T-shirt and leggings for fast walking. I'll be ready in one minute.'

'Bubba,' she yelled, throwing her arms around his neck, 'get offa her, ye big stupid wolfhound. What are ye? You're a wolfhound. What are ye?'

I'm a person who believes it is important to be appropriately dressed for special occasions and I didn't want to be the laughing stock of Clonoulty. I had no idea what turning the hay meant but followed the procession of animals across one field into another. Honey-coloured cut hay was lying all over the ground and we leapt into the tractor with seating for one, we and the dogs fighting for space for the next few hours of bumping and grinding. The tines on the hay bob slowly turned the cut hay so that it could dry out, releasing a delicious sweet essence so you wanted to get down and lie in its softness. When we managed to chuck the dogs out, Tricia would yell 'Rabbit!' and they dashed wildly into the nearest fence yelping and barking with canine/hunter conviction.

Turning the hay had to be done twice a day for three days, a mind-numbingly monotonous job and I was grateful it wasn't the good old days when they did it by hand with a hay pike.

The cigarette in her lips and the noise of the tractor did nothing to distract Tricia and me from catching up on a lifetime of not knowing each other. I found out that she owned and ran the farm, originally bought by her grandparents and which she inherited from her parents. Her mother was Agnes Long, my mother's cousin. She had 20 to 40 dry heifers depending on the season and seven horses she used for hunting and breeding. Her boyfriend Seamus, who lived there also and ran it with her, had a garage at nearby Ballagh, a village with all the necessities of life — three pubs, a grocer and a butcher.

> Ballagh is a village without church nor steeple
> And in every door there stands a whore
> To mock the deacent people.

At seven o'clock on the first evening Seamus came into the meadow to meet us. He had on jeans, a white shirt and a great smile behind his rimless glasses and trimmed dark red beard. His friends said he had not changed a day since they'd met him, always relaxed and youthful looking — a quiet, gentle man, thoughtful and tolerant. He immediately set to fixing the tines that had slipped out of their position. At the sight of mechanical activity I immediately lost interest and trailed my way back through the meadows to the house to unpack.

Huge discipline had gone into packing my one suitcase. It is like a hairdo to me now. I can put it together and take it apart in a flash and always know where everything is. Unlike all my hair decorations which I have kept for 20 years, I am now ruthless about discarding used research, sending books and shoes I don't need back to New Zealand, and hanging my clothes in a hot shower to steam iron them. When Random

House make me rich, my whole travelling wardrobe will be Issy Miyake Pleats Please, which dry in a second, take up no space, don't need ironing and always look stunning. You would think a normal person wouldn't wear Issy Miyake on a farm and to the local pub full of farmers, threshers and mechanics but I was complimented on my colourful, no-care clothes, especially by young girls who observed, hawk eyed, everything I wore. The night I wore feathers in my hair to the local swept-up restaurant gave cause for great philosophical discussion on the merits or demerits of expressing oneself. But back to Tricia's house.

The front vestibule as you walked in the door had an antique stand wearing coats and hats, shamrocks and plants in pots and a fine old weather barometer by which Tricia swore. When she was 'in the hay' she studied this instrument almost hourly because the worst thing that could happen was for it to rain on your nicely drying hay and in early July, as it was, the weather couldn't be trusted. In fact an Irish summer is an entirely capricious set-up — it can change not only from day to day but from hour to hour.

On the right side of the entrance was the parlour, the prettiest room in the house and never used of course, the door always shut. Dark polished floors, brocade-covered furniture, ornate antique French rosewood dressers full of family china, a gold-framed mirror over the marble fireplace, a little walnut writing desk, shiny mahogany dining table and horsy, animally paintings on the walls. The pale lemon striped wallpaper lightened the room but because there were so many valuable things in it, the heavy cream curtains with rose-coloured pattern were always drawn.

On the left the real house began with the comfortable flagstoned living room where Seamus watched TV, which after I got to know him better I turned down as I walked through and he turned up as I walked out. Family photos decorated the mantelpiece above the fireplace, a piano hid in a dark corner with the vacuum cleaner, armchairs had bright yellow cushions on them and the couch was covered with a cable-knit blanket. This was a dim room with a low ceiling, one small window framed by a tasselled blind and green Marie-Antoinette print curtains and more horsy pictures on the walls. The best part of it was two exquisite small doors with ovals and rays engraved on them, one of which led nowhere and the other to Tricia's office, a little room stuffed to overflowing with books, papers, family photos, horse certificates, a crucifix, statue of the Virgin and two antique desks. Walking out of this room you came to the bathroom on the left and the large kitchen ahead and up a step. Everywhere in the house were vases of multicoloured flowers — on the floor, in cubby-holes, in the kitchen, on the landings, in the bathroom.

The kitchen was a real farmhouse kitchen and the centre of the home, where everything happened, everyone gathered, animals tirelessly tried to enter, food got cooked, late-night sessions were had and Charles the cat reigned. He only left the kitchen when the other animals had been put out to bed. This room held the heart of the place as it had done for generations in its continuing warmth and affection by an oil-fuelled Aga that never went out, night or day, winter or summer. In the old days if you moved house you took the glowing embers from the chimney of the previous house with you to the next, thus giving continuity and love to the new house. Tricia's was kept at mark 2 and was always in action for one reason or another. The top oven was very hot and the bottom one just warm, neither of which was suitable for cake making I was to find out. The two large round elements on top of the stove were covered by heavy padded stainless steel lids that you lifted up by handles when you wanted to cook. The left one was very hot, the right one warm and all other areas on the large stove-top had varying degrees of warmth to house a teapot, a huge kettle for washing-up water and dinners being kept warm.

My books *Fête Accomplie* and *Salut!* were in the bookshelf above the TV, along with all the other cooking books Tricia had never read: classics like *Farmhouse Cooking*, *Little French Dinners* and an original 1888 edition of *Mrs Reeve's Cookery and Housekeeping.* The 60cm-thick walls of stone and mortar had been plastered and the tops of them bordered with a flower pattern. The walls were covered in paintings, one of which was Christ with the bleeding open heart, and kitchen implements and across one side of the room above the Aga was a washing line. Tricia's snowy white knickers and bras hung on horses' bits and meat hooks over the stove. Every so often I whipped them off because I couldn't bear the cooking fumes going into them any longer. Her riding hat was slung over the cooking utensils in an earthenware jug. Along one side of the kitchen was a long table with a radio and tray of breakfast condiments and mugs on it, and in the centre of the room another table covered in a green check cloth on which Charles sat. On either side of the room were large cabinets, or presses as they called them, full of linen and crockery.

Upstairs were three bedrooms, but as Tricia had so many guests there was also a bed on the landing and one in the antechamber to her and Seamus's large bedroom. When she redid the upstairs of the house and reinforced it, Tricia discovered the huge thick walls were made of a weird mixture of turf, mortar, horses' hair, straw, clay, animal blood and general scraps. The landing had a little alcove with a statue of the Virgin and a perpetual lamp. She had decorated the bedrooms in the same style as the rest of the house — generous designer curtains, flowery wallpaper with contrasting borders, antique furniture, cushions, dolls, ornaments, plump duvets on double beds covered in pretty bed linen.

It was in the kitchen and front bedroom that I wrote this book, looking out onto the fields through the white-shuttered little windows with rosebuds peeking in. On a fine day the laundry was dried on the line over the kitchen garden, giving it the smell of herbs and grass and pure country air. It was a house overflowing with her personality and sense of home and comfort. So imbued was the house with Tricia's charisma that when she went away to a funeral for a few days it seemed as if she had taken the soul of the house with her like wind out of a tunnel. Bubba bleated plaintively, the dust gathered and I found myself keeping the kitchen very tidy just like she did. But when I came downstairs in the morning, no one was standing there with their hands on their hips saying, 'Well! Hello there!'

On my first evening I was taken out for dinner by Tricia and her friends Theresa and Marie to the Anner Hotel in Thurles. Tricia had emerged from the shower transformed by a blue denim dress on her cute little figure, blindingly white platform sandshoes and clean, shining hair falling in thick waves to her waist. She had on a little makeup which made you very aware of her piercing green eyes and how pretty she was with her high cheekbones. She smoked continuously, never stopped talking and considered God didn't give her enough hours in the day. In the car I was made privy to the mysterious world of rural problems such as the hay and the stress of choosing the right day to cut it; cows breaking into Theresa's garden, a crime for which she could think of no punishment vicious enough; and how Marie was going to keep her lads (children of either sex) occupied in the holidays.

In rural Ireland you get invited to everything that's going as you come across people in your day; the day I arrived I was invited to a wedding and a funeral and was disappointed by the end of the day that a christening hadn't come up. Dinner was three kinds of potato — mashed, creamed and chipped — all way beyond their first blush of youth, and cold overcooked fatty chops. We moved on to Monk O'Gorman's pub for their Wednesday night session and enjoyed the company of a gazillion sweating, elated people all squeezed into two rooms. And they kept pouring in all night. We ordered our drinks and listened to the session, which was going great guns. Musicians come from all over Ireland to play in this pub and there's even a CD of their sessions called *At the Monks*.

A smiling dark-haired man left the group of musicians, came up to me and said, 'You're the New Zealand woman writing a book about Ireland, aren't you?'

'I am, unless there's two of us, in which case I hope their publisher isn't Random House.'

'I met you at the céilí in Dublin — you had just come home to Ireland and we talked about the bodhrán.'

'Oh, yes, I do remember. You had your boy with you who also played it. Is he here tonight?'

'Here he is. Now I think if you want to understand the bodhrán you have to play it. It's time you learned. Here you are in Tipperary and you're still an onlooker.'

I sat up very straight on my stool. 'I didn't think you would let me. I didn't dare ask but I'd love to.'

'Okay. Are you ready now, Peta?'

'Ready.'

He showed me how to hold the cross piece at the back in my left hand, resting the rim of the drum against my left shoulder and on my left leg. Then he put the stick or 'tipper' in my right hand and instructed me to hold it like a ballpoint pen but in the middle. Then you turn your wrist inwards and strike to the beat of the tune. It's not very hard — you just have to listen to the rhythm and keep your wrist loose. Once I had more or less got it, he showed me how to place my left hand against the back skin of the drum, lifting it on and off at intervals to alter the tone. It was thrilling to be part of the session if only on the periphery and I thought one day I might get up the courage to sing.

There are two theories on the origins of the bodhrán. The first is the 'someone took the kitchen sieve and played it' theory, in which the ancient skin tray used for winnowing (separating chaf from grain) could also be used as a sieve through the simple process of punching holes in the skin. Was it a drum that became a work instrument or the other way around?

The second theory is that it came with foreigners via the Roman Empire or Arabian traders. This one appeals to me because you see similar drums in many other cultures, especially Arab, Chinese, Russian and American Indian. It seems believable that ancient wanderers handed the drum from race to race, culture to culture. According to the respected bodhrán maker Malachy Kearns, who is based in Connemara, two very good players in Ireland are Ringo McDonagh and Tommy Hayes. They'd be the boys to hang out with.

In the meantime some sexy Spanish students had taken over the session, singing their songs and doing their ardent, hot-blooded dancing. We suffered the longwinded attentions of a local bachelor who interminably asked us all if we were married and didn't we want to go off with him and did we know we were the most gorgeous, fair fresh women he had ever seen. We got out of there at 2am. Pub closing time in Ireland is 11.30pm and we were by no means the last to leave.

The following evening Tricia came in from the meadow covered in hay, flung back her long hair, took a good suck on her fag and said, 'Pip, I'm taking ye to Jim o' the Mills tonight.'

'What about taking me dancing?'

'Wha?'

'Dancing.'

'Be Jaesus no. My legs weren't graced with steps but ye'll get a real country session at Jim o' the Mills. Quit wit your bawlin' and squalin', Bubba.'

'I'm still tired from last night. I have to have an early night tonight, Tricia — four hours' sleep isn't enough.'

'An early night? Sure the real craic doesn't start till 1am. Be ready at 10.30 so. We'll have a drink at Bridgie and Jim's pub up the road, then move on to Jim's. The music will keep ye awake.'

My other cousin Jim Mulhall, Tricia's brother, and his wife Bridgie had Mulhall's pub in Clonoulty. Recently renovated, this pub became like a second home to me as time went by, a home where I could gas with family, see Tricia's friends who became my own and always feel welcome. Seamus was already there so we sat with a group of Tricia's friends who laughed all the time and swore we were the spitting image altogether of each other. Jim and Bridgie were a wonderful, generously proportioned young couple who worked very hard in their new pub — he friendly and generous but strict enough to make you not wish to cross him, and a good singer I found out; she gentle with a Madonna-like face and soft voice. They had two teenage daughters, one sweet and earnest like her mother, the other an extrovert with the most extraordinary head of long, naturally many-hued red hair, hanging thick like velvet curtains to her waist.

Time and glasses of burnt barley went by, and just as we were leaving Seamus quietly asked me if I'd like a whiskey before they closed.

'No thanks, Seamus, I'm fine and I've still got my Guinness to finish.'

'Go on wit you.'

'No thanks. My body is a temple.' Roars of laughter.

'What kind do you want?'

'Stop already.'

'Jameson's? Right you are.'

Seamus couldn't be talked into coming with us because he knew Tricia would be out till all hours, no matter what she said. We jumped in the comfy solid Merc in which I felt I could come to no harm and drove for half an hour along unlit country roads, turned off at Drumbane and stopped on the side of the road in pitch darkness in what appeared to be the middle of nowhere but was Ballyboy. This was a family farmhouse that had a one-day-a-week licence to sell liquor. Every Thursday night of the year, come hell or high water, there was a session there. It was called Jim o' the Mills because it was Jim Ryan's house and there was a working mill on the property until recently. There had been sessions in this old house as long as anyone could remember — seven generations in fact. Before Jim it was his uncle.

There used to be establishments called síbíns (pronounced shee-been), pubs without a licence, very few of which still exist, but this was different. The downstairs was cleared out and one small whitewashed flagstoned room was for singing and music, the next one was for talking, and the third, over-crowded one was the bar. The window frames and stairway were painted red, old photos and prayers in Irish graced the mantelpiece and dresser full of crockery and there was a large fireplace with a peat fire on the floor of it. When we arrived at 1am people of all ages sat chatting on hard-backed chairs around the room and up the stairs.

There were three fiddlers, one of whom was a slight man in grubby farm clothes and big boots with dishevelled curly hair — this was Jim. I got my Jameson's and sat halfway up the stairs. Quietly a man began singing 'Tipperary So Far Away' by Sean Tracy, either looking at the floor or with his eyes closed, then someone else sang 'Where the Mulcair River Flows' by Ryan Malachy and 'Slievenamon', weathered hands on knees, head thrown back and eyes closed. This man had a rich, colourful voice with lots of depth and he sang in the old way with what they call ornamentation, going in and around the notes rather than singing them straight. Ornamentation was originally done in Gaelic songs, giving the movement between main notes a logic and inevitability that it would not otherwise have: it smooths the musical texture in a very subtle way. Also it allows the singer to express their personality and means you hardly ever hear the same song sung the same way, which keeps things varied. His name was Billy, he was a specialist in Tipperary songs and we were to have the pleasure of many more from him that night and on subsequent visits.

Some of his songs were very long (they can go up to 30 verses or more), harking back to an era when time was more plentiful and memories longer. These songs are not intellectual — they come directly from life, springing uncensored from the soul of the people, and from certain singers you really get that feeling of warmth and spirit.

Alone all alone by the wave-washed strand,
All alone in a crowded hall.
The hall it is gay and the waves they are grand
But my heart is not here at all.

It flies far away by the night and by day
To the times and the joys that are gone.
And I never will forget the sweet maiden that I met
In the valley near Slievenamon.
— 'Slievenamon' by Charles Kickham, 1828

Sheila, an older woman dressed nicely in a suit and polished shoes, was asked to sing and she gave beautiful, heart-rending renditions of 'It was Only a Bunch of Violets' and 'Down by the Sally Gardens' in a high voice with lots of sliding up to the note. All through the singing, people quietly muttered 'lovely' or 'tis grand' to encourage the singer and the room often joined in for the chorus or last line of the verse. Sheila stopped in the middle of her song because the people singing the chorus with her were singing a different version, distracting her. When they ceased, she started up again. There is a tendency in traditional Irish singing to alter the material by the process of oral transmission, or vary the melody in successive verses. This is considered acceptable — even essential — in the tradition because even though it's an old culture they are open to change and innovation within it, which is probably why it is still so vibrant today. They allow it to breathe — the 'commodious vicus of recirculation' as Joyce called it. I also quite often heard tunes with two different sets of lyrics and vice-versa.

It seemed the people there were talking to one another through song and this was the closest I had come so far to the real thing — not a tourist in sight and untrained people singing in the real old, peasant way, voices quite different from modern ones. People also sang some sean-nós, an old-style complex form of unaccompanied Gaelic singing derived from élite mediaeval bardic poetry, which you don't hear often because it's fiendishly difficult. I was too transfixed to move so Tricia kept me supplied with whiskey passed up the stairs from hand to hand.

Needless to say, not everyone was there for the session — lots were there to drink and be rowdy so periodically someone would shout, 'Will yes shut the feck up out there!', to which no one paid the slightest attention. I got talking to a priest from America who had grown up in the region and was back visiting — he met people he hadn't seen for 40 years that night.

'Where are you from then and how long are you home for?' he asked.

'New Zealand.'

'Do you know, when I visited Jim's a few years ago there was a woman from New Zealand here. She had long blonde hair and a very fine voice. She was from Auckland. Beautiful voice.'

'She didn't by any chance have a harp with her did she?'

'No, no. No harp. Her name was Cathy Harrop. Do you know her at all?'

'I went to school with her — we had the same singing teacher.'

'Will you look at that now!' And the whole room had to be told the story.

This was when he asked me to sing and I thought, it's now or never, so I sang a Piaf song in French, thinking they would throw me out for not being staunch but they were very appreciative and begged me to sing a few more. Irish people love their own music with a very emotional intensity but they are also open to 'foreigners' contributing. They just love music, no matter where it's from, and like the rest of the world they have a special place in their hearts for Piaf songs. Even the diehards at the bar were moved to emigrate briefly and listen. I sang an old Irish song called 'Love is Teasing' and they all joined in — I felt I had been baptised.

Tricia was very happy I had turned out to have some talent and I was rewarded with another whiskey. She then sang 'Black is the Colour of My True Love's Hair'. I had no idea she could sing but there she was with her fierce, deep, strong voice, her shyness finally being overcome at 2.45am. People like to be invited to sing if they lack confidence and if you don't think to ask they may never sing and it would be a loss to the evening.

Billy told us the story of an old couple lying in bed together one night. They had never got along very well if you know what I mean and she asked him, 'If you woke up in the morning and found me dead, what would you put on my gravestone?' He thought for a while then said, 'Here lies my beloved wife — cold as ever.' After a while he asked her the same question to which, after thought, she replied, 'Here lies my beloved husband — stiff at last.'

Jim o' the Mills was prevailed upon to sing 'The Wild Reparee' and it was then, as I watched him and listened to his fine, poetic voice full of subtlety, that I saw what intelligent, beautiful eyes he had. Listening to him was a pleasure because he took his time and had a lovely country accent. He had huge knowledge of the history, both local and general, of Irish music. A gentle, whimsical man, I couldn't imagine him ever raising his voice and no matter how rowdy the drinkers' end got he was always polite with them. One night I was there and a drunk trying to do a jig fell into the fireplace. Jim just gently helped him out and ushered him outside. The trouble with falling into the fireplace was that there were people on stools right inside it and they ended up wearing their Guinness and screaming with laughter. When the Irish have an accident, they don't get angry — they laugh.

The pace of a house session is quite different to a pub one — it's much slower, more intermittent, chilled out and low key. At 3.30am Jim asked me if I'd like a daecent cup of tae. The Irish drink tea all the time — with their dinner, at a party, in the heat out in the field, in bed, when they're hot, when they're cold, when they're happy, when they're sad. Quarter of an hour later a sister-in-law emerged from the kitchen with two plates of freshly made ham sandwiches cut in triangles and pots of steaming tae. These were passed around to the grateful faithful. Jim looked at mine, said, 'Sure, Pip, that tae's too weak to travel altogether. I'll get you another one.' In France they have the same tradition of feeding people at the hind end of a party but with onion soup. They sang patriotic songs like 'The Bold Fenian Men', 'The Green Fields of France', 'A Nation Once Again', betrayal songs like 'I Know My Love', 'A Bunch of Thyme', and emigration songs like 'The Shores of Amerikay' and 'Mary from Dungloe'. Most of the sad emigration songs related to America:

Oh, then fare thee well sweet Donegal,
The roses and Gweedore.
I'm crossing the main ocean
Where the foaming billows roar.
It breaks my heart from you to part
Where I spent many happy days.
Farewell to kind relations.
I am bound for Amerikay.

I wish I was in sweet Dungloe
And seated on the grass

And by my side a bottle of wine
And on my knee a lass.
I'd call for liquor of the best
And I'd pay before I'd go.
I'd roll my Mary in my arms
In the town of sweet Dungloe.

This idea of a journey is a recurring theme in the history of Irish music and the journey is often perceived as exile, even though the leaving meant an improvement in life. And the songs of leaving always lament in deep emotional terms the love of landscape and describe the hills and valleys of the home. There is actually a word for it, dinnseanchas, or the lore of place names, which also harks back to the ancient practice of writing poems and songs in praise of place. Aos dána (meaning Ireland's treasures) was a term encompassing all the travelling musicians, poets and storytellers who turned up at feasts, celebrations and courts of the constantly warring Gaelic and Celtic chieftains. They wandered freely across bogs, mountains, forests and islands telling stories, singing, playing the harp and pipes, reciting satirical poetry and relaying scandal from court to court. The Celtic monks wrote with jewel-like perception of weather, bird-song and plants. Seamus Heaney is a dinnseanchas who writes about Ireland not as a geograph-ical place but a 'country of the mind'. It is easier to leave the geographical country than the interior landscape and many Irish 'exiles' never did; also the exile is an internal one: the feeling that for historical reasons the Irish person is a stranger in his own land and longing to 'come back' is the theme of many songs. When a piper is playing a port na bPucai or slow air, the loneliness, heart memory and belief that rocks, rivers and mountains are inhabited by spirits and are part of you is very moving. They also sang plaxys, which are songs or tunes written in honour of someone.

We went up to Jim o' the Mills many times and it was the

night I heard a loud thumping on the ceiling from the bedroom above that I realised Jim's wife and five little daughters were 'sleeping' upstairs. His wife had heard the Gardai coming but so had we by that time, because they were upon us before we had breath to finish the poem in our mouths. I was shocked beyond words that the police would defile the hallowed ground upon which Jim stood, a farmhouse in the middle of nowhere, disturbing no one. People began to leave — it was only 2am — but my friends and I stood our ground like true heroines, the stuff of staunch Tipperary blood, the blood of the great kings of Munster. I decided there and then to approach the Pope for a dispensation and told one of the Gardai he ought to be ashamed of himself for disturbing a person's home in the middle of the night and what was he thinking of? Fortunately he was charming and easy going and fortunately I was a visitor or I would have found myself saying my poems to the jailhouse rock. Once they had left along with the other guests, we drew the chairs up to the hearth, locked the door and gave up the night to settling one another's genealogy. By 3.30am everyone agreed that:

(a) The Garda was a very nice young man from a good family;
(b) We were all related; and
(c) There's nothing like a ham sandwich to settle the stomach after a fright.

When the cock crowed to announce the soft light seeping over the mountains and the music lifted away into it with the remains of the peat smoke, we reluctantly left; after all this was a Thursday night and everyone had their farming and jobs to go to in a few hours' time.

Tricia was up again at 8am in the hay. The Irish don't appear to need sleep. Before she hit the meadow she put dinner on. Lunch was called dinner and was a large hot meal of spuds, carrots, meat, peas and gravy; dinner was called tea which was a sandwich or salad with ham. The potatoes were boiled in their skins and served in a big bowl on the table. Everyone had a side plate on which they peeled their potatoes, which then went on the dinner plate to be topped with half a pound of good Tipperary butter.

Tricia put dinner on a slow part of the Aga in the morning so it would be ready for Seamus and anyone else who wandered in. When I asked her why she was making a big cooked meal in this heat she said, 'Ah, you're fierce innocent, Pip. Sure ye can't give your farmers rabbit food for lunch — they'd tink it was the starter.' At midday I was still throwing zzzs to the ceiling, as Tricia says, when I was awoken by a man's voice downstairs repeatedly yelling 'Hello! Hello!' which I obviously ignored. Ten minutes later he was still doing it, determined that whoever was upstairs was *going* to come down. In a fury I jumped out of bed, flew down the stairs in my black slip and wild hair and shrieked, 'ARE YOU HAPPY? I'M AWAKE NOW.' There before me stood a tall man and a gobsmacked teenager.

'Is Tricia here?' he asked quietly, mouth sort of gaping.

'Obviously *not*.'

'Okay, that's fine, that's fine now,' backing out the door. 'I'll come back later.'

I got dressed and settled myself at the kitchen table to write. It was now the fourth day of turning the hay and the tines of the machine had been turned inward for 'ranking' or drawing the hay up into rows of high walls for bailing. If it had rained at this point the hay would have to be dried out again. Hay fast dried in the hot sun with all the green and moisture gone is much better than hay that is soaked in rain and brown. Haymaking automatically means sunshine so everyone's happy because you don't get a lot of it in Ireland and it's a great cause for celebration.

It was a glorious day so I decided to sunbathe and read on

the lawn. Within half an hour I was covered in animals, specifically Bubba who head-butted, tried to mount and sat on me, and finally defecated little round balls in my personal space. Tricia bent over with laughter and told me I had to go up onto the roof 'otherwise they'll ate ye'. We both climbed through the bedroom window and stretched out up there on the roof of the bathroom. I called it the Riviera and so did everyone else from then on. Friends and neighbours like Majella and her four beautiful daughters often dropped in to have a sit and a yak up on the Riviera.

'By the way,' I told Trish, 'a man came to see you and I was asleep and I think I was short with him.'

'Who could that be, now? Was he tall?'

'Yes.'

'Did he have a dog-collar on?'

'How do I know? I was in no mood to study his apparel.'

'No! Ye didn't scream at poor Father Brenhan! That's the parish curate ye're after givin' out to. What did ye say to him, tell me again, sure you're a tirrible woman, what are ye?'

So I told her and she bellowed with laughter. Within a day the whole parish knew the story and thereafter whenever I answered the phone, no matter what time of the day it was, the caller always said, 'I haven't woken you up, have I, Pip? — I'm very sorry if I have.' Once a person in rural Ireland has met you, they know you, so when they phone they just start talking and you have to catch up on who they are as best you can.

That night I was determined to get some sleep and was reading on my bed at 11pm when Tricia threw herself into my room all tight jeans, skimpy white crotcheted top, makeup, hands on hips, look of horror.

'Well! Are ye ready so?'

'Ready for what? I'm in bed.'

'We're off to Jim and Bridgie's pub for a quick gas.'

'No thanks, Trish, I'm going to bed early tonight.'

'You're jokin' me.'

She ran down the stairs and I heard them coming in again at about 3am after the Gardai had shown them the door, an action she was quite indignant about but no stranger to. Another night they were at a pub at two in the morning having 'great aul' craic'. The old mother who slept in the kitchen was well known for rampaging out into the pub in her nightgown to order her daughters to close the bar, so when the Gardai knocked on the door they quickly turned the lights down, laid the mother out in the bed and pretended she was dying. The mother, who wasn't well anyway, put on a suitably wan countenance and everyone stood around looking morose. The Gardai offered their respects and left, at which point the party continued.

At 9am Tricia and Seamus were up checking out the horses and feeding the squawking, barking, baaing, honking family who raced out of their night quarters as if they'd been locked up for a week. They were all embraced and talked to and kissed by their mother as she ran around putting on her daily load of washing and doing 'housework', which was a lick and a spit with the broom and mop. She had the same attitude to housework as me — either do the minimum or pay someone else to do it.

This weekend was to be baling day and of course the baler who had said he would be there bright and early was three hours late. Now the hay smelled more aromatic and complex but equally wonderfully clean somehow and as the day went by, various relatives and friends turned up to help. They worked all day in the meadow doing the heavy job of stacking the oblong bales the baling machine spat out, already tied, onto the long truck, then driving over to the barn and stacking them to the roof. As they got sweatier and thirstier and more and more covered in insects, the haystack got higher and higher. And what did they beg for in the middle of all this? Not a cool drink but tea — so they sat out in the fields on the bales and drank the cup that cheers, but not inebriates, ate sandwiches and told stories.

Tricia donned a bikini top and shorts for this operation and tied her long hair up in a big knot on top of her head. They came in for lunch which was spuds, two giant slices of rump steak that had been cooking for four hours in the slow oven and an onion and whiskey sauce I had made. This was wolfed down with brown soda bread and more tea. Tricia's friend Sheila and her mother Mary popped in to visit and Mary said to Trish, 'Blessed Mudder in heaven, you're not out in the hay with men dressed like that, are ye?'

'Course I am, Mary, it's a feckin' heatwave. Sure I'd die if I had more on and this way I can get meself a tan as well.'

'No wonder you've got so much help. Ah, Trish, isn't this heat brutal, so? I can't hardly sleep nor breathe at night and sure I don't know whether to call the doctor or the priest. May God preserve us all. How long is your cousin home for?'

'Ages and ages. She keeps sayin' she's off at the end of the month but sure, she only just got here, she's in a divil of a hurry. She's desperate — we're going to teach her how to relax.'

In the evening Trish studied the barometer in the hall feverishly. If the weather turned now with only a few more bales to get in, it would all end in tears. She told me: if the ash blooms before the oak, it's the sign of a soak (sunshine); if the oak blooms before the ash, it's the sign of a splash (rain). On Sunday morning we woke to find it had rained earlier on and Tricia ran straight out from her bed to her meadow in her nightie to discover it had rained everywhere *but* on her field. A miracle was pronounced and if they hadn't been so busy they would have gone to Mass. The rest of the day was balmy and clear. That night we celebrated by going into a pub in Cashel 'for a quick gas', from which we were requested to leave by the Garda at 2am.

Tipperary folk drive along narrow country roads at great

speed with no seat belts and frequently stop to talk with people who are walking or in vehicles. They line up their cars side by side so no one can get past, roll down their windows, stick their elbows out and have a good old yarn. Cars queue up behind them, no one toots and all wait patiently for the conversation to finish. As they often say in Ireland — when God made time, he made plenty of it. Tricia also stops the car to talk to pusheens (cats) and dogs.

Once in Thurles I went straight to a pub called Dwan's I had heard about where they brew their own beer. The Dwan family are actually old and respected producers of mineral water and bottled beer since 1921 and now grandson Bill has opened up a very smart restaurant/bar and micro-brewery. Their signature and award-winning beer is Rich Ruby, a fruity aromatic ale produced by a combination of crystal and chocolate malts, wonderfully smooth and rich. My personal favourite was An Dubhain (the Dark One) stout with its complex dry-roast flavour and that hint of bitter-sweetness that might have seduced me away from Guinness. The beers are made from the best of Irish ingredients — Irish water, Irish malted barley and wheat and their own yeast. Hops from the United States, Britain and Germany are flown in in small amounts to maintain their flavour and aroma. The beers are brewed in small batches so they don't need to pasteurise them, which means the beer is always fresh and needs no additives or preservatives.

Bill Dwan got £1.5 million from somewhere (probably at least half of it came from the government, which throws money at new businesses) to create the development of brewery, restaurant and bars and it looked very cool. You could see the brewery within the restored and updated 800-square-metre granary, which was all New York New York stripped-back stone redefined with perforated steel and pale rosewood. There was a large plate-glass wall looking out onto the street and lines of galvanised ducting softened by light from high glass panels and mirrors.

In Ireland, beer is an intrinsic part of the social structure but over the years the product has been tainted by mass production and heavy marketing. Lots of micro-breweries have started up in an attempt to create faithful versions of classic brews in the traditional style and because people want to taste beer the way it should taste. And this, folks, is how you should taste it: pour the beer into a wide, wine-style glass to allow it to swirl and the aroma to escape, then drink slowly, allowing the beer to release the flavours, passing it over the tongue before swallowing. Then observe and appreciate the aftertaste or finish. As master brewer Michael Dobin says, 'Beer is about flavour and aroma, not to be forgotten but enjoyed, used in moderation and repeated daily.'

The next visit was to the cousins on my grandmother Margaret Shanahan's side. Eileen and Jim Shanahan had the family farm at Curraghnaboola, Borrisoleigh. A farmer will never tell you how much stock they really have but I gathered there were about 50 cattle, 100 sheep and 15 horses. They brought up the first four of their children in the thatched farmhouse my grandmother was born in and when it burned down they built a new house across the driveway and made four more children for good measure.

The Long boys always married good women and Eileen was no exception — she reminded me greatly of my darling Aunt Edna in Sydney, married to Uncle Pat. Edna had the perfect death: after a lifetime of simplicity, devotion to church and family, extended family, the world — everyone was encompassed in her love, kindness and humour — she sat up one night in the bed she had been born in, sighed and floated away to the God she believed had guided her life and given her all her beautiful children. Eileen was a carbon copy — small, flowery frock, bright eyes in an animated face and funny. She and quiet Jim ('Ah, I got myself a good man there, I was very lucky') farmed the property together and brought up their eight children in the little three-bedroom farmhouse

I found myself in now. She often rested her hand on his leg or arm as they talked. The Irish have in general cut down on their big families but you still see young women with five kids. I heard of a local traveller family who had 20, all apparently wanted, and the mother seemed to be in perfectly good shape. Theresa and her sister Geraldine were from a family of 10 and Theresa's husband from a family of 20. Eileen and Jim considered it an honour and a gift to have had a large family and such a solid marriage.

'Sure, Pip, I can't understand these couples who split up after three or four years, breaking the hearts of their poor little children, the innocent creathurs. Why is this happening so much now?'

Being an expert on the topic of marriage and long relationships I put forward the suggestion that it was very hard work to keep a marriage together.

'No, it's not 'tis not at all,' she replied.

'Oh, well, you know, Eileen, the romance in a marriage doesn't last long. You don't feel the same way about a person after a number of years. You can't tell me your marriage is exactly the same as it was at the beginning.'

'Yes I can, Pip. Yes I can. Our relationship is exactly the same as it was in the first year in every way.' At this she gave me a meaningful look. I glanced over at Jim who had his face resting in his hand, looking at her peacefully and nodding.

They still had a couple of teenagers at the house; the others visited home every Sunday and they all went to Mass together. She had made them wait all day to meet me, which neither Trish nor I had realised and as Trish works on Irish time rather than world time, they could have been waiting till midnight. As her children left to go back to their various homes, Eileen followed them out, sprinkled them and their cars with holy water and said, 'God bless you, God bless you, travel safely, dear, and watch yourself.'

Jim looked like a farmer — solid, red faced and tanned

from hard work, dressed in the farmer's day-off uniform of dark trousers and white shirt with the sleeves rolled up. He was a nice man who was lucky if he got a word in edgewise with Eileen's constant merry chatter occasionally interspersed with a sudden swipe of the fly swat and a 'Feckers! Ah, Jaesus, Mary and Joseph, wouldn't you know the feckers would come just because I have important guests. The shame of it. I haven't seen a feckin' fly all day and now lookit.' While Jim put on a daecent cup of tae, Eileen dragged out the photo albums, lit up another cigarette and identified a cast of players who mostly bore no relationship to me. There were old black and white photos of a tricycle, ones with people's heads cut off, ones where the occupants were so tiny they could have been plants in the garden and ones gone yellow from time. The best were the photos of their brothers and sisters, parents and grandparents in horse and cart and their wedding photos.

Along with the tea, little plates of salad and cold cuts were presented to us with homemade soda bread. Like the Maori, the Irish love genealogy so Trish and Eileen were in heaven going over every single person they both knew, who was related to whom, who they married, what they did, which widow was getting her leg over both brothers (few good sucks on the fags), which ones could sing and on and on. As Irish people have such huge families it's a lot of information to take on board; also within families they use the same names over and over again, so that both the Shanahan and Long families had Margarets, Marys, Jameses, Johns, Michaels. If you listened to Eileen and Tricia you would believe everyone in Tipperary was related. I have a fault in that I have a limited interest in genealogy; when it comes to fourth cousins, step-siblings and remote village connections I glaze over. I would have been happy just to meet someone who had known Margaret Shanahan and Jim Long but Adam and Eve I didn't need. Once they had exhausted all possibilities they moved on to farming and horsy matters while I tried to get some information out of Jim about my grandparents, of whom he remembered very little save that Jim Long was a good-looking charmer known to like a drink from time to time. As we left we were roundly kissed, hugged, sprinkled, blessed and even given the bottle of holy water to take with us for good measure.

Now that Tricia and Seamus were no longer in the hay there was time to relax and hang out talking. People would come in and out all day with the golden weather continuing, and sit outside on the lawn drinking tea and Coke and sunning their legs. Sometimes we went down to the lazy Suir River at Ballycamus and lay around in the cold, clear water which smelled deliciously of mud, stones and weeds. Majella with her high cheekbones and nonstop talking and laughing, Father Peter Brenhan (peace had been established between us), Theresa with her perfect tan and figure, easy-going Marie of the three beautiful daughters and one son and sometimes Sheila, the statuesque young postmistress with an infectious giggle and a stunning head of long golden/red hair. Sheila loved everything that shone and frequently wore gold nail-polish to set off her engagement ring — a huge flower of diamonds. Her wedding dress was to be gold and cream with a tiara and thick golden lace veil.

Theresa often popped into our kitchen talking fast and hard in her husky voice, hands flying, eyes dilating, telling some shtory, as she called them. For some unfathomable reason she loved cleaning, in spite of our making constant jokes about it. She would sit ramrod straight and tell us you could lick her floor, her hedges were trimmed to within an inch of their lives, and every time her windowsills got a scratch she painted over it. 'Me oil tank has split and sure I was almost ruined and wasn't it lucky I was dere in the yard sweeping up the leaves when it happened. Oh stop! [head in hands] Jaesus, the leaves is driving' me mad, mad I tell you.' If Theresa could have had a house full of appliances all for cleaning, she would have been in heaven. She was famous for cleaning up a party around you as you tried to get your pint down. One night at her sister Geraldine's place we were having after-dinner drinks and talks and she couldn't stand the idleness of it, so got out the ironing board in front of us and beat the creases out of three baskets of her sister's washing.

On a sunny afternoon I went into town with Sheila and was entranced by her mother, Mary, who made me laugh every time she opened her mouth. After our shopping we had a coffee together at Dwan's.

'Now, Pip, have you a husband and children?'

'I had one but he died on me and I have no children, Mary.'

'Glory be to Jaesus but isn't that a terrible story now, and you such a happy person in yourself like. Ah, but you're a Catholic and that must be how you cope. Prayer is a great ting, so it is.'

'A recovered Catholic, Mary. I lost my faith when I was 19.'

'Get away outa' here now. How do you get trew life witout praying? Sure I pray about everyting, morning, noon and night — me knees are ruined from it — but I suffer from the nerves you know . . . my whole family does. Mind now, at the same time I envy you. I couldn't do witout my children and sometimes I like my dogs better but marriage is a hard row to hoe. Sure I didn't know anyting about anyting when I got married and I don't know how I stuck wit it. But Pip, even though you're a strong person, if you don't believe in praying then you don't believe in God. Who do you turn to?'

'I don't need mysterious outside influences to help me, Mary. I help myself, I believe in myself and I use my own head and common sense to guide me through life.'

'Oh,' she laughed, 'is that so? And where do you tink you're going to go when you die?'

'Why, straight to heaven, Mary, where I belong, and I'll be waiting there to negotiate a good seat for you.'

'Oh, Pip,' clapping her hands together, 'you're mad altogether, so you are.' The conversation ended on an examination of each other's rings and clothes.

Not even heaven and hell are what they used to be. Just when you thought it was safe to sin again, you are reminded 'hell hasn't gone away, you know'. I asked an old man in a pub where he thought he was going when he died and he said, 'I don't mind. I have friends in both places.' Now the Pope has declared that hell is not a place but a state of mind. I'll never forget the pages and pages of raving descriptions of hell in James Joyce's *Portrait of the Artist as a Young Man* — 'the fire of hell, while retaining the intensity of its heat, burns eternally in darkness . . . amid which bodies are heaped one upon another without ever a glimpse of air . . . all the filth of the world, all the offal and scum of the world . . . a pestilential odour . . . the immortal soul is tortured eternally . . . an eternity of agony . . . the damned howl and scream at one another.'

This was how the visiting Jesuits used to thunder on their yearly hellfire missions to our church in Auckland. They were scary and hugely entertaining at the same time so I suffered from nightmares of eternal blisters, pain and hopelessness but admired their dramatic and oratorial ability. The whole parish looked forward to their visit as a chance to pull up their spiritual socks and see a new face on the altar for a change. I always felt sorry for non-Catholics because of the lack of ostentation and over-indulgence in their religious diet.

The concept of evil and the devil began to fascinate me when I was working as an alcohol and drug therapist in Canada. In my nightmares in the first month at the treatment centre where I trained, I regressed straight back to childhood. Along with the guilt nightmares, the being-late nightmares, the rejection nightmares, came back the evil nightmares. You will go to the devil, to hell, you are born in a state of sin and only true conversion and purity will save you from damnation. It was Ben Hur bloody and ripped from the chariot race all

over again. Night after night I woke up shaking, with palpit-
ating heart and drenched body. I had no language or training
to connect my inner life with the horrors that I listened to
all day in my outer life at the treatment centre. My secular
imagination was reaching for old religious metaphors to cope.
At the same time as I was repelled by both the addicts and the
methods of the therapists, I was attracted by the negativity of
drugs and the possibility that I could actually bring some light
into these people's lives.

Revenge rather than guilt is probably why we like to believe
in hell — we want to see those who got away with murder in
this life get their comeuppance in the next (that's why we have
to invent a next, otherwise it would be too unfair), and not just
a comeuppance but a permanent punishment. Also such
obviously unproven threats as hell served as a way in the past
of controlling rebellious people. In *The Rebel* Albert Camus
wrote: 'Rebellion is form of asceticism, though it is blind.' If
you can't keep people in line by persuasion or killing them,
you resort to the crude and desperate imagery of terror. But
it doesn't work any more (it's amazing it worked for so long).

The Pope says you still aren't permitted to make your own
mind up about these things because if you make the wrong
decision, hell is still a state of mind of those who freely and
definitively separate themselves from God. But in fact there is
a huge backlash against Catholicism in Ireland, with veritable
witch-hunts hitting the headlines periodically. In one month
alone there was the trial of a nun convicted of rape for holding
a schoolgirl's ankles while a man raped her; her extraordinary
reprieve by the courts the following day with no one being left
with a clue as to what had actually happened; and the drama
of a priest in Cork denouncing a well-known and loved Irish
athlete for having a child out of wedlock. From the pulpit he
named her and called her a common slut, causing a national
outrage that quickly evoked a public apology. Even closer to
home I heard of a girl in Tipperary getting pregnant and her

father throwing her out of the house. The village disapproved strongly and she was eventually welcomed back into the family to be cared for.

Another evening we went over to Mary's to pick up Sheila for a night on the razz at Mulhall's pub. Even though Sheila was in her late twenties and her fiancé 20 years older, they still lived with their respective parents. Sean's mother was capable of calling around the neighbourhood if he didn't come home to take her to Mass in the morning. One approached the Heffernan home, a large old rectory, by a subtly grand entrance and long road through land and trees. The large Georgian, ivy-covered house seemed to go on for ever, with three floors overflowing with stupendous antiques, colourful decor, expensive armchairs with the stuffing peeping out of them, paintings, grand pianos covered in photos and cards, plush rugs, raggedy rugs, expensive wallpaper, chipped hallways, beautiful double bathrooms, fabulous mirrors . . . and animals everywhere. We were ushered down to the back of the house where Queen Mary reigned in her large yellow and green kitchen. She poured us glasses of Baileys topped up with a great dollop of Powers whiskey, then topped her own up with more Baileys. She had four dogs and eight cats in the house, this being evidenced by the eau de chien that immediately greeted you as you walked in. She and her husband had constant arguments over these animals — he said out and she said in. Collectable plates covered the walls; cabinets, shelves and stands were spilling over with kitchen supplies; and the Aga had clothes drying over it in piles. Jesus was there with his open bleeding heart; so was the Virgin with the everlasting lamp and so were Mary's poor knees wrecked from praying.

'Sure, what do ye want me to do with the animals, Tricia — I can't put the poor creathurs out in the winter and in my life full of problems and my heart breaking with the nerves, they're a source of comfort to me. That is when I'm not praying,' she winked at me.

'Don't start on me, Mary. There have been many prayers said on my behalf. My grandmother and Aunt Peg used to say novenas for me for years and send me the cards to Paris to prove it.'

'Well, they did a bad job of it so, heathen that you turned out to be. Why didn't you get down on your knees when you received those novenas?'

'Mary, honey, I was far too busy learning French in bed to be praying.'

'Jaesus, Mary and Joseph but you're a divil, aren't you? Have some more Baileys.'

Sheila sat at the other end of the table laughing. Mary had on a brightly patterned dress which she disliked and described as resembling a tinker's apron. She was a fine-looking woman with lovely eyes, hardly a line and a good firm jaw, with her blonde hair loosely tied in a knot at the back of her neck. She and Tricia shared a weakness in that they couldn't resist an auction or an antique shop. Mary was always scandalised about the price she had to pay for something but then again how could she live without it altogether. Then we got onto recipes. I told her about pushing sliced lemons, garlic and herbs up under the skin of a chicken before roasting it, and she told me about the difficulties of feeding a large family and farm hands who all had different tastes and wouldn't eat this and wouldn't eat that.

'By crikey, sounds like they need a good slap. You're too nice. They need a dose of the Long no-choice-think-of-the-starving-millions catering method. You need Trish and me in here to sort them. Which brings me to my next point, Mary — I'm expecting an invitation to dinner here any day.'

She threw her hands up.

'Is it mad y'are? Sure, I wouldn't cook for you — I couldn't bear the look on your face at all.'

'Mary, I would be so good and so grateful.'

'A bottle of wine is all ye'd get and I'd give ye plenty of

it. If ye're too good for Inch House [a grand country house with whose cuisine I was unimpressed] ye'll be too good for me altogether.'

Eileen had suggested if I wanted to dance I should go to Irish night in Dundrum, which was why Trish, Theresa and I found ourselves one night sticking out like lollies in a tackle shop, surrounded by older ladies dressed in pleated skirts, pastel blouses and polyester dresses. The entire older male population in the tatty lounge noted our arrival with a rustle of their beer glasses and a shifting of feet around the bar. Couples were doing waltzes, foxtrots and de-sexed tangos, and most of the men had not been graced with steps, as Tricia would say. This music was interspersed with country and western tunes from a drummer on automatic, an accordionist who moved not one muscle save for his fingers, and the singer with a guitar. Within seconds I was on the dance floor and within minutes came the usual question: what's your name and are you married? I wanted a good thumping set dance and I got one — the 'Siege of Ennis'. We lined up in long rows facing one another, holding hands all the length of the hall, then danced a few steps towards one another and a few steps sideways. You found yourself in front of a different man briefly but you always kept the same partner for the stepping part. Then you took hold of each other by criss-crossing arms and swung around for four bars. These swings ranged from arthritic to gymnastic to fast enough to sweep you off your feet. I always had to turn around in reverse to unwind when I had been placed back on the earth.

We escaped after a few more dances to Gleeson's pub in Ballagh. They say in Ireland that the only possible way to walk down a street without passing a pub is to go into each one. I liked Gleeson's because it was small, clean and pretty with its green and red walls, had lots of atmosphere, and Mary Gleeson was a no-nonsense blonde with a heart of gold. Here Theresa set to baiting her old drunk friend Festy. Mention hurling to him and he became obsessed but tonight he was distracted.

'Who's that then? Is she married do you know?'

'No, she's not, Festy, she's a tragic widow.'

'Sufferin' Jaesus, will ye get away outa here and isn't she a fine-lookin' woman. I could find room for her on my hearth but the eyes'd be leppin' outa my head all day. Ask her if she'd take me, go on, go on.'

Theresa was paralytic over these exchanges and provoked him tirelessly all night. Mary told me I was of great interest to the men at the bar, although in the three months I was in Tipperary not one of them ever spoke to me. When I said I didn't think they were my type she smiled and said, 'Ah, Pip, you know, there's an old stocking for every old shoe.'

Theresa's sister Geraldine was another woman in Tricia's retinue who became one of my favourites. When I met her in her restaurant, Ryan's Daughter in Cashel, she was a red-haired charmer with a gorgeous smile and very attractive face, and the next time I saw her she was a streaked blonde, which suited her even better. Ryan's Daughter was a pretty little cottage with flowers hanging outside, specialising in old-fashioned home cooking. I had bacon and cabbage, a great Irish speciality, which Geraldine served with turnips, carrots and parsnips mashed together, and spuds. Her food was hearty, warming, no nonsense and simply good, as all country cooking in Ireland should be. I thought with her good looks, charm and vibrant personality she should have been out front of house but I most often caught her in the kitchen and the restaurant was full all day. Sometimes when Tricia and I turned up we did what my friends used to do in my restaurant in Paris on insanely busy days — take to the dishwashing and serving for half an hour to ease the congestion before we felt able to order a meal. On these days Geraldine would put a bowl of soup on the kitchen table and make us sit down and eat it. Then she would join us in the restaurant for a fag, slump in her chair and say what I always used to say when I'd had enough: 'If another customer walks in that door I'll feckin' shoot him.'

To make boiled bacon and cabbage you put a good kilo of bacon in one piece in a pot, cover it with cold water, then add a couple of bay leaves, a dozen peppercorns, a celery stick, a halved onion and a couple of carrots. Bring this to the boil, cover and simmer for an hour. In the meantime prepare a large savoy cabbage by discarding the tough outer leaves, quartering and coring it. The Irish don't usually do this but I would blanch the cabbage first. Now you add it to the bacon pot and simmer for another hour. Remove the bacon and slice it thickly, drain the vegetables and reserve the cooking liquid. To serve, arrange the bacon on top of the vegetables, garnish with chopped parsley and pour a little of the cooking liquid over. *Of course* you offer spuds on the side. They usually make a white sauce to go with it, which I assume is an English affectation. There are those who drink the cabbage water for good health and the keeping of the horn in working order if you get my drift.

Geraldine rivalled Tricia in unbridled generosity, capacity for hard work and tendency to burn the candle at both ends. As Tricia said, 'All she wants is the wind of a word of anything happening and she's off.' She could whip up a sumptuous meal in the flicker of an eyelid and had an eye for anything beautiful: clothes, perfume, food. Like Trish, she also had an eye for a good man, specifically in the person of her partner, Gary. Gary was a gentle giant, a rugby player who had produced two huge professional rugby sons and worshipped the ground Geraldine walked on. He always seemed to have a sweet smile and greeted you as if he were thrilled to see you. An easy-going, good-looking man with fine-rimmed glasses, he loved indulging in stimulating conversation and telling stories and when he had enough under his belt he took to the song in a big way. He had to be talked into it but then he wouldn't stop. He actually had a fine baritone voice that sounded trained but he swore it wasn't.

In Tipperary there was no such thing as an early night even if you were just at home. If I suggested the concept to Tricia and Seamus they would say, 'What for?' Going upstairs early was seen as a shocking waste of time — even watching rubbish on TV was a lesser fate than going to bed and dying of boredom. One evening Geraldine, Gary, cousins Richard and Kathleen, Tricia and I went to a performance of Brú Ború — traditional singing and dancing in a performance setting. It was very good if a little syrupy and we quickly moved on to Jim and Bridgie's pub. Tricia and I had bought books of Irish songs at the Brú Ború centre and out they came — 'Black is the Colour of My True Love's Hair', 'Raglan Road', 'She Moved Through the Fair'. Geraldine sang 'Grace' in her husky sensuous voice, Jim sang, even Seamus sang a song by 2.30am. It's only a matter of time for an Irishman — eventually he'll sing, then he'll get into the car and sing all the way home, then when you hit home at 3am everyone is invited in for tea, reheated leftovers and soda bread, because sure, yes can't drive home in that state. Gary got into his marching songs, I jumped up on a table to conduct and the others stood up and marched. Gary loved a finale and it always took a long time to finish 'I Did it My Way' because he did it his way over and over. We would have a dramatic finale wherein Gary would raise himself to his full height — which was considerable — and throw out his chest, we exhausting ourselves with the emotion of it . . . do it his way . . . then start over again.

the
wild west

There's a little spot in Ireland where fairies can be seen
To frolic in the meadows and dance upon the green.
It's a place of tranquil beauty, of fame and wide renown.
Oh, I must deeply love it, it's my dear old Galway town.

It has walks all strewn with fragrance and gardens that are
    rare.
It has trees that bloom with lilac, its waters are so clear.
No other place can match it, a haven on this earth.
To death I'll always thank my God for this my place of birth.

Its Colleens they are graceful, no others can compare.
Their smiles are all so radiant, their beauty is so fair.
God grant that it may flourish and ever please look down
Upon this earthly paradise, my dear old Galway town.

— Found on a pub wall in Galway

I decided to rent a car and gallop off on my own to discover the wild west of Ireland. The one-hour drive from Shannon airport in Limerick took two hours along backed-up country roads. The road on which I came into Galway was a one-lane road overloaded with articulated trucks, tour coaches, bicycles and hundreds of cars, one of which had me and my tape of 100 Irish songs blaring in it. As I crawled through postcard-pretty villages with white-washed houses and countryside that was much less green than Tipperary and wilder, I amused myself by learning 'Raglan Road', a song that had captured my vocal cords.

The west of Ireland was the old province of Connacht and is predominantly bogs and mountains. It was and still is the last bastion of pure Irishness because no one wanted it and was basically dragged directly from the sixteenth century straight into the nineteenth. The vicious and rampaging Oliver Cromwell so detested the area he gave the Irish chieftains who resisted English rule the choice of 'going to hell or Connacht'.

Galway is a pretty, walled, seaside city that still thinks it is a fishing village and by a miracle of improbability the car drove itself straight to my hotel. Jury's is just a regular hotel chain but the service was striking. Through hopeless communication skills on my part, my room was booked by the marketing person from Millennium Festivals for only one night rather than three. But the hotel not only slipped me into the first cancellation that came up for the next night but arranged for me to stay at another more expensive hotel at the same price the third night. This in a town that was bursting with visitors to the Galway Arts Festival and all because the manager liked my dress and felt sorry for me over my email problems. And my room overlooked the tranquil River Corrib which ambles through the town.

Kathryn MacDonnell of Millennium Festivals had invited me to a function preceding the big drum concert. I tripped out into a chilly but pleasant summer's evening and found my way through the happy throngs to the reception at the university. One is always tempted to ask directions in Ireland simply for the pleasure of the exchange and it is your loss if you can't get into the spirit of the game.

'Hello. Am I going in the right direction for the university?'

'How would I know? Sure that depends where you came from.'

'I don't know — I'm lost. Over there somewhere.'

'Ah, now I wouldn't have come that way.'

'How do you know which way I came?'

'Because if you'd been coming the right way, you wouldn't be standing in my shop now. Don't be going down that road there on the left, it'll be doing you no good at all, that's the road there to the right. As you go past the cathedral, say a Glory Be and turn to your left.'

Kathryn was busy so I sat down to a glass of wine and made myself privy to a flurry of cocktail sausages with big bowls of ketchup to go with them, wedgies and sandwiches. The drum concert had as its centrepiece the largest drum in the world, standing at a phenomenal five metres. It was designed to represent a bodhrán on one side and a lambeg (Northern Ireland version of a bodhrán) on the other, symbolising the different traditions. It was an enthralling, powerful concert with about 30 performers singing, dancing and playing brass, strings, guitars, xylophone, uilleann pipes and drums of all shapes and sizes. And who played the pièce de résistance — the millennium drum? Why, a bronzed, oiled, hair-full-of-gold-paint Maori gentleman by the name of Ken Samson. When I got him on the phone he answered with a familiar 'Gidday, man, kia ora' and went into loving detail about exactly where he came from up north. Hailing from and still living in the Hokianga, Ken lived in Ireland for five years and learned to drum in Africa.

The next day was a heatwave in Galway (Irish for not raining) and I hit the colourful streets armed with anticipation and my green basket housing recorder, camera, umbrella, cellphone and notebook. No one can say I am an unprepared writer. I am equipped to the hilt night and day; no one raises a fiddle or eats an oyster without my knowing about it. Galway is young like Dublin — hip, offbeat, progressive, charming and insanely good looking. Maybe the attitude comes from the proximity to the coast but it's very easy going, fun and pumping day and night. This general area is the music and arts centre of the west and has remained quite traditional due to its closeness to the Connemara gaeltacht (Irish-speaking region). Finding a pub that doesn't play traditional music would be like finding a nun at the sceptics society weekly lecture on logic.

I ducked into Sheridan's Lane and found the fish shop at the back of the famous McDonagh's fish and chip/seafood restaurant. This dear little place has really fresh local whiting, haddock, salmon, Pacific oysters, crab, lobster and scallops, kedgeree and fish salad, and in the evening they put out a few tables in the shop for diners. They buy whole catches from the fishermen and within hours it's on your plate. Open since 1902, the restaurant has its large main entrance on Quay Street and you can sit at the seafood bar or have your generous portion of freshly battered fish and chips from potatoes cut on the premises. They oak smoke their own fish and if you bring in fish you have caught with your own fair hands they will smoke it for you to take home. Extraordinarily, in the middle of tourist season, they were closed on Sunday — I suppose they were all off at Mass.

The real gastronomic find in Galway was Sheridan's Cheesemongers further around on Kirwan's Lane, a small but perfectly formed haven of decomposing milk and cured flesh. Kevin Sheridan, who also has a shop in Dublin, is mad about cheese and knows most of his cheesemakers personally. My eyes immediately fell on some Mine Gabhar from Wexford, a goat cheese Tricia and I had found in Nenagh.

'Oh,' I gasped, 'this is the best cheese. I tasted some of this a few days ago.'

'Yes,' he said, smiling. 'I've been in the cheese business for years and it's the finest soft goat cheese I have ever eaten.'

'Well, I lived in France for 10 years, goat cheeses are my favourite and I agree with you. How could a person in Wexford make such good cheese?'

'I know the guy — Luc van Kampen — he's a genius. His abilities are magical.'

Sheridan's had a lot of their cheeses in huge blocks and rounds right there in front of you on wooden tables — Parmesan cliff faces, farmhouse rounds called Durrus from Coomkeen, the well-known Milleens and Ardrahan soft cheese from Cork, bries and camemberts and a raw-milk cheese called Coolea. There were also lots of perfectly finished French cheeses, extra virgin olive oils, marinated olives and caper berries, baskets full of fresh basil, Italian and Irish salamis and cured hams from Parma and Tuscany. The staff were very friendly and behaved as cheese experts should behave — that is, they gave the endless flow of customers who crowded into the shop tastes of other cheeses to try. Not pathetic smidgits but generous dollops and scrapes.

Kevin told me about the market down the road situated on, wait for it, Market Street. Whoever named the streets in Galway suffered from a spectacular lack of imagination — Dock Road (guess where), Shop Street (which is also Williamsgate Street, William Street, High Street and Quay Street depending on where you are standing), Canal Road, Middle Street, Station Road, College Road. The Galway market happens every Saturday; the street leading into it is lined with flower sellers and so is the street leading out. Just like a French village market only smaller, it was overflowing with happy people and beautiful produce — turnips and swedes (the Irish love them), fresh farm eggs and vegetables, apple pies, breads, crafts, grilling sausages, steaming crêpes, big fat organic broad beans practically bursting out of their jackets, new potatoes, blackcurrants, gooseberries and little green Irish apples.

Back on High Street I came across Kenny's Bookshop, a place I had read about in New Zealand in connection with their Irish Book Parcels. Now this was quite a good idea, especially for Kenny. Every couple of months they select a package of books by Irish writers and send them off wrapped in brown paper to the subscriber. You fill in a form and decide how often you wish to receive a parcel and how much you wish to spend and you never know what you will receive — like an Irish literary Christmas cracker, you pull it open and words fall out. The shop was beautifully laid out, with the walls covered in photos of famous Irish authors and at the back an art gallery topped by two mezzanine floors of second-hand and antique books, prints, maps and paintings. In my research into the connections between Ireland and France for another project I had heard about the romantically named

Wild Geese (Les Oies Sauvages) and found some books on the subject in Kenny's.

The Wild Geese were Irish who migrated to France over two centuries from 1607 and became winemakers, soldiers and statesmen. The Hennessys of Cognac, the O'Mahoneys and Butlers of northern France, the O'Neills and de Plunketts of Paris were but some. These Wild Geese are very highly thought of in Ireland and their descendants, although French in all but name, are proud of and knowledgeable about their Irish ancestors, easily able to trace their lineage. To this day the French feel a deep sentimental connection with Ireland. I'd always wondered why a lot of them were named Patrick. Descendants of Les Oies Sauvages still harbour Catholic, Celtic, anti-English sentiment. Interestingly, it was not the poor who emigrated but the aristocracy, who are still celebrated for their nobility, sacrifices, love of Ireland and Catholicism. The Marquis de Goulaine said, 'Every time I go to Ireland I feel at home. It is probably the Celtic style — we are faithful, courageous and unpredictable. The Irish are probably even more so because of the terrible life they had.'

In principle when one thinks of a goose one thinks of someone flighty or foolish and it has been suggested the term meant Irish Jacobites who fled to France when James II abdicated. Another theory is that they were recruits for the Irish Brigades on a ship's manifest as it returned to France from the south and south-west coasts of Ireland after unloading its cargo of wine and brandy. Around 50,000 people emigrated and most of them never returned. In fact the sons of wealthy, educated Catholics left Ireland for political and military reasons and because being a Catholic slammed all the doors to higher education and upper-echelon careers. Most people thought the Wild Geese left because they couldn't stick the English in Ireland but in fact they had much better career opportunities in France; it was a sort of eighteenth-century brain drain. They married into other Irish families already there and into French nobility and gentry, and there was a fertile trade going on with salt, wine, cognac and silk being sent to Ireland and fish, butter, beef, wool, linen and leather going the other way.

Hennessy cognac was started by Maurice Hennessy in 1765 and merged with Moët et Chandon in 1970. Seven generations later they still describe themselves as Irish. In Bordeaux, the Anglo/Irish Anthony Barton of Château de Langoa produces one of the finest wines in the world, a Médoc, is one of the only growers to own both a second and a third growth, and has an Irish passport. The Johnstons are still highly regarded as négotiants in Bordeaux, as are the seventh-generation brothers Hugues (négotiant) and Daniel (broker) Lawton. Many Irish names are found on buildings and streets in the city of Bordeaux, testifying to its Irish past. The Marquis de Goulaine in Nantes makes a very good Muscadet from the château owned by his ancestors, the O'Briens and the Galweys. This family are probably the oldest wine growers in the world as they have been there for a thousand years and all that time have grown vines. The Duc de Magenta, otherwise known as Philippe de MacMahon, lives in splendour in the Château de Sully near Autun in Burgundy and can trace his line back to the Bourbon kings of France and Brian Ború, High King of Ireland. He has five hectares of vines producing the commercially very successful Duc de Magenta burgundy red and white wines.

The pub where I found 'My Dear Old Galway Town' written around the walls in red ink was like a lot of Galway buildings — two faced, which the Irish say is just like their politicians (indeed Parliament Building in Dublin actually has grand entrances and façades on opposing sides of the building). In this particular case you walked into Tomas O'Riada pub from High Street and exited from the Front Door pub on Cross Street. People kept telling me about a great session at the Front Door and pointing to it, but trawl the street as I did I couldn't find it. Eventually I settled on the first door my feet walked into and crossly ordered a pint of Guinness. The barmaid laughed her head off, informed me I was in the Front Door and confessed she had no idea why it had two names. This dog-legged pub was only two years old but you'd swear it had been there for centuries and in a way it had. It was composed of two shops and a courtyard between, all turned into one huge space with odd angles and mezzanine floor out the back. The High Street part used to be a drapery and still has the original counter, now the bar, tongue-in-groove walls and built-in drapery drawers.

There are many restaurants in Galway catering to tourists and festival-goers, none of which I wished to defile my tastebuds with. The easiest way to find the best eating places is to ask someone in the food business like Kevin Sheridan. Without hesitating he pointed to Spanish Arch and said the Long Walk wine bar, which of course has another name — Nimmo's. Spanish Arch, built in 1594 to shelter stores of Spanish wine unloaded to the docks, was where all the fishing boats used to come in and there used to be a fish market in the square. Anyone who's anyone knows it is there, even though when you look through the arch all you see is rubble from a building site. But if you fearlessly advance, over on the right by the water is a little inconspicuous bar. Quiet, very few tourists, mostly locals and selected referees such as myself. I sat at the bar and had the menu explained to me. It showed that the chef/owner had travelled and was over white sauce. I was advised by the couple at the end of the bar to order the Finnish chef's fish soup, which came crowded with chunks of salmon, cod, leeks, tomato and dill. I checked the wine list and rumbled and snaffled at the lack of New Zealand wines. They were mostly French, Australian and Italian, like on every other wine list in Ireland, and shockingly few of them were by the glass, which is strange for a wine bar.

'Aha!' exclaimed the barman. 'I do have some New Zealand wine but it's not unpacked yet — Wander or Pender or something like that.'

'Don't tell me. I refuse to believe Diane and Mike Ponder have found their way to this little restaurant in Galway.'

'Yes! That's the one — Ponder Estate — great wine.'

'I'll have some.'

'Haven't unpacked it yet.'

'Oh, and I who thought the Irish were so hospitable.'

'No, no, no. The most hospitable, friendly people in the world with the most beautiful country are New Zealanders.'

'Ireland is beautiful.'

'New Zealand is much more beautiful and varied and people invite you into their homes to stay. I would go back there in an instant and live if I could.'

White sauce is the scourge of the working class in Ireland; it will be their downfall yet. It is possible to make a delicious white sauce but you have to have a playful, light hand — use the best butter you can find and cook the roux gently stirring with a wooden spoon for at least five minutes. You don't want to colour the sauce by browning the roux but you do need to cook the flour as there is nothing more desperate than a sauce tasting of flour. Have a garlic clove peeled, maybe half a small onion with two cloves stuck in it, salt and freshly ground white pepper, a nutmeg and cayenne pepper. Throw all this in except the nutmeg and cayenne, pour lots of milk on top, turn the heat right up and whisk in a committed manner. Don't stop whisking till the sauce is the consistency of pouring chocolate. Turn the heat off and remove the onion and garlic if you can find it. Taste for seasoning — the reason you use white pepper is to retain the white colour of the sauce. Grate in some nutmeg and flick in a suggestion of cayenne. The French sometimes stir in an egg yolk at this stage to give the sauce a gloss and richness. If you're not serving it immediately, rub butter over the surface to prevent a skin forming. Irish cooks now throw in parsley which I can't stand — finely chopped chives which cousin Tricia does or chervil is much finer. If you make white sauce or béchamel thus, you will be cured of every traumatic boarding school Sunday roast and tripe for breakfast on the farm experience you have ever suffered. A good béchamel on a simply boiled, free-range chook is incomparable accompanied by a perfectly chilled riesling.

Upon emerging from the Long Walk I was just in time for an outdoor performance by the Australian troupe Strange Fruit doing a take on the story of Icarus and Daedalus in mid-air. The idea was to explore our longing for the freedom of flight and the tension created between flying and falling. The Aussies have always been tops at street theatre and costumes and although I am unable to warm to magicians, I find myself enchanted by clowns for their pathos, rubber bodies and truly magical qualities. Clowns have no gender — they are ourselves reflected with humour and affection. In this unbridled visual fantasy the performers were dressed as golden angels, people in black with umbrellas, ladies in white with white umbrellas and a man on elevated shoes with a Frankenstein head-dress. They danced an aerial choreography, each perched atop a four-metre flexible pole. Each pole would bend enough to allow the actors to lean in and embrace one another and the fluidity of their movement was truly beautiful and very moving.

In the evening I went to a stupendous performance by a Russian mime company called Derevo. Their play, called *Once*, was a love story, a kaleidoscope of inspired lunacy combining mime, clowning, acrobatics, dancing, great music and even pyrotechnics. A sinister aristocrat and a clowny tramp vied for the love of a bubbly café waitress and of course was desperately funny and sad because she was charmed by the incompetent tramp but seduced by the suave aristocrat. It all ended in death and destruction, rampant symbolism billowing off the stage in clouds of smoke. At the end of the curtain calls the troupe opened a bottle of champagne on the stage, toasted the audience who were by this stage all on their feet screaming and stamping, and went out to a pumping rendition of 'Love Hurts'.

As I wandered from pub to pub to find the best session I discovered that some of the most interesting music was coming from the streets. Lots of New Age prophets and wandering hippies accompanied by dogs slouched around beating drums and looking vaguely as I did 30 years ago except I always brushed my hair and teeth no matter how much dope I'd smoked. In the middle of this was a clean-cut group of musicians who all looked exactly like one another — blond, blue eyed and wholesomely good looking in plaid shirts and new jeans. They all seemed to be able to play upright bass, guitar, banjo, fiddle, mandolin, dobro and flute interchangeably and were, in fact, all brothers and sisters with one brother-in-law. The Dutch Intveld family strangely enough played bluegrass gospel despite being classically trained — they told me they went to the Grand Ole Opry in America and have never looked back.

An Irish boy was playing African drum with an exotic trio of Nepalese mountain men. They sat on the ground cross-legged in their traditional costume and hats playing mesmeric music on two string instruments and a sort of bongo. Later on I passed them again; they had been joined by a bodhrán player and were dancing wildly and ecstatically. Then there was Robbie, the littlest man in the world with the biggest voice who hurled out his songs like a newspaper seller or a ball from a cannon, grounding himself with his accordion and castanets attached to his right foot. He had on his midsummer outfit of thick maroon jumper, woollen scarf and cap. Behind him leaning on the wall was his bicycle, with tweed jacket thrown over the handlebars in case of a sudden chill, and a plastic bag full of flowers.

Apparently the best sessions of all are at the Crane bar on

Sea Road (guess where?) on Wednesday nights but this was Saturday. Taaffes pub on Shop Street was reputable so I slid in there — nothing starts before 9.30pm — and peered through my Guinness at three flute players, a bodhrán and a keyboard, which I thought was a bit upmarket, but as soon as you think you've sussed the rules they slip away from you. At Jim o' the Mills I saw young people with sheet music and words, which is very unusual. In the old days nobody could read music; you learned by listening and watching.

One of the few non-moveable rules of an Irish pub, however, is the no-ventilation rule. Here's how the rule goes: find a sunny day, have standing room only, everyone smoking, dim lighting and not a door or window open. It has crossed my mind to wonder about the effects of smoke on precious instruments but they've survived hundreds of years thus far and the only degradation seems to be in the tarnished complexions of the players. What I love about about traditional musicians is the utter staunchness — no expression, looking at the floor for the most part and little if any acknowledgement of the appreciative 'lovely' or 'grand' from the adoring faithful.

Traditionally you don't get paid to play in a pub — you get free drinks — but overwhelming tourism has put an end to that, except maybe in winter. In high season the musicians are paid and the music is for tourists, not true music-lovers. The Quays on Quay Street is Galway's most impressive pub aesthetically speaking, with a never-ending, stained-glass, church-like wood-panelled interior. It pumped contemporary music out the back but had a good session going on in the front window with a squeeze box, fiddle, bodhrán, accordion and Irish bazooki which was strummed.

Raining and windy again — heatwave over. In one of those truly great demented leaps of faith I resumed my traveller's brutal, uncompromising search to get to the heartland of Ireland. Everyone tells you Connemara on the west coast and specifically the Aran Islands are the quintessential, staunch Ireland. Here I would find my rugged rural stereotypes and unlimited supplies of the famous Aran jerseys.

What I found somewhere in the Atlantic between Inisheer (Inis Oírr) and Rossaveal was the bottomless pit of agonising gastric spasms that my poor body became. I was desperate to escape the scourge of tourists in Galway and get some peace and quiet to write so chose the smallest and, I hoped, least visited of the three islands. At the dock a rugged type with an attractive burnt-barley flush wordlessly grabbed my case and slung it onto an clunky old plonker of a boat with few takers (not built either for comfort or speed, it transpired). He showed no emotion regarding the hugeness of my suitcase when everyone else was clearly carrying shoulder bags. A woman must always be prepared for a lifetime. Who knows where two days on an island will lead?

Inisheer had three pubs and I tried them all. I braved one of the pubs for a lunch of fresh cod (no white sauce, thanks), frozen veges, a spud and some dead lettuce leaves. Dessert was a soggy apple pie and mug of coffee with a spoon in it. The food of a cook who no longer cares, if he ever did. The pubs and restaurants there had the annoying practice of asking you to pay in advance so if you subsequently ordered a dessert, coffee or another drink you had to root around in the depths of the green basket and find more money each time. How this could be considered an easy system of payment on anyone's part escapes me.

This was the heart of gaeltacht, the mother language being Irish, the secondary one English. Islanders spoke English only when addressing a visitor. I listened to the men around the bar and to me their Gaelic sounded like a Nordic language. Profusely idiomatic and diverse, Irish is as fiendishly difficult to learn as to pronounce, although there are only nine irregular verbs, past tenses sometimes being completely different words. Owing to its peculiar anatomy of 'broad', 'slender', aspirated' and 'eclipsed' consonants, it has about twice the number of sounds that other European languages can boast. The softening and eclipsing of initial consonants, according to complicated and uncertain rules, cause the words to dissolve and change their appearance like shape-shifters in mythology. Irish is a lyrical language without a modern literature, originally devoted to mythological sagas, poetry, works of devotion, philosophy, medicine and science. Free Gaelic was used in classical and mediaeval literature, songs and folklore. Such is its warmth of expression, it has been described as 'the language for your prayers, your curses and your love-making'. You have to have a fine ear and a mobile larynx to speak Irish but fluently spoken it is very beautiful to listen to.

Inisheer has 300 people, one church, a graveyard and a school with 50 pupils. It also has three cars, half a dozen tractors, a shop and a craft shop. There is no policeman, no crime, no one locks their doors, kids roam free and the likelihood of a traffic jam is as remote as the island itself. Over the centuries the islanders have had to put up with a lot — grinding poverty, winds from hell and the English to name a few — but the most recent indignity, an event from which they have barely recovered, pushed them to the limit. A few years ago, for the first time ever in the history of Inisheer, a policeman visited under cover. He infiltrated in darkness cleverly disguised as a tourist, observed the both-ends-of-the-candle pub hours, went back to his tent, put his uniform on and revealed his dastardly purpose to the incredulous publicans. So shocking was this sight that the islanders took to their Guinness with even greater purpose. Convictions followed which have resulted in zero change in the drinking hours, in fact Ned of Ned's pub had a clock installed that goes backwards. Said Ned, 'People like a drink, a singsong and the craic and sure sometimes I have to throw them out and they just stand under the stars and drink what's left in their glass and sing.'

Rumour has it that a few wives had complained to the police on the main island of Inishmore that they never saw their husbands, but no one's talking. Well, you wouldn't.

I went for a walk with the express purpose of shredding my blue plastic raincoat and deforming the spokes on my umbrella by seeing how many times it could turn inside out. After some time I noticed the islanders ignored the rain as if it didn't exist — they never used umbrellas and hardly ever pulled up the hoods on their coats. Inisheer is 3.5km of limestone rock and one of the loneliest, most barren places in Western Europe, life here being a 52-weeks-a-year battle with nature. It is, however, affectingly beautiful with its endless stone walls, ancient ruins, thatched cottages and rare plants and flowers — you see wild thyme, harebells, brambles, wild strawberries, daisies and maidenhair fern. The sturdy currachs they used for fishing, lobster work and transport were pulled up on the beach. These wonderfully light dancing boats were originally covered with hide which has now been replaced by tarred canvas. The framework, with its raised bow like a pointed spoon and broad square stern, is sometimes still made with rough hazel saplings but more likely with light sawn slats. The oars, which are only 7cm wide, are fixed, there is no keel and believe me, if you try to row one of these things you just spin in circles. In the hands of the islanders however, they jig over the waves like corks and go incredibly fast in weather a larger boat wouldn't consider putting to sea in.

The TV series *Father Ted* is set in a place called Craggy Island which is in fact Inisheer. The real-life priest is a caring man called Father John Keane, who's very busy with all the children they have on the island, what with births, weddings, deaths and other social commitments. The children receive a completely Celtic education in terms of language, music and arts and visiting kids can join in with their summer cultural activities like the nightly céilís and Irish crafts. A fisherman can't always get out to do the job so tourism and Father Ted have saved the island to a large extent. The people work as much as they can in the summer because there's nothing happening in winter.

I had been given the false information, a form of Irish communication commonly called blarney (something the islanders specialise in), that if I dined in the restaurant of the pub where I'd lunched I would get a much better meal. By the way, the word blarney comes from Lord Blarney who refused to will his castle to the crown of Elizabeth I. She complained that 'what he says he rarely means', what with his eloquent excuses and soothing compliments, and she declared it was all blarney. I partook, in between unsuccessful calls from 97FM in Auckland, of a tough steak, potatoes done three different ways (one of which was the supreme sophistication of new peeled spuds) carrots, broccoli and turnips. This fortified me enough to go down the hill to another pub to check out the music. Here at Ned's I finally found someone playing the uilleann pipes. Michael O hAlmhain told me the pipes are so valuable, no one has the courage to bring them into pubs. The oldest parts of his date from 1830 and they're worth about £2000; a new handmade one would cost £3500. Michael has been living on Inisheer for 10 years, is one of Ireland's leading musicians on many instruments and is three times All Ireland champion on the concert flute.

There was a young woman from Dublin playing a button accordion and some children on holiday playing mandolin, flute and tin whistle. A strawberry redhead from Quebec, dressed in a short tartan skirt, maroon tights and a black cardigan, knew many tunes on the fiddle. Every time someone started up a tune, the others knew it — it seems there is no tune that is unheard of and there are thousands. Maybe they have an inherited collective memory or maybe the tunes are instilled from birth.

Even here there were lots of tourists, Irish and foreign, but you could tell the islanders for their florid, weathered complexions and reticent, quiet manner. They stuck together. Getting a conversation out of them was quite difficult as they took a while to move on from one-sentence answers. If you dropped it and sat quietly they would come back to you and open up voluntarily but one could never call them loquacious. But within an hour everyone on the island knew you were there and why and where you were staying. The afternoon of my arrival I met a man on the road who saluted as I passed and asked how my book was going.

As in most rural areas and especially the west, there is a shortage of women on Inisheer. The girls go away for adventure, excitement, romance, jobs and education and the boys stay to inherit the land. You can't buy land or property on Inisheer unless you're an islander — the only way for an outsider is to marry in. This is why Inisheer has retained its essence and integrity and places like Doolin in County Clare have not. Old photos in the pubs show the men in their Aran sweaters dragging seaweed up from the beach to create growing soil and sustenance for the livestock and women in their traditional red flannel skirts. Originally, while the women spun wool from untreated fleece, the fishermen knitted the sweaters, using goose quills for needles. They evolved patterns of great beauty that were symbolic and also designated the family they came from. For example the cable stitch symbolises the fisherman's rope — safety and good luck when fishing; the double zigzag stitch symbolises the marriage lines — the ups and downs that make life worthwhile; the diamond stitch symbolises success, wealth and treasure.

The next day I had been assured that the one and only restaurant on Inisheer, Fisherman's Cottage, would give me a good meal and so it came to pass that I ate six huge fresh crab claws served simply with a little mayonnaise, lemon wedges and brown soda bread. The apple pie was light and fine with lashings of good Clare cream. It was perfect. This was a pretty, clean little place with a wonderful sunroom where I got gloriously up to my elbows in it. Lunch was simple but in the evening they raised themselves to chicken with tarragon and cream, monkfish with lemon, garlic and brandy and red pepper, and basil tart with cucumber pickle, and happily, everything was organic.

The boat trip back to Rossaveal made *Moby Dick* look like a bathtub frolic, the voyage of the *Titanic* a long lunch. I threw the lovely crab straight back into the heaving Atlantic whence it came and continued to retch violently and painfully for the next hour and a half. My body, as I clung to handles on the deck, was wracked with sweat, immediately wiped off by cold sea spray as the boat lurched through the wild Atlantic sea. Okay, here is the big tip of this book: don't get the boat to the Aran Islands, get the plane. Better still, don't go at all — read the book and watch *Father Ted*. I met an old fisherman afterwards who said to me as I lay green and prostrate in the car on the side of the road, 'I tell people not to go to the islands because they haven't the faintest idea what the journey involves, but sure they won't listen — they are mad to go. I spent my life fishing and got sick often but I had no choice, it was my job.'

Now I know I suffer from seasickness and I've known that all my life but somehow I am unable to learn. I have learned never to buy another restaurant, I have learned not to wear short skirts, I have learned not to talk to men who say 'trust me', but I haven't learned not to get on boats. I don't recall a worse boat trip or worse vomiting in my life but I might be making that up . . . in any case you'll be interested to know that even though I thought I was dying, the Blessed Virgin Mary didn't enter my head once. The second tip of this book is: carry lots of cash with you. Many places don't have Visa and deal only in cash, and most villages don't have a bank.

I somehow drove up into wild, desolate Connemara which may be where my name came from, who knows? Connemara is beloved among Catholics because in the fifth century a captured slave later known as St Patrick arrived from the west coast of Britain during the break-up of the Roman Empire. *And* in the early seventh century a monk called St Mathias founded an important monastery on the remote and rugged island of Inis Ni. This may explain my name even though my father, Harvey, is of Welsh stock, because monks travelled from outpost to outpost a lot in those days.

I was on the trail to stay the night and eat at a country lodge called Garraunbaun House. They were booked out but said they would arrange for me to stay down the road if I would like to have dinner with their guests. I had read about Delia Finnegan's cooking and was very disappointed I couldn't stay there. It was way up in the hills and hard to find and by the time I got there it was 8.30pm, but worse than that — I was still sick and couldn't eat, so I missed out not only on the big bed but on the entire reason I had driven so far. In the morning I went over to have a look at what I'd missed out on.

One arrives by a rhododendron-, camellia- and hydrangea-fringed drive leading to a rather grand Georgian manor house. Set in six hectares of woodland, the house faces Ballynakill Bay and Lough Garraunbaun on to the Twelve Bens mountains beyond. It's a very comfortable house full of the scent of flowers, Victorian furnishings, squishy sofas, grand piano, beds like fields, rooms like houses with charming ensuites.

Garraunbaun (meaning white garden) has acquired cult status in just a few years and is now considered one of the best places to stay in the west. Delia made it clear she was busy and probably not too thrilled by my absence at dinner. I wasn't too thrilled with her either because when she took me around the house I saw there was a small bedroom free where I could have stayed. I did, however, get a sniff at the portion of Irish stew that would have been mine. Her Irish stew is quite sophisticated by normal standards — she uses olive oil for a start and chunks of Connemara lamb leg rather than cheaper cuts, then in a large Le Creuset pot she layers lamb, onions, carrots, potatoes, mint, thyme and sage from her garden, lots of garlic, pepper and salt till it gets to the top. Adding no water or stock, she simmers it covered for three to four hours.

Delia, who is from County Mayo, has a French assistant, speaks fluent French and German having lived in both places for long periods, is well travelled and a language teacher by trade. She's blonde with glasses and dresses in a white smock, pearl earrings and a gold necklace. Her famous food is about reproducing the flavours and memories of her mother's cooking. The secret to her success is the primary product, which is of the utmost integrity — her vegetable garden is organic, producing a large variety of lettuces, vegetables and berries which she snap freezes with great success. All her meat is free-range organic, she gets deliveries of fresh wild lobster, salmon and crab from the Atlantic and has an orchard of organic apples and crabapples from which she makes 600 wine bottles of apple juice every season. Delia cooks a different menu every day in consultation with her clients, which could include steamed salmon with beurre blanc, Pacific oysters which she says are good all year round, apple tart cooked with sugar and lemon, almond tart and lemon tart. The wine list is small but very good and entirely French with some rarely seen clarets, for example, Haute Médoc and St Emilion, and also my favourite Sancerre, Pouilly Fumé and Chablis.

What you do in Connemara is walk, pony ride and fish and the place is riddled with hearty outdoorsy types with thick socks and muscly calves getting in your way on the roads. I drove down to the 'capital' of Connemara, the pretty market town of Clifden, one of the last to be built in Ireland. The town is perched on a forested plateau above Clifden Bay and is graced with numerous 'Walk Centres' with the afore-mentioned types heading purposefully toward them. I smoothed down my J.P. Gaultier dress and smartly walked the other way to food and the music shop. Clifden is obviously an unlikely gastronomic centre but on the main drag, Market

Street, I did find a wonderful little food shop called the Connemara Hamper run by Eileen and Leo Halliday. They have hit on the bright idea of doing up tramping and picnic hampers full of good things like smoked Connemara salmon and eel, salamis, marinated olives, home-baked Connemara ham, stoneground and olive breads and Irish farmhouse cheeses like Lavinstown, a semi-soft cheese with a strange piquant flavour, and a hard and soft goat cheese from Ennis called Bluebell Falls. The soft one tasted of the salty Atlantic grass on which the goats were grazed — slightly sweet and herby.

Eileen suggested I lunch at a restaurant on the main square called Destry's so I did and watched the world — including ponies — go by. It was a little whitewashed and blue café with French doors that opened out onto the square, presumably only during a heatwave, as the doors were closed on the windy, chilly day I was there. As I was on the coast I was salivating over visions of the fresh seafood and oysters I was going to order but couldn't see any on the menu so chose the prawns with brown soda bread, all of which I would tear apart with my bare hands, the saline juices dribbling down my chin. What I got was frozen shrimp in a pink sauce on a piece of bread with wedgies and salad. To say I almost wept is perhaps overstating it but I was feeling emotional. Throwing it on the floor in a tantrum is what the appropriate reaction would have been. When I opened the weekend paper later I saw to my astonishment the chef of Destry's, Dermot Gannon, featured in a big story on Irish chef power, profiling the four best Celtic cubs of cuisine. The words genius, imaginative and mouth-watering were used. Go figure.

I decided to drive the coast road to the most famous village in the republic if you're talking music and song — Doolin. Doolin's fame is of mythical proportions and anyone who's serious about traditional music does a pilgrimage there. Many big names in Irish music have done their 'apprenticeship' in

Doolin, playing with any musicians who might have dropped in. The Connemara/Clare coast is the most beautiful, breathtaking drive I have ever done, somehow very heart-rending and dramatic. The air on the west coast is moist and dewy smelling even on a fine day and is quite mesmerising, making you drowsy and alert at the same time. The clouds drift in from the slate sea and the light is bewitching and moody in a way that seems to colour the landscape so that it's not only green but all colours, changing as you drive through it. People get this wild harsh scenery into their souls and can't get it out — it has been written about endlessly by many poets, composers and novelists. I passed small farms, white sheep with black faces and legs, piled-up stacks of peat which is still used for heating, haystacks in old-fashioned mounds rather than the modern square or round bales, lakes and rivers, wild sea, mountains. All this on one-lane country roads where you rarely get above third gear. I never used fifth the whole time I was in Ireland, what with the winding roads, hideous tourist buses, bicycles, walkers and ancient ruins I had to stop and look at. I ambled through villages with gorgeous names like Ballinderreen, Burren, Ballyvaughan, Boherboy, and Beala-clugga that made you want to melt them down into a sauce and spread all over toffee. Every so often I stopped to pick wild flowers from the side of the road — fuchsia, berries, daisies, ferns, bluebells, lavender and white convolvulus.

When I arrived in Doolin I thought it was a sort of pre-hamlet to the real thing, knew that couldn't be it and drove right past. When I got to the dock at the beach a few minutes later I realised that the cluster of a dozen houses and three pubs in the middle of nowhere actually was Doolin. It is in fact very close to the Aran Islands (which would have meant an hour less of emetic activity) and you could see the currachs (fishing boats) plying their trade. Irish was the only language spoken here until quite recently but I didn't hear it while I was there. In fact I was fortunate to hear an Irish person speaking any language as there are only 40 natives in Doolin — the other residents are foreigners who fell in love with the place and stayed, buying houses, setting up little businesses and marrying in. Even O'Connor's pub, an establishment mentioned in the same breath as the Blessed Virgin, is no longer owned by the O'Connors.

Cars and tourists on foot crowded the little road so I parked the car and went on a tour of the B&Bs closest to 'town'. I found Mrs Shannon's house which I really liked for the bright, kitsch décor, but I would have had to share the bathroom with the six other residents no thank you. Then I visited a place up behind, renting a little bedroom with shared bathroom for an outrageous £30, and finally settled on a place with an ensuite for £25, which is still a lot of money but in Doolin it's a seller's market. Any poor farmer who happens to have a family home in Doolin is now creaming it. The money in this poor fishing village is staggering — the outskirts are dotted with large new houses, almost all of them B&Bs, with lots more in construction.

Upon making my decision to stay at his place the owner, a burly middle-aged man with a gravelly voice and a beard that appeared to have declared itself an autonomous region cried with open arms: 'Ah sure, I knew you'd come back. Good-looking women always come back to me. Come in, come in now. You won't regret it, you'll be very happy here.'

'Thank you. If I wanted to stay another night would that be okay?' I asked as he brought my suitcase in.

'God almighty, God bless you but you can stay the rest of your life if you want to. My wife, who God rest her soul died tree years ago, was American and didn't she come here for a holiday and didn't she marry me so? Dat's her photo on the wall up dere and didn't I nurse her to the end when she got sick? Ah but I had 10 happy years of marriage and two beautiful children and I'm a widower now.' He spoke in a sing-songy voice and put a terribly sad look on his face as his eyes fell to the floor, a look I felt obliged to mirror.

O'Connor's pub was so hideously crowded I went up the road in the rain to check out the two other pubs, McGann's and McDermott's. I perched myself at the bar of McDermott's, ordered a plate of bacon, cabbage, spuds, white sauce and lashings of butter, and settled in with my pint of burnt barley to see what the evening would bring. As there were few Irish people to be had I got into a conversation with an Australian couple who were downing Baileys Irish cream like it was springwater. They were as disappointed as I to be surrounded by Americans, Germans, Australians and now, to add insult to injury, New Zealanders. The hired musicians with sound system on a little stage at the other end of the bar got started up with some truly beautiful singing of love songs like 'Peggy Gordon' and 'Carrickfergus' so I moved down closer to the action.

Oh, Peggy Gordon you are my darling, come sit you down upon my knee
And tell to me the very reason on why I am slighted so by thee.

I'm so in love that I can't deny it. My heart lies smothered in my breast
But it's not for you to let the world know it. A troubled mind can know no rest.

I put my head to a glass of brandy; it was my fancy I do declare
For when I'm drinking I'm always thinking and wishing Peggy Gordon was here.

There was a fiddle being played by an Irish Adonis with blond wavy hair tied back in a ponytail, the well-known Kevin Griff on banjo, an old guy on the bodhrán, a guitarist and the singer, a one-legged man called Ted McCormac. He was playing bass on the old-style Hoffman guitar like the one John Lennon used, and as usual the music was accompanied by floor-splitting foot stamping. Most of these musicians were locals which was reassuring, and to be fair, the upside of all this commercialisation is that you get a top-level concert basically free. I moved on to McGann's to find a more low-key session with no sound system, comprising a melodeon, an accordion, a guitar and, frighteningly, a digeridoo. On my way back I stopped in at O'Connor's to find a marathon session going on between a young woman fiddler and an even younger accordionist. For the first time I saw people spontan-eously dancing jigs in a pub and understood immediately why they don't move their arms and why the steps are so complicated and compact — there's no room to do otherwise.

The story of Irish dance is an ancient one, every history book mentioning how much the Irish danced and played music. In the beginning there were the Druids, who did circular dances to the oak and the sun, then the Celts turned up from central Europe bringing with them their dances and songs. When the Normans invaded in the twelfth century they introduced a love-song dance called the carol, associated with May Day rituals, wherein the leader sang a song and the six couples replied as they danced around him with simple steps. Early in the fifteenth century the English were doing a maypole dance which seemed to be a copy of Irish round dances. In the 1500s people were dancing the rince fada (long dance), the hey (women wind in around their partners in the forerunner of the reel), jigs and sword dances but to the tune of repeated attempts by the English to suppress Irish culture, including a ban on piping and the arrest of pipers. These draconian Penal Laws forced a decline not only in dance but also in customs and language that lasted for over a century. Neither was dancing the preserve of the ordinary people;

there were great knees-ups in castles, such as the Trenchmore, a big free-form country dance like the long dance where people formed two straight lines. On St John's Eve the dancers would dance in a circle around the bonfire and sometimes the cattle would be driven through the fire to purify them.

In winter or in bad weather when you couldn't do cross-roads dancing, people moved into the kitchens, which were small but had good hard flagstone floors for tapping. Crossroads dancing involved using the large area around a crossroads to do group dances in the summer evenings. As I suspected, I read that more recently the clergy saw dancing as an occasion of sin, so it had to be hidden. They were up there in their pulpits raging against it and in their spare time searching hedges for courting couples. In fact the Catholic Church put an end to crossroads dancing, bringing it inside to the more formal, controllable location of dance halls. Bishop Moylan of Kerry went so far as to threaten excommunication for the sin of unsupervised dancing. At the céilís a form of social dancing was devised by having boys and girls face each other in two lines to perform the double jig. Between each step the facing couples changed places by linking arms and turning, so that every second step was performed in the dancer's original positions. Today there are about 6000 Irish dance tunes including jigs, hornpipes, sets, polkas and step dancing.

The other important historical reason for not moving the arms and keeping the torso rigid in solo dancing was a question of grace and control. The only arm movement that was practised was a threatening gesture with a clenched fist, seen in the jig danced to what was known as a 'Tune of Occupation'. Originally all dancing was done barefoot and soft shoes only came in 1924.

Looking into the history of traditional dancing I found out about the fabulous, flamboyant, itinerant dancing master of yore. In the old days poor country people had a lot of time on their hands, especially in winter, and they spent hours telling stories, dancing and singing to pass the time. The dancing master and his fiddler began to appear in the middle of the eighteenth century and he was eagerly awaited by the village, who set up accommodation for him in one of the houses. He wore brightly coloured clothes and a tall hat called a Caroline, a long-tailed coat and white knee breeches, white stockings and turn pumps. He carried a cane with a silver head and silk tassel, indicating that he was a cut above the normal wandering musicians. Swish as a switch he would set up his classes in a kitchen, classroom or barn or even a makeshift building made specially for him.

The charge per pupil was sixpence, half of which went to the fiddler. The top masters were assigned to the 'big houses' where they would be treated like royalty, getting the best of accommodation, food and clothes. They often gave private lessons to the children of the household. The standards were very high and the steps intricate, including rounds, jigs, reels and solos. Soloists were the crème de la crème and tables were cleared to give them a suitable stage. When dancing masters came across each other at fairs they would issue a friendly challenge to dance in public on upturned barrels and sometimes they kept on dancing till only one was left. They survived right into the early twentieth century, especially in Clare and Kerry, but were gradually replaced by the formal dancing schools you see all over Ireland today.

When I got home at 1am (anyone who leaves a pub before 2am in this country is a loser) the owner of my B&B was still up in the kitchen and he invited me in for a tipple of homemade poitín, which he got down on his knees and begged me never to mention in my book. He was a farmer with horses and sheep, used to buy cattle from the Aran Islands but didn't any more — probably too busy creaming it in the B&B his wife set up.

'You know, Peter, da Doolin which became famous 20 years ago no longer exists . . . ah, I could tell you stories . . . I was brought up in dis house wit my nine brodders and sisters . . . dat's my mudder's God rest her soul photo on the wall . . . and we were poor and times got tough but weren't we happy at all . . . we were happy . . . life was so different den. Tirty years ago da villagers here and on da islands only married each odder.'

I took a sip of the generous glass of poitín, which smelled of wheat and barley and was absolutely delicious and refined, not at all the firewater I had expected.

'Poitín is very good for you, Pete — you rub it on your joints if you have de artritis like.'

'I have to know how this tiny isolated place, of all the other tiny isolated places on this coast, became so famous,' I said.

'Well, you know, in da sixties and seventies dere was very high unemployment, people had a lot of time on dere hands and dey sat in the pub all day and all night playing music and socialising like. Dey were big powerful men — farmers and fishermen and sure nottin' was written down, dey just learned da tunes from dere parents. Da west has always had da best musicians and been da most Celtic place in Ireland and dey all seemed to come here. Da musicians who made Doolin famous are all gone so and now da music in da summer is for da tourists, not for each odder.'

I shifted my chair back. He shifted his forward.

'But when the tourists go, what happens in the off-season?'

'Well, now you've got it. You're a very nice lady, you know. I'm not married, you know. You have to come from October onwards, dat's when you get only Irish, or even September when dey have da matchmakers' fair. Oh, you'll have to go up and see Willie Daly — he's da matchmaker. You'll get some good craic dere, now.'

'Right. I'll go and see Willie and I think I'll be off to bed now. Goodnight and thanks for the drink.'

'Ah, you're a very nice lady and I'm a widower, you know [kiss on the cheek]. God bless you and watch yourself now. I wish you da best of everyting.' Another kiss on the cheek.

The huge international popularity of Irish music is a relatively new phenomenon. For most of this century Irish music and songs didn't have broad appeal even at home, except among certain small groups. But some families kept the music and song traditions alive by singing them at home and learning them orally, and among these were the Keanes of Caherlistrane in east Galway, whose enormous collection of music and song first brought them to national attention in the 1950s when the family of four brothers and four sisters established the Keane Céilí Band. The father was a musician and the mother played concertina and melodeon and sang but never in public — women didn't in those days. Two of the sisters, Rita and Sarah Keane, who are now in their seventies, are well known and loved in Ireland, and the most famous Keanes now are a niece, Dolores, and nephew, Sean. The family farmed 30 hectares as well as travelling the length and breadth of the country with their Céilí Band, sometimes leaving home in the evening after finishing the farm work and returning, after concerts, in the early hours of the morning to be ready for another day's work. As I've said, the Irish don't need much sleep. In the Keane household there was always singing, music and set dancing going on till all hours, never mind the travelling to concerts. Sean's most recent album, *No Stranger*, went platinum in Ireland and Dolores has recorded many albums, such as *A Woman's Heart, Lion in a Cage* and *The Best of Dolores Keane*. She has a deep, husky, mesmerising voice with instinctive interpretations — very untainted and unaffected.

The next morning I did a recce of the village, made a booking at the only good restaurant in town and knocked on the door of a house that had a large sign on one side of the building pronouncing

CATHERINE FLAVIN O'LOUGHLIN MD
ORTHOPAEDIC SURGEON

Another on the other side pronounced:

TELEMEDICAL MARITIME STATION

This so mystified me my hand couldn't stop itself tapping on the door. It was opened by a statuesque blonde woman with grey eyes, a firm chin and a confident American voice. It was a sunny day so I said in a sunny way, 'Hello. I'm sorry to disturb you but I just have to know the meaning of these extraordinary signs and see who lives here. Would you mind talking to me for a few minutes?'

She smiled a big open Colorado smile and said, 'Of course I don't mind. As the Irish say, when God made time he made plenty of it. Sit on this stool. What would you like to know?'

'Well, who are you and do you really do these things?'

'I'm an American of Irish descent from this area. I had been living on Santorini in Greece for many years and two years ago I felt the urge to connect with my Celtic roots. I decided to set up business here and absolutely love it. I have a degree in science and engineering and I also have a project at the moment to open up an ancient Celtic spa in Fanore, not far from here. In my research on ancient European Celts (they were the Kettoi from Northern Greece), I found out about their preparation for war in the springs. They got seaweed from Ireland and made saunas that were like beehives. Mine is going to have big tubs made from whiskey barrels. It will be heated by turf and I will use seaweed for pharmaceuticals and medicine and treatments. I'm studying diseases of the joints and turf will also be made into mud for treatments.'

Mrs Shannon from next door came to sit in the sunshine on the other stool.

'Can I reserve now and for ever once a year to come and be looked after by you?' I asked.

'Yeah, yeah. The best part is, I'm going over to the Aran Islands with a film crew to shoot the gathering of seaweed.'

'Is there a restaurant in this spa?'

'You bet. We will serve seafood, fresh fish, sea vegetables and seaweed pasta and we'll make elderberry, parsnip and blackberry wine. It's going to be fabulous.'

A voice near us said, 'Are you Peta?'

'No. Okay yes.'

'You'll hate me but may I take a photo of you with me? My name's Bev. I watch your show all the time and I just can't believe it's you here in Ireland.'

This business of people sensing their Celtic roots is all the rage and a quite extraordinary phenomenon — sing them 'oh Danny Boy' and they come over all foolish, lacrimose and preoccupied. Lots of people in unlikely quarters suffer from Celtitude and you find most of them at the annual Inter-Celtic Festival in Lorient, Brittany, leppin' about in cable-knit jumpers and suffering from hangovers. The eight Celtic nations are Ireland, Wales, Scotland, Cornwall, the Isle of Man, Brittany and — madly enough — Asturias and Galicia in Spain. I came across lots of Spanish students in Ireland and it was truly uplifting to watch them trying to do rigid, foot-stomping Irish dancing when their bodies were so clearly made for passionate, sensual movements. Even though these people are all Celts, of course they no longer have a language in common so the thread that ties them together, the language that knows no barriers, is music.

When I lived in France I would sometimes mention the Irish mother whereupon suddenly they loved me more, and the business of Irish people asking me how long I was 'home' for, as if my being born and raised in New Zealand was an aberration, I have to say, did touch a whakapapa chord somewhere. It helps to know who you are if you know where you came from. Sometimes the cultural thing can go too far, though. While I was in Connemara there was a drama involving a summer Irish College that sent home a 15-year-old student because she spoke English (four sentences to be precise). Said her father: 'Marian was in tears all the way home after her dismissal. As soon as she realised she had spoken English, she apologised straight away with tá brón orm. Many of us learned Irish through fear in our day but we wanted our children to learn it through the medium of understanding.' The administrator of the school said rules is rules and thems the breaks. If you come to these summer schools to seriously learn Irish then you don't speak English.

In the evening I snuggled into a corner of Doolin's little reservations-only Ivy Cottage restaurant on Fisherstreet. The food was fresh, organic, had no preservatives, used only local fish and meat, and the menu was small but perfectly formed. I ordered a dish of the famous Connemara lamb and it came in the form of juicy tender chops with carrots, cabbage, potatoes (and white sauce of course). It was simple in the extreme but in the best way — the sort of home cooking you would eat if your mother happened to be a good cook. The cakes were set out on a table to tempt us to the sin of gluttony and wine was served in pottery goblets. The owner, Ilsa Thielan, arrived from Germany 20 years ago, just out of art school, to photograph the wild untouched landscape of the Burren, fell for it and never went back. She was a gentle, lovely woman whose passions were food and Irish music, a poet and photographer with long wavy pale red hair and a soft, nurturing voice. Her manner and attitude to life had affected the staff because the food was presented as if it were a gift. The little ivy-covered thatched cottage had a garden full of flowers and suitably cottagy decor of red window frames and flowery tablecloths. And get this: I heard from another source that she had bought it as a ruin for not even £1000 and just sold it for £400,000. That should tell you about what's happened to Doolin.

I had to visit Lisdoonvarna simply for the beauty of the

name (Lios Dúin Bhearna: the enclosure of the gapped fort) and because it had the only operating spa in Ireland known for having sulphur, iron, magnesia and copper in the springs. On my way I drove through the Burren. A more mystical, moon-like landscape you couldn't imagine — white, crevassed and barren with gentians, geraniums and orchids growing in the earth-filled fissures. In spite of its apparent aridity the Burren is profuse with unusual examples of both northern and southern plants. Irish saxifrage covers the white boulders, maidenhair ferns grow in the damp clefts and Arctic alpine mountain flowers hide in the passages and caverns.

In Lisdoonvarna I discovered two important things: the Burren Smokehouse and the Matchmakers' pub. Irish salmon is highly sought after all over Europe and the biggest treat you could get when I lived in Paris was to have an Irish friend bring you over some. The secret to the salmon is the source — the clean, pure waters of the freezing Atlantic. When it reaches the smokehouse it is cleaned, salted for five hours, washed then dried in the kiln for eight hours, then red oak is lit and the fish is smoked for eight hours. To sample it I walked up to the Roadside Tavern, a smoky, quaint little bar with diehards inside scoffing stew and a few tables outside in the fresh air. I ordered at the bar.

'Can I sit outside, please?'

'Sure you'll catch your death of cold, so you will.'

'But it's a heatwave out there.'

'You wouldn't be havin' a bit of fun with me, would you now?'

I was served a huge portion of fragrant smoked salmon with a bright crispy salad, lemon wedges and grainy brown soda bread. Absolutely glorious.

I passed the village of Kilfenora and the ruined Lemaneagh Castle, which belonged to the legendary Celtic clan of O'Brien. Connor O'Brien was married to the powerful and gorgeous Maura Rua or Red Mary, many of whose exploits have passed into folklore. When he died she did what a lot of Catholic landowners had to do in those days, she remarried a crony of the evil Cromwell to ensure the inheritance of her son, Donat, and the retention of her lands. He soon got his just desserts, however, when she got sick of him and chucked him out the window of the castle.

The Matchmakers' pub in Lisdoonvarna, where Willie Daly, the king of lonely hearts, runs the Matchmaker's Festival for the month of September, was closed so I drove over to Ennistymon, where he had his own pub, to find him. Having negotiated the endless tail-backs, tourist traffic jams, potholes, boreens and byways, I had a great afternoon in his stained, ancient little pub, met lots of people but never saw Willie Daly. The people holding up the bar went into hilarious detail about matchmaking and was I looking for a husband myself and this man here found his wife at the Matchmaker's Festival and oh it's great craic and here's Willie's number but sure you won't find him at home, he's that busy with his Romantic Riding School and his farm and his seven children and did I know there were 27.5 fellas per woman in the county? It seems if you can't find a man here you never will. It's the old story — women are such adventurers, much more so than men, who are attached to home, land and hearth. All through history the vast majority of those who emigrated were women. And the misunderstanding so sadly outlined in the song 'After the Ball is Over' often meant the ruination and thwarting of two people's lives.

The bulbous, jolly man at the bar had married his wife after a whirlwind courtship of five years and said it was too soon to tell yet if it had taken. A woman told me how it works. From the end of August till the beginning of September over 25,000 people gather in Lisdoonvarna every weekend for barbecue championships, dances, sessions, outings, meetings and you come and go as you like. Local cynics call it the sex and sangria conference; romantics call it a bit of the soft emotions between the stirrups.

All the grand hotels are full with people there for the matchmaking but lots also there just for the craic. The people requiring Willie's services are normally over 30 and they can even enter the Mr Lisdoonvarna and Queen of the Burren competitions. She told me Willie, who had been matchmaking for 33 years, believes God meant us to find a mate. He takes a few details from the people, such as number of acres, size of the milk yield, quotas etc, chats to them, gets a feel of them and doesn't believe in showing photos. Then he makes the introduction. He likes putting opposites together, such as a shy man with an outgoing woman, or a small man with a fine tall woman. It's like a spring in a mousetrap that hasn't been released — all you need is that moment of magic to set it off. Men want the same in a woman as they've always wanted — a good-looking honest girl and a companion, but what women want has changed. These days they are not looking for money and a home, they're wanting romance. Willie believes there's a lot of unharnessed love in the world and romance is the best thing life has to offer.

When I got back to Tipperary I called Willie, who'd just got in from his riding school, to talk to him. He had a gentle, lyrical Clare accent and comforting sort of voice.

'Would you mind calling me back, pet, I'm in the middle of a match at the moment. She's 72 and he's 34 and he's mad to have her.'

'Willie, you're just telling me this.'

'Ah sure, I swear it's true. Isn't it grand? She's a gorgeous woman — dead spit of Elizabeth Taylor [I wondered which era]. She's waiting in the car outside now.'

The next day I called back.

'Willie, how do you become a matchmaker? Is it inherited or did you get a calling or did you learn it?'

'My father and grandfather were traditional matchmakers and my daughter Marie is one. I wasn't sure I was going to do it as well, but in my twenties I started to notice bachelor farmers all alone on their farms and the farms having to be sold because there were no heirs. I knew they needed wives.'

'I assume the men who come to the Matchmaker's Festival are Irish but where do the women come from?'

'Mostly they're Irish but also a lot from America and England. I work on the 29-year-plan, pet — you don't rush the first 20 years and after that the following nine lose their urgency. Are you married at all?'

'I'm a tragic widow.'

'Ah now, maybe I could find someone for you.'

'No one would want me for a wife, Willie — I'm never at home and I wouldn't cook meals to order.'

'I can get around all that. There's someone for everyone. A lovely friend of mine who recently died had 20 children in a little cottage. A few years ago Irish television did a documentary on large families in Ireland and came to the house to interview them. The wife was too shy to speak to the cameras so they asked her husband why they had so many children in such a little house. He replied, 'Well, it was this way, like. My wife is partially deaf and every night we would go up the stairs and we would get into the bed. I would say to her, "Do you want to go to sleep or what?" She would say, "What?" So you see, pet, you have to be careful how you answer an Irishman.'

A pretty young woman sitting next to me, way down the road to sottishness, confided her two major problems in life.

'I'm suffering,' she smiled.

'A man,' I shrugged.

'Of course. He's not here and as you can see by my condition, I've been waiting a long time. You think I'm a fool, don't you?'

'Don't you know the rule? Never wait for a man longer than half an hour. If he's more than half an hour late, either he's never coming or he's rude; either way you don't need him.'

'I know this and I can't do it. This one is special.'

'They're all special.'

'He's not my only problem. My mother.'

At the mention of the word mother I screamed with laughter.

'Oh God! Not the mother. The two biggest problems in the history of the universe. The man and the mother. If I were a doctor I'd give you pethidine.'

'We don't get on. She doesn't understand me.'

'She's not meant to. She's your mother. The day you stop trying to please your mother is the day you will grow up and do something with your life. Metaphorically and psychologically you have to kill the mother.'

'You could be my mother.'

'Yeah, I could, so listen carefully and watch my lips.'

Her black-eyed smile was so endearing and she was so intelligent and funny and sarcastic, I loved her and wanted to play word games with her all day. She ordered another Guinness and berated me for not drinking fast enough.

'And another thing. I heard you talking about the traditional fleadh [music festival] on in town this weekend. You should know all this traditional Ceoltas stuff is very Catholic. You have to be Catholic to belong — it's all quite reactionary in a way. You have to toe the party line. What you need to listen to is contemporary Irish music, not all this passé, marching bands, set dancing crap. Hip young people wouldn't be seen dead at these fleadh and my advice is get out of town fast. Go back to your cousin. Where does she live?'

'Tipperary.'

'I live in Tipperary. Where?'

'Near Cashel.'

'I live in Cashel.'

'Near Clonoulty.'

'Oh, in the sticks.'

'That's where farms tend to be.'

'Tipperary is the best county in Ireland — you'd be much better off there.'

Chapter five

the
south-west

I returned to the bosom of Tricia, Seamus and the farm in Clogher to write at the kitchen table and allow their life to sink into my veins. After a few weeks it was time to hit the road again and this time I went south. If anyone says to you 'Don't go to Cork City, it's boring' don't listen to them. Cork (Corcaigh — meaning marsh) City is sexy, alive and ribald and I had the best meal there of the whole time I was in Ireland. It reminded me of Marseilles, that other tough, southern, ancient port town. Like the Marseillais, Corkonians have a thick, distinct accent — a blunt and guttural lilt that Dubliners maintain reeks of the farm and field. Cork has slums and bleak warehouse districts like Marseilles and is surrounded by hills. Eating there and going to their fabulous covered market was almost as much fun also in terms of flirty, informative and hilarious exchanges.

Dubliners, who consider themselves to be the centre of the universe in terms of intellectual and literary skills, still think a trip to Cork means hurling, Gaelic football and televised ploughing competitions. The oldest of the many jokes about people for Cork goes like this: a Corkonian arrives to work in Dublin and brings with him a stone from Cork. Tradition has it that he drops it in the Liffey and if it floats he goes back to Cork. Then of course there is the definition of a Corkman: he is really a Cork City man — anyone from outside the city boundary was a Kerryman with shoes. All this is jealousy — they have a tradition as aristocratic as that of Dublin and they are very clannish. For centuries they intermarried within their own walls and it is still said today that if a Corkonian buys a business, Cork people pop up in it immediately like daisies.

But Cork is in now, in a big way. At the time of writing Cork had just won the Rose of Tralee contest, Gardener of the Year, Tidiest Town and the All-Ireland Hurling final and they were feeling very good about themselves. I liked it as soon as I got there; I even liked the train station and the look of the town as I drove to my B&B. It's not a city of hotchpotch styles — the architecture seems homogeneous and equally old. On my street alone there was a Catholic church, a bikie bar, a vegetarian restaurant and a pub where farmers, hippies and gays drank placidly together. Cork has some of the country's best traditional song and music culminating in a big folk festival in September, they have a progressive university, lots of art galleries and a cool café culture. It's a bit like a southern Galway really, but with better food. I was to discover that the south-west of Ireland is where it's at, gastronomically speaking.

The first place I hit was the huge English Market on Grand Parade. This truly marvellous old Victorian covered market had many entrances from different streets and was a wonder world of produce with beautifully kept stalls. Meat stalls filled with half pigs' heads, Clonakilty black and white puddings, giant round steaks, rows of pigs' tails, smoked rashers, spiced beef and tongue and drisheen. Drisheen is the Cork variation on black pudding and looks like a chocolate python, being a sort of sausage of jelly-like consistency made from sheep's blood and milk. You boil it lightly in milk and serve it sliced, with a rich buttery white sauce whereupon it resembles a muddy blancmange. You can also slice it and fry it in butter and a common Cork dish is tripe and drisheen together — native Corkonians are mad for it.

There were cheese stalls stacked with handmade cheeses like Gubeen, a semi-hard cheese which can also come slightly smoked; Ardrahan from north Cork; Ardsallagh, a fresh mild goat cheese; Gabriel, a Swiss-style cheese from Schull in west Cork; Killarglin, Milleens and Cooleeney goats' milk brie. I found out they also hand-churned country butter in Cork. Each year Bill Hogan of West Cork Cheeses packages his butter in light wooden boxes and sends them off. He says the finest butter is a result of pastureland, the climate, bovine breeding and well-being. Here also I found lots of buttermilk, that sweet/sour by-product of butter making, so essential to good soda bread. Buttermilk is the liquid squeezed out when cream is churned to make butter and makes a very good alternative to drinking a glass of milk. It has less fat, tastes less gloopy and is good for the system, thanks to the bacteria in it. There were troughs full of shining olives and wooden buckets with reddish-green carrahgeen moss (seaweed) bouncing out of them. For generations the inhabitants of Ballyandreen village have gathered and sold carragheen moss, picked from the farthest rocks at low water during spring tides in June. They lay the beautiful fan-shaped fronds out on the cliff top to dry and bleach in the sun. It is what agar jelly is made from and used to be fed to calves and made into cough syrups and milk puddings.

Myrtle Allen of Ballymaloe House is famous for her pudding which she makes thus: soak ½ cup of carragheen in tepid water for 10 minutes. Put in a saucepan with 3¾ cups of milk and a split vanilla pod, bring to the boil and simmer very gently for 20 minutes. Pour through a strainer into a mixing bowl, pressing all the thick jelly well through. Beat in 2 tbsp of sugar and an egg yolk. In a separate bowl whip the egg white till stiff and fold it gently into the carragheen mixture. Serve chilled with a fruit compote and lashings of whipped Cork cream.

I discovered something I had never seen or heard of before — trays upon trays of buttered eggs. As soon as the eggs are laid and while the shells are still soft they are dipped in hot butter, which preserves them longer — up to 6 months — and gives the eggs a creamy taste. This preservation technique was created originally to ensure a winter supply of eggs when the hens were not laying a lot. There were duck eggs, new potatoes from Ballycotton, organic vegetables, berries, beautiful fruit and grocery stalls laden with fancy products, local and imported. In one corner of the market was the fish department, surely the most important place in any market but especially here in the south-west, where everyone agrees the best seafood comes from. Long stalls of shining, slithery, sylvan goodness of many hues, almost all from the pure coastal waters nearby — red mullet, mackerel, monkfish, salt cod, kippers, mussels, crabs, oysters, Atlantic prawns, all kinds of seaweed and tuna from near the Bay of Biscay.

The restaurants serve things like traditional tripe chowder flavoured with Murphy's stout, smoked Irish salmon, spiced Cork beef with apples and cinnamon, lamb's liver and bacon in red wine, and fish and chips in stout batter. I was told the restaurant to polish my molars on was the Ivory Tower, an upstairs place on Princes Street. According to my sources the young eccentric chef, Seamus O'Connell, was a virtuoso who could do anything with anything, throwing out heady, intense menus that were, not to put too fine a point on it, thrilling. On a Tuesday night he wasn't doing anything with anything, with no explanation and no hours announced on the front and I was, not to put too fine a point on it, not thrilled. Now what? In a starving huff I wandered into a bookshop where I got into a conversation with a seller who said yes, but a friend of O'Connell's had an equally good outfit called Café Paradiso and wasn't his wife a New Zealander and hadn't she been in the shop not one minute ago and wasn't there a pile of his recipe books sitting in front of me to prove everything. As luck would have it, Café Paradiso (yes, the name is inspired from the Wellington restaurant) was just down the road from my sterling B&B so I had two top-notch experiences in one night, but I'll get to the B&B later.

Café Paradiso on Western Road was off the dreaded tourist/student/backpack track so unless you were staying down that end of town you wouldn't come across it. It just looked like a nice café from the outside — nothing to prepare you for what was inside. I soon discovered it was acknowledged as the best vegetarian restaurant in Ireland and should have a waiting list of three years. Now I know what you're thinking and I hate vegetarians too, because of their social problems and their desperate need to attract attention to themselves by forcing you to cook special meals for them, but this place was not like this. I love vegetarian food but have inherited my mother's attitude of eat what you're given and thank God you're alive. At no point did you notice there was no meat or fish, so stunning was the skill of chef Denis Cotter, and the wellish-heeled but not conspicuously fashionable cust-omers were generally non-vegos — who came for the cuisine. It was a small, utterly unpretentious place with buttercup and leafy green walls and good-looking, charming waitresses in hip black who remembered your name.

The wine list was idiosyncratic for several reasons — its size (about 50 wines), its lack of French wines (Denis's New Zealand wife Bridget banned them after the bombing of the *Rainbow Warrior* in Auckland in 1985), and the inclusion of many good New Zealand wines. All the biggies were there — Montana, Aotea, Selaks, Milton, Spencer Hill, Rippon, Ata Rangi, Matua and Cloudy Bay. Denis's cooking showed he had lived and cooked in New Zealand. 'In New Zealand I first experienced seasonal eating as a physical reality rather than a fashionable concept. One day we pulled over at a roadside stall and bought two kilos of asparagus. We scoffed the lot for dinner as my London learned food concepts did somersaults in my head. When the asparagus glut was over there were new bounties to be exploited, and that continued through the summer until the high point of the sweetcorn pick-your-own frenzy. Bags of the stuff for a pittance, eaten within minutes or, at worst, hours of being picked. New Zealanders loved food in a way I had never encountered before. They loved to grow it, buy it and sell it in vast piles of outrageously fine quality at insanely cheap prices; and of course they loved to cook it with generosity and with a sense of freedom that seemed to come from the fact that they were throwing off their colonial culture and owed their allegiance, culinary or otherwise, to nobody. It is I think something that Ireland has in common with New Zealand.'

I started with ravioli of leek and artichoke with fresh tomato, basil and olive sauce. The smell alone sent me to heaven — a summery, golden cloud of a meal, light and fresh as sitting in the garden and picking a ravioli off a tree then sucking a tomato whose sugar had not had time to convert to starch. The main was goat cheese, pine nut and roasted tomato charlotte with spinach, polenta croutons, Puy lentils and basil oil.

I know I might get thrown into the Liffey for this but I preferred this food to Conrad Gallagher's at Peacock Alley. This was the food of a grown-up man disencumbered of an ego problem — restrained with total understanding of method. It was 100 per cent balanced, sane and fresh to within an inch of its life and almost nothing was prepared in advance. I'm sorry to pull rank but you can only really know that if you are a chef. It was Mediterranean in feel and passionately Irish in the use of seasonal produce (without going over the top in the description department). Never in a month of apple pies could I fit in a three-course meal and feel comfortable but I could have eaten 10 courses at Café Paradiso three times a day. I would go so far as to say that if I lived in Ireland I would have to drive down to Cork regularly to eat properly. This being the case, I launched into a little summer pudding with poached nectarines and vanilla custard (note the self-discipline in not using the term crème anglaise).

To make the charlotte you start with the tomatoes. Slice 6 beefsteak tomatoes thickly, remove the seeds and place on an oiled oven tray. Lightly spray with oil and bake till partly dried, crisp and a little caramelised. Meanwhile purée 6 cloves of garlic, 450g goat cheese and 2 whole eggs in a food processor, then add 3 egg whites one at a time with the motor running. Transfer this custard to a bowl and stir in enough cream (100–150ml) to give a very thick pouring consistency. Stir in 50g of pine nuts, some chopped fresh basil and freshly ground black pepper. Preheat the oven to 175°C and lightly oil 6 large ramekins, putting a piece of greaseproof paper in the bottom of each. Put a tomato slice in each, then a tablespoon of custard, repeating till you have 3 layers of each. Cook in a bain-marie for about 30 minutes. To turn out, run a knife around the outside of the charlotte, then invert the ramekin over a plate and tap the end. While this deliciousness is happening in the oven, boil the lentils in salted water till just tender, drain and return to the pan with basil oil and a finely chopped red onion. Reheat before serving. Wilt some greens, such as spinach, kale, rocket — whatever, and place some in the centre of each dinner plate. Scatter the lentils around, then invert the charlottes onto the greens. Garnish with fried polenta croutons. For home, the charlotte could be made in one large dish and the whole lot served up the same way on a large platter.

My home for that night was Garnish House on Western Road. There's a lot of talk about how dignified and hospitable the Irish are and how they'll always take time for you and have a pint or a cup of tea. There is a historical explanation for this. I often asked myself how they could be so nice and polite after all they'd been through. The answer lies in the question — at least three times the native aristocracy was conquered and dispossessed. Those who did not flee remained to be forced down by poverty and penal legislation to the economic level of the peasantry. Up until the famine it was not unusual to find poor peasants making elaborate wills for huge estates long ago confiscated. That figure of fun in Victorian days, the Irish beggar who was always saying he was descended from kings, was often speaking the truth. They say Irish good manners and hospitality are less and less evident especially in heavily tourist-burdened areas but in general I disagree, especially in the B&Bs. Staying at Garnish House was like being on retreat, with Hansi Lucey as the kind, polite, solicitous mother superior. All her staff were the same — unaffected, helpful and caring in their no-nonsense black skirts and white blouses.

Breakfast was stupendous, many splendoured and the best in Ireland — and that's saying something because B&Bs specialise in outdoing themselves on breakfasts. Mrs Lucey herself helped serve and personally asked everyone if they had slept well and how they were enjoying their breakfast. There was much gentle consternation over my bird-like meal of fresh stewed rhubarb, stewed dried fruits, fresh fruit salad, applesauce, poached peaches and pears, homemade yoghurt and muesli. She placed a basket of scones, danishes, croissants, toast and chocolate loaf on my table in case I fainted clean away. This is what people normally start with before they move on to breakfast proper, which is the cooked Irish break-fast of tomatoes, black and white puddings, eggs, bacon, beans, potato cake and sausages. If that's what you want. But you could also have porridge with cream, honey and Irish whiskey, an omelette, poached fish in lemon butter sauce, soufflés in tomato cases, avocado stuffed with smoked salmon soufflés, salmon and dill tart, brioche with scrambled egg medley *and lots more*. Mrs Lucey then came around again and asked if anyone would like more sausages or bacon or whatever. Unfortunately I just can't put food in my mouth in the morning but I think a lot of people stay in Irish B&Bs for the express purpose of making this the main meal of the day. When I reluctantly left that household Mrs Lucey gave me a hug, a God bless, a baby teddy bear with a Garnish House sash and a specially blessed ribbon to carry with me and keep me safe in whatever home I was in.

One of my sisters, Keriann, is batty about Ballymaloe (pronounced Ballymaloo) House and seemed consumed with envy and pilgrimage passion at the thought of my getting there before her. It is outside Cloyne on the Ballycotton road and they have a cookery school down the road. I had tried to contact Darina Allen of the cookery school several times and when I finally got her she was lukewarm, but I decided to go anyway. If she was there she was, and if she wasn't she wasn't.

If all else failed I could call Keriann from my bower in the hotel and gloat about my surroundings. As it turned out I never even saw Darina but that was more than made up for by meeting the gentle matriarch Myrtle Allen, who had started it all with her late husband Ivan, and hanging out with her son Rory and his wife Hazel.

Ballymaloe is rather grand as you drive into the 150-hectare property through a large stone-wall entrance up a long road . . . past signs that say 'drive slowly — lambs' . . . past the little golf course . . . past the well-kept pastures, and sweep (as much as you can sweep in a rented Fiat) up to the main entrance of the château/hotel. My room was the panelled room with an ensuite bathroom of the same size, accommodating a bathtub that was so much longer than my five foot four inches that I kept sliding under the waves. There were no locks on the doors but you could use a little slide lock from the inside. That one little thing symbolised to me what the place was about — here was an atmosphere of honesty, trust and simple homeliness. For all its greatness and legendary reputation, this grand house felt casual and unpretentious.

Ballymaloe is part of an Old Geraldine castle, rebuilt and modernised through the centuries, the fourteenth century keep remaining in its original form. It is truly a lovely old house with 32 rooms of varying sizes for families or couples, and Myrtle lives in a flat on the top floor. The blue halls, bedrooms and communal rooms are covered in paintings, some great art works by Jack Yeats (brother of the poet), Mainie Jellett, Patrick Scott, Louis Le Brocquy to name a few, creating a sophisticated aesthetic of both modern and abstract. You could spend all day looking at the paintings if you didn't have to take yourself to the dining room.

The tables had been dressed in blue gingham and silver cutlery for lunch and one had to pass by a groaning board of starters — smoked wild salmon and mackerel, soused mackerel, mushroom salad, garden tomato salad, beetroot salad, quiche, homemade bread, patés, stuffed eggs and fresh country butter. It was simple fare — they made no pretence to modern fusion ideas — but the thing is, it was all so desperately fresh, straight out of their extensive gardens that morning. The colours were bright and inviting. And thus you sat with your plate of taste treats and contemplated the menu. A waitress in navy blue uniform and white frilly apron brought me monkfish fresh from Ballycotton down the road, napped with a chive beurre blanc sauce — beautifully tender, sweet and garnished with a side bowl of green beans, potato and tomato concassée. The dessert trolley wound its wicked, many-layered, many-splendoured way toward me, jumping with meringues, apple crumble, stewed plums, chocolate cake, jelly and bowls of whipped cream. Coffee was served with dark demerara sugar and thick cream.

They always come back and ask you if you want more of anything, be it main course or dessert, because the Irish are terrified you will die of hunger on them. They are hospitable in a way that is not overbearing or garrulous like the Italians (adorable as those fine people are), and they don't take it as a reflection on their culinary skills if you refuse; they just don't want you to feel unpampered in any way. Cousin Tricia was exactly the same way in her home — she would provide a meal for anyone, any time of the day at no notice, and always worried that you hadn't had enough.

In the afternoon Hazel, who ran the hotel, took me on a tour of the properties. She was an easy-going country woman with a soft smile, curly chestnut hair and no makeup, dressed in white pants and pale blue cotton jumper. At the tiny village of Shanagarry we turned off. Shanagarry had one yellow pub, one cream pub, an amateur boxing club, a petrol station, a church and a shop.

Darina Allen's world-famous Ballymaloe Cookery School, which has spawned cookbooks and television shows, was not as I expected. It had a big demonstration kitchen and two large get-in-and-do-it-yourself kitchens with long well-equipped tables and all that, but the entrance hall, which was large and open, was decorated with brilliant fun colours — and I mean kindergarten orange, turquoise, canary yellow, sweet pea, red and fairy lights. This was a school where you didn't only learn to cook but could take courses in gardening, basket making, paint finishes and seed saving, *and*, if you still felt you hadn't grasped the meaning of life after 40 years of banging your head against a brick wall, you could also do such navel-gazing courses as the Power of Relationships, the Power of Negative Thinking, the Wisdom of Vulnerability. The power of negative thinking was the most useful of the lot in my opinion. I remember a psychologist friend of mine trying to get over a deception in love, so she made herself a list of all the dastardly things that annoyed her about the guy — he farts in bed, interrupts me, dumb haircut, skinny bum, not as brainy as me etc — and read it every time she felt weepy.

The Allen dynasty continues into the third generation with Darina and Tim's son Isaac and his wife Rachel having set up a large café/restaurant next to the school. Again it was very colourful with large Italian-style tiled floors, looked idyllically out onto the fields and served up organic, beautifully cooked food using local ingredients. This was a family who seemed to get along together, a family who had turned a lifestyle into a very successful industry. What was their secret — how could they all be good looking, hard working and nice? I found out later when I talked to Myrtle.

Walk out the doors of the dining room of the cookery school and your eyes fell upon the luscious sight of the herb garden with its ancient beech hedges, inspired by the design of the Château Villandry gardens in the Loire Valley. The kitchen garden was hidden inside a screen of trees and laid out in a series of diamonds and squares containing all sorts of vegetables. You really just wanted to sit down right there and start grazing. Hazel and I kept walking and came to the ornamental fruit garden with plums, pears, old varieties of apples, quinces, greengages, peaches, apricots, almonds and, unbelievably, an olive tree. They were not going to stop there either — they were making a water garden and an allegorical yew maze on three-quarters of an acre. The best thing was the shell house — a little temple or folly-type construction covered inside with an intricate design of shells — like a mermaid's doll house.

Tim and Darina and their family lived in a Regency home on the property, beside which there were six cottages to accommodate the students, which were rented out to holiday-makers when no courses were on. They were converted, whitewashed, eighteenth-century farm buildings, absolutely gorgeous and covered in honeysuckle, clematis and roses. On the way back we visited the pottery studio of Stephen Pearce, who makes his distinctive cream and brown ceramics and he ended our conversation with 'goodbye Peta Pleats Please'. I stared at this man in the forest wearing sandals, socks and work clothes. 'How on earth would you know about Issy Miyake?' He gave me a huge smile.

'I do travel, you know.'

In the evening I sat myself down in the Ballymaloe House dining room again. The gingham tablecloths had been whipped off to favour starched white ones and the candles were lit. The story goes that the chef sees what's in the gardens and what the sea has provided and makes up the menu in the afternoon. Irish country houses always serve four courses and mine started with a fruity and light French onion and tomato soup. This was followed by fresh shrimps and crab on the best brown bread I tasted in Ireland with fresh mayonnaise — once again you can see all this food is very simple but I can tell you the sweet, soft taste of really fresh seafood is something one rarely gets in life. Honesty is the word that kept meandering through my head. Tender roasted organic lamb was served plainly with a rosemary and garlic jus, spinach timbale and garden vegetables on the side. The waitress served everything with the word 'now', as they do in Ireland but her skills did not stretch to bringing me the cheese trolley, the only thing I was really looking forward to. I gazed mournfully as the trolley was wheeled to everyone else but no amount of asking, salivating or Marcel Marceau imitations worked, so 20 minutes later I slouched up to my room to tie myself to the laptop for a few hours.

In the morning I prepared myself to depart but Ballymaloe was a microcosm of Irishness — you can't get away. I got into a conversation with Rory Allen, Hazel's husband, who not only farmed the land there but was a fine musician. He taught a winter weekend Irish music and culture course at the cooking school, wherein students made music, swapped ideas and techniques, learned from experts and hooned around the local session pubs. I got his knowlege for free that evening when he discovered I was interested in traditional music and singing.

'Ah sure, you can't leave, then. There's a great session on tonight out in the country not far from here.'

'No, no,' cried I. 'I've planned to go to Kinsale — you know, the gastronomic centre of Ireland.'

'Don't be talking like that. I've yet to have a good meal in Kinsale and I've lived here all my life. You can't leave. If you're really interested in music, you have to come to this session with me tonight.'

'But . . .'

'Look, what's your hurry? Sit down here in the lounge. I'll help you make out an itinerary of places to visit today, you'll have tea [dinner] at Spanish Point restaurant in Ballycotton which is better than anything you'll get in Kinsale, then be back here by 9pm and we'll drive over to Walls pub in Ballinroskig.'

'But . . . where am I going to sleep? There are no more rooms free here.'

'Don't worry about that, you can sleep at our place, there's always a room somewhere. You might have to find it yourself but it's there.'

I did my tour and ate at Spanish Point as ordered. The seagull-guarded cliffs of Ballycotton were covered in heather and wild flowers and dropped straight down to the sea. The houses were on one side of the street and their gardens on the other, the sea side. It was blessed with fishing boats, colourful nets, clotted accents and burnt barley faces, with people breakwater fishing for mackerel, flat fish, dogfish and codling. The young waiter commented on the beauty of the afore-mentioned view from the restaurant, adding that his father was a fisherman and his grandfather manned the lighthouse on a little island in front of us. As was common in the country-side, there was a set-price four-course menu. Soup was usually included and sometimes they got it spectacularly wrong, like the place in Tipperary which started it all off with a sorbet. Anyway, there we all were in this seaside setting with an unsurpassed supplier outside the door and guess what? They couldn't cook fish. The haddock, which had recently been free-range frolicking in the sea, was fried rigid and dry as a Welsh sense of humour. I almost wept when the waiter asked if all was in order and had to tell the truth. With the cheese plate arrived the chef and owner — an attractive young woman who apologised profusely and refused to let me pay — explaining that an underling had committed the crime. If she had seen the dish she would never have let it go out.

It was a beautiful drive back to Ballymaloe past rocky inlets and lonely headlands, along roads umbrellaed by trees, through lush fertile farmland. I got there on the dot of nine. Rory was just pulling up on his bicycle, pointed to the three-storeyed tower attached to their house and said, 'Second floor; hope the bed's made.' I wandered into their large sprawling home, always full of people, always comfortably in disarray, always welcoming. The inhabitants of that moment included some of their children, a visiting family, a Brazilian friend of the daughter and moi. Rory said he built the tower because he was a farmer and wanted to be able to count his sheep without getting up too early. Of course the bed was beautifully made up, as was the ensuite, and breakfast was a cuppa and homemade jam on homemade bread grabbed from the leftovers on the dining-room table.

We all flew off into the night to Walls pub for their Thursday session, which turned out to be very decorous compared with the anarchistic Jim o' the Mills, whose sessions Rory had also been to. He maintained Jim used to give folks onions to eat on their way out to put off the Gardai. People were acknowledged, introduced and asked if they'd like to sing along with the squeeze box, guitars, fiddle and tin whistle. Rory played the guitar and sang, with a marked predilection for American folk music. I have always been easily seduced by the tools of the trade and the insouciant, confident way the practitioners wear them . . . finger picks on the tips of a loosely relaxed guitarist's hand as he sips and talks . . . a knife in a chef's hand held casually downwards as she listens to the radio . . . a rifle half cocked under the arm of a hunter . . . a belonging, a complacency. Session performers Kathleen ni Lordain and her husband were a wonderful couple, very staunch in their Irishness and music, who sang in Irish and English, such songs as the patriotic 'Song for Ireland' and 'Ar Éireann ni Neosfainn ce ht' and love songs like 'Sweet Rose of Allendale'. It's heresy to say you prefer Guinness in the south so I began ordering Murphy's, which is nice but not as strong as Guinness. I sang some songs in French and it turned out there were lots of froggies there so they all joined in passionately and told me it was cute to hear Piaf sung with an English accent. At the end of the night (it's always the way) the most beautiful voice I heard in any session anywhere piped up from the back of the room. Paddy Powell gave us some Scottish songs in his strong, deep, mellifluous voice and it was truly like listening to the angels. At the end everyone stood up and sang the national anthem. For one terrifying moment I thought we were going to pray.

*Walking all the day near tall towers where falcons build
    their nests.*
*Silver winged they fly, they know the call of freedom in their
    breasts.*
*Saw Black Head against the sky where twisted rocks they run
    to the sea.*
*Living on your western shore, saw summer sunsets, asked for
    more.*
I stood by your Atlantic sea and sang a song for Ireland.

*Dreaming in the night, I saw a land where no one has to
    fight.*
*Waking in your dawn, I saw you crying in the morning
    light.*
*Lying where the falcons fly, they twist and turn all in your
    air blue sky.*
*Living on your western shore, saw summer sunsets, asked for
    more.*
I stood by your Atlantic sea and sang a song for Ireland.

The biggest Fleadh Ceoil or traditional music and dance festival in Ireland happens a bit further around the coast — up in County Wexford in the town of Enniscorthy in the last week of August. Thousands of people come from all over the world to participate, learn, exchange and get into the craic. It's a week-long extravaganza of workshops, classes, recitals, dancing, singing and sessions, and also performances of mumming, an entirely nutty and eccentric sort of folk drama, which came from Cornwall with traders. In the Wexford version of the mummers' play, the 'captain' introduces characters from Irish history, praising each in turn. It is written in verse and the main theme is a combat between two heroes, the fall of one of them and his revival by a doctor. This is said to symbolise the end of the old year and start of the new. The mummers' play goes back to at least the Crusade and is often followed by the even nuttier morris dancing, which is thought to have pre-Christian origins. In Ireland the dancers were called Straw-boys, and the dancing involves figuring, step-dancing and the striking of wooden swords in unison to music. A mumming performance consists of 12 men rigged out in white shirts, green and gold sashes with rosettes attached, dark pants, tall colourful hats that look a bit like bishops' mitres, and straw masks. In the eighteenth century they visited weddings and other celebrations and expected to be rewarded with food and drink. In Ireland there had also been a tradition of young, well-educated but homeless men looking for hospitality in return for music and song, which may also have lain behind the Strawboys.

A recent addition to the classes are workshops in story-telling, which I would love to have gone to because there are very few good storytellers left. It is an ancient oral tradition and a form of highly skilled entertainment from the days when people were illiterate. Originally fairytales, they were complex works of art that went on and on and mixed the real world with the 'other' world. The story was vivid and exciting and quite often was about real people in real places — what we would call today 'magic realism', which is fashionable in novel writing now. Storytellers (seanchaí) used vivid imagination, craft, style and elegance to suspend disbelief, and the sign of a good one was when they managed to triumph over the scept-icism of the listener. The stories were also a form of education — historical, geographical and cultural — and required great feats of memory to carry them down from generation from generation. People would travel long distances to listen to a good storyteller mingle riddle, humour and paradox. More recently the stories and poems have had less of a fairytale component, being more like morality tales or true stories, but told with the same skill. Like Catholicism and paganism before it, storytelling gave people an out for things they could not explain or had no control over.

There is a significant academic life within traditional Irish music and in an attempt to make sense of such a carnival of activity the newly published book *Crosbhealach an Cheoil — Tradition and Change* makes available 32 provocative papers from a 1996 Dublin conference on the subject. Georgina Boyes, who wrote 'The Imagined Village', slags off the under-qualified, self-appointed instigators of folk and traditional music revivals who have caused all sorts of problems of selection and rejection, favouritism, elitism and marginal-isation. She says it is the intentions of the singer and the circumstances of the performance that define whether it is traditional. Reg Hall goes so far as to assert that the heyday of actual traditional music (1850–1960) has come and gone. Tony MacMahon argues that in spite of traditional music's trivialisation by Irish society, its nobility and vitality have a relevance within the spiritual desert that covers much of the western world today. He is seriously critical of the 'Irishness' of material put forward by the TV series River of Sound and damning of the use of the music as aural carpet — ear chocolate to soothe people's nerves in pubs, traffic jams or shopping centres.

In the morning I talked to Myrtle Allen over breakfast in the glasshouse extension of the dining area, a glorious black and white tiled space with wicker chairs and a view of rustling trees and the duck pond. A great place to write while watching the rain. When someone is very well known you always imagine them larger than life and this was the case with Myrtle — she was actually a small, trim, attractive woman in her seventies (unbelievable to look at her, must be all those unpolluted veges). When I remembered that someone had told me they were a Quaker family, the feeling in the house and the family in general all fell into place. The simplicity, honesty and calmness were all encompassed in this quietly spoken, intelligent woman. Sitting there in a pretty flowered skirt and cotton jumper belted around the waist, Myrtle was not a person given to grand gestures; her soft, refined accent was most unlike the Cork twang.

She told me she and her husband had bought the house at auction and farmed the land. She had always cooked good food for her five children and dreamed of having a restaurant in the house, cooking exactly the same kind of meals made from high-quality produce, and in 1964 she did it. She had no time for cans and packets, cooked with the seasons and feasted on free-range birds, freshly smoked fish from down the road, eggs, milk and pork from the farm and berries and nuts brought to her by local children. The jaded palates of the world still hang their tongues out for her wild fraughans (whortleberries), sea kale, carragheen moss pudding, simply poached sea mullet and green gooseberry and elderflower compote. But we all know you can't make money from a restaurant, especially without a liquor licence, so she and Ivan opened up accommodation and the rest is history. Two generations and 18 grandchildren later the family enterprises, which also include a craft and kitchenware shop, a café in the Crawford Art Gallery in Cork City and a chutney business, employ over 200 people.

I zoomed off in the sunshine/rain/sunshine/rain to visit Ballymaloe's fish man in Midleton. Dick Walshe, sometimes known as Coffee — which is his grandmother's name — because everyone agreed there were altogether too many Walshes in the area, was a dear treasure of a man. His small, jaunty, nautically decorated fish shop had been there for 15 years. Dick himself had been fishing for ever, his father and grandfather before him, his sons and daughters after him. There was a photo on the wall of the famous Tommy Sliney who used to sell fish from his donkey in Ballycotton. He died five years ago actually selling fish, God love him, as they say here. Dick used to own fishing boats but doesn't go out any more, buying from five big boats that fish all along the south-west coast. He supplies all over County Cork and the day I was there the shop was stocked with conger eel, lobster, oysters (two of which he dropped down my gullet as I was speaking to him), brill, turbot, smoked haddock, ray and prepared dishes made on the premises. He insisted Irish summer plaice was the best in the world. I put him out in front of the shop to take a photo and a very little old priest wearing black suit and beret, a transistor glued to his ear and a blissed-out smile, walked right through it.

Starvation drove me to the Farmhouse in the middle of town. I really like these places and you see quite a few of them in the south-west, where the left side is a pastry and bread-making kitchen and the right side is a shop selling beautifully presented local fruit and vegetables, cheeses, wines and deli products. You walk through to the restaurant at the back, past the dessert table (which is like swimming against the tide) and thence to your communal table to partake of grilled goat cheese on a sparkling salad.

A brand new sunny day took me to Cobh (pronounced Cove), the port of departure for all those people who left Ireland for whom all those sad songs were written. Until 1849 it was called Cove, being located in the cove or harbour of Cork, then Queen Victoria visited and the name was changed to Queenstown, and in 1920 it got its old name of Cobh back. I was still suffering from post-traumatic stress syndrome from my Inisheer sea voyage, the sight of boats and water immediately instigating in me a retrospective heaving and hot flush. Maybe this is where I got my nonsensical sea-sickness from — maybe it's an inherited memory from that tedious, nauseating voyage in that previous generation when my grandmother and her nine children sailed the waves to Sydney?

I expected Cobh to be dreary and depressing considering

they used to call it the town of tears and joys — people were either weeping with grief because loved ones were leaving or weeping with joy at arrivals. It was the last port of call for the *Titanic* and had the ghastly task of receiving the survivors of the *Lusitania* when it was torpedoed in 1915 by a German submarine off the coast. Of 1959 passengers, 1195 perished. But Cobh isn't dreary — it's a very pretty, busy port town built on a hill and looks more or less the same as it did in the old days. All the buildings are nineteenth century, looking out to the ornate white iron fencing around the port, and closer to the wide main street are big hotels where emigrants stayed the night before leaving. The grand mansions are further up and the houses in town are ablaze with colour, painted forget-me-not blue, mauve, peony pink, terracotta, buttermilk, racing green, canary yellow, burnt pink, cerulean blue.

In the past 150 years Ireland has had more of its people leave the country than remain in it, which is unique in the history of emigration, and it was the port of Cobh that served as the departure point for 2.5 million emigrants. The Cobh Heritage Centre, which should really be called the Emigration Museum, shows in graphic detail the boats, conditions and reasons for leaving. The convict hulks from the middle of the eighteenth century were obviously the worst, with 'criminals' who hadn't done much more than commit the crime of trying to feed their families actually chained in the hold for the whole horrendous journey to Australia or America. Some were indentured servants or actually kidnapped for labour in the colonies, a practice that was basically white slavery. At least a third died on the way in these 'coffin ships', people were whipped publicly on deck for minor infringements, and by the time the survivors got to their destination they were raving lunatics and ready for anything. In regular third-class travel conditions were marginally better because they weren't actually chained, but they had no air, no sanitation, disease and sea-sickness were rife, they had to cook their own meals in pots and give birth in the madness below deck. The one piece of baggage they could take with them that cost nothing, weighed nothing and couldn't be taken off them or lost was their music and their songs. Their hearts were broken but at the same time there was excitement at the possibility of the new world, and in a way the ones who left became more Irish than the Irish.

I think it is a common assumption that emigration from Ireland had always been poor Catholics from the south but in fact it all started in Northern Ireland in the eighteenth century, with farming Presbyterians of Scottish Ulster plantation stock, pushed out by religious persecution, bad harvests and high rents. Seventy-five per cent of Irish emigrants were Protestants, three-quarters of which were Presbyterian, the remainder being Anglicans and Quakers. They sailed to America, some-times in entire communities with the parish curate and all, and the huge archive of Irish emigration songs started from this time. The words of 'Slieve Gallion Braes' show their Scottish heritage.

It's not for the want of employment at home
That caused all the sons of old Ireland to roam,
But those tyrannising landlords, they would not let us stay.
So farewell unto ye bonny bonny Slieve Gallion Braes.

I had heard people talk about the 'American Wake' and asked around for an explanation because it seemed that once the decision had been made to go, the homesickness and melan-choly had set in immediately. It was with the emigration around the middle of the nineteenth century, which saw more single women than men leaving, that the last night before sailing turned into a wake or watch just like a funeral. Singing, drinking, music and dancing went on all night in an orgy of grief and emotion as neighbours and family farewelled those leaving. The lifestyle of the rural Irish was communal not individualist, interlocked and bound by tradition, so the leaving was a terrible wrench — a sort of death — and was treated as such. Young girls preferred emigration to being married off to an old husband, the nunnery or spinsterhood and looking after the ageing parents. Between 1856 and 1960 over six million left, mostly for America and England. The impact of emigration, like the great famine, is an integral part of the Irish psyche — they still talk about it as if it were quite recent, they still sing about it and they welcome you home as if it were only an accident of birth that you were born in New Zealand. I have never spent time in a country where they are so reluctant to see you leave. Of course now everyone is coming back, the population is going up and they are welcomed with open arms, with financial help in setting up businesses and huge tax incentives. Recent figures show that in 1998 alone about 10,000 English people came to live and work in Ireland.

One of the saddest Irish songs ever written (called the suicide song by my friends) is 'The Fields of Athenry' about a young husband and wife calling to each other over a prison wall, speaking their last words, knowing they will probably never see each other again.

By a lonely prison wall
I heard a sweet voice calling,
'Danny, they have taken you away.
For you stole Trevelian's corn,
That your babes might see the morn,
Now a prison ship lies waiting in the bay.'

Fair lie the fields of Athenry
Where once we watched the small freebirds fly.
Our love grew with the spring,
We had dreams and songs to sing
As we wandered through the fields of Athenry.

By a lonely prison wall
I heard a young man calling
'Nothing matters, Jenny, when you're free
Against the famine and the Crown,
I rebelled, they ran me down,
Now you must raise our children without me.'

On the windswept harbour wall,
She watched the last star rising
As the prison ship sailed out across the sky.
But she'll watch and hope and pray,
For her love in Botany Bay
Whilst she is lonely in the fields of Athenry.

Further south around the coast, zooming past rolling fields, dipping into woods, winding around estuaries, I came upon the supposed gastronomic centre of Ireland: the Celtic St Tropez, the haven for rich yachties — the beauteous Kinsale. West Cork has become a hideaway for big shots in the British media, politics and entertainment darling, for peace and calm darling, and Kinsale is the top player. It's full of art galleries, antique shops, fish tackle shops and money. The accents you hear in restaurants are not your riffraff, they're élite, cosmopolitan yachties, well-heeled Irish from up country, northern Italian tourists. Here again the Georgian houses on the cobbled streets are painted gorgeous colours of ox blood, Mediterranean blue, vermilion, purple, emerald green.

It's a well looked after, proud town and there are lots of food shops, delis and highly recommended restaurants. Ireland's *Food and Wine Magazine*, which I kept close to my breast, didn't mention any of them in its list of the top seafood restaurants in Ireland and all the ones I had been told about were, unbelievably, closed for lunch. It's a really lovely town to walk around, right along the pier and up the hill around the eighteenth-century street called the Mall and Rampart Lane, then down again to end up in the old marketplace. There I spied people sitting outside a fish shop sucking on huge scampi, getting garlic and juices all over their upper halves and knew I was home.

The Gourmet Store & Seafood Bar was located at Guardwell, adjacent to the twelfth-century Church of St Multose, and was owned and run by the entirely charming and friendly Martin and Marie Shanahan. The fish shop and deli were open from 9am to 6pm and they served food between 12.30pm and 4.30pm. This bright, happy place housed lobsters with their huge pincers and crayfish in a tank, wines, still warm apple pies made by Martin's mother every Friday afternoon, preserves, cooked delicacies and wet clear-eyed fish. Behind the fish counter was the kitchen where Martin did his California-style cooking and made his own bread and desserts. At 4.30am he rose to buy fish from Skibbereen so that you and I could eat a huge plate of chilli garlic scampi so fresh it sort of just melded with your soft palate. Why this place was not on any of the 30,000 recommendations I was given was mildly mysterious. They sure didn't need the publicity — I had to wait an hour for my table and the people next to me looked entirely desolate at being told there was no pie left.

Everywhere you go in Ireland you can find Clonakilty black and white puddings. They only make so many a day and when they run out they run out, so cousin Tricia used to get to the supermarket early to get them. I drove into the village of Clonakilty to drag their secrets out of them and found a humble little butcher's shop on the main street. Started by the Harrington family in 1890, the business is now run by Edward Twomey. The butcher on duty gladly told me the black puddings were made by getting lots of ox blood and soaking pinhead oatmeal in it overnight. Then they mixed beef, onions and *secret* natural spices in. This witches' dinner was then secreted into synthetic casing and cooked for 20 minutes. To make white pudding they used pinhead oatmeal, onion, pork, water and *secret* spices. To eat puddings, normally you slice and fry them and Clonakilty had some suggestions that I thought sounded quite nice and French-inspired.

Make potato cakes by grating potatoes, squeezing the juice out, seasoning and frying on both sides. Sauté some peeled apple wedges, throw in a shot of sherry vinegar and add a knob of butter. Fry your pudding and serve it up by placing the pudding on the potato cake and pouring the apple wedges and juice over.

Another good idea is to make a warm salad. Have a bed of greens ready on a plate. Fry some pudding and smoked rashers (bacon), then put them aside to keep warm. To the juices left in the pan add a dash of balsamic vinegar and cook till syrupy. Place the pudding and bacon on top of the greens and pour the cooking juices over. Can you imagine that with a thick slice of brown soda bread and a glass of Murphy's? Black pudding is probably the oldest of all sausages — in Homer's *Odyssey* they roasted a stomach filled with blood and fat. Cereal is used in all Irish black puddings but in ancient recipes you can find all sorts of innovations like chopped hard-boiled egg yolks, pine nuts, onions and leeks flavoured with pennyroyal and ginger. A lot of village butchers in Ireland make their own puddings, very moist and succulent I might say, and sell them fresh rather than dried. The mother loves black pudding and we always ate it as children. She told us stories of making it on the farm outside Sydney where she grew up, of standing next to the stuck pig and collecting the warm blood in the bucket as it poured out. I couldn't find anyone who still home-made puddings but farmhouses usually make it themselves for special occasions like Christmas. Sheila told a story of how she had to go home on Christmas Day to a bucket full of blood and do her job.

On my gastronomic way to Castletownshend further around the coast I stopped at the brightly painted village of Rosscarbery to look in on an acclaimed seafood restaurant called O'Callaghan-Walshe, a most unlikely name for a village food shrine. Although I only rushed through, I loved this village and it captured my romantic imagination with its mountainous Provençale-like feeling and central square. It traces its foundation to a sixth-century Benedictine monastery and the famous patriot O'Donovan Rossa. The restaurant was on the square and it too was Provençale looking, with its rustic sea-shanty decor, check tablecloths and holiday feel. The space was originally owner Sean Kearney's grandmother's general store, thus the name and he did simple but exciting things with Rosscarbery oysters, poached haddock, wild Atlantic salmon, rack of West Cork lamb and seafood platters.

On I vroomed around the Celtic Riviera through gay towns festooned with flags strung up across the roads to the one-steep-street village of Castletownshend. The famous women writers Somerville and Ross came from here and there was a lovely old Church of Ireland that contained stained-glass windows made by Harry Clarke. Mary Ann's Bar and Restaurant, halfway down the steep street, was painted salmon pink with flowerboxes in little black-silled windows and festooned in awards. Fortunately I had reserved because it was a packed Friday night. I chose to eat outside in the rustic back garden to enjoy the lovely evening — there were tables and flowers and a large stone hut roofed with grapevines for big parties. I ordered chef Patricia O'Mahoney's seafood platter, not realising it would feed a family of 10, and got into a conversation with four women who had joined my bench. They were all from the area and came back here on holidays with their husbands and kids. They told me lovingly about the village and area. My platter arrived with ramparts of fresh and smoked salmon, excavations of gigantic crab claws and scampi, clusters of mussels and soft beds of crab flesh, accompanied by a temple of glistening homemade mayonnaise, meltingly good brown bread and a collection of serious-looking surgeon's tools with which to extract the morsels from their carapaces.

Right when I was up to my eyeballs in it with crab meat halfway to my elbows, the air temperature dropped suddenly and host Fergus O'Mahoney rushed out, grabbed half my paraphernalia and upgraded me to the restaurant upstairs. The transition didn't work as I lost my intrepid pincers, my crab crackers, my finger dip — actually everything. Eventually I gave up asking for these things back and did a Diane Cilento imitation from the eating scene in *Tom Jones*. It was desperate to be without a young Albert Finney in such circumstances — bit like wearing a Dior dress to a cattle auction. Mind you . . . no, I won't go there. I quickly got bored with the fat, over-indulged, wealthy Irish and English patrons in the belfry and went downstairs to the pub for my coffee, where I found my companions from earlier on. They were in fine form by this stage and entertained me all evening with local gossip. That's how it is in Ireland — you enter a pub alone and you leave with four new friends. I saw Edith Somerville's nephew in the pub — an old man with white hair, a great smile and a walking stick. Telling someone I was off to Kerry in the morn I was met with: 'Ah, Kerry people are cute [meaning crafty] whores — they'll take your money but they're very charming. They would rob the eye out of your head then come back for your eyelashes.'

Tricia, Seamus, Sheila, Sean and I had agreed to spend the weekend together in Killarney. I met them in the afternoon propping up the bar and immediately announced my intention to dine in one of Ireland's longest-established seafood restaurants — Gaby's.

'Ah sure, there's no soakage in fish. I'm not eating fish,' said Sean, pointing to his drink.

'We need steaks, Pip. We are men and we need steaks and spuds.' I raised my eyes heavenwards.

Everywhere Tricia went she accumulated objects, animals, promises, purchases and human beings. The more the merrier was the catch phrase oft repeated in her dialogue. There was already an extra couple in our entourage and we were to pick up more.

'I've temporarily converted to Murphy's stout,' I announced, sliding onto a bar stool.

'Murphy's is for starters, Pip. Guinness is for hard core,' said Seamus out of the side of his mouth.

'I'm getting into the spirit of the south-west, thank you, and yes, I'll have a Powers whiskey while I'm on the topic.'

The well-known MP Jackie Healy-Rae walked by, whose most remembered statement according to Seamus was: 'I want to serve the ordinary people of Ireland.' 'Who are they?' asked the interviewer. 'The people who eat their dinner in the middle of the day.'

Gaby's was booked out so Sean didn't have to worry about lack of soakage after all.

Killarney town is a horse dung-infested Babel — very tourist polluted and commercialised with the locals having been practically pushed out of existence for the tourist dollar, *but*, outside Killarney town the scenery is spectacularly, heart-breakingly beautiful — resplendent with lakes, waterfalls, mountains, broad valleys, wooded peninsulas full of oak, arbutus, holly and mountain ash. It's like being in Canada and New Zealand all at once. There are lots of walks and drives you can take in the pristine national park, around the 180km Ring of Kerry running along the perimeter of the Iveragh Peninsula, which I did in parts. Most dramatic was the wild and mystical Gap of Dunloe. We all piled into the blue Mercedes and bravely drove into a no-man's land of tranquil windswept blue lakes, rocky islets, isolated farmhouses, craggy blue mountains and sheep and goats that seemed to be able to walk sideways up cliffs. This ancient, mythical area has inspired many poets and writers, in fact the earliest writing in Ireland probably began around 300AD and was found on stones right here. The stones are inscribed in the alphabet called Ogham, after Ogmios, the Celtic god of writing.

The gang went back to Tipperary and I continued my adventures down into the heart of the Gaeltacht to the Dingle Peninsula, that spectacular land mass jutting out into the sea in the most westerly part of Europe. As it was August I thought I might catch the Dingle races, considering my spectacular luck last time I found myself at such a betting establishment, but they were over by the time I got there. Why only in January I had won $10,000 worth of diamond earrings at the Boxing Day Derby in Auckland, and all because my friend Astar had made me the most beautiful hat. I had been told that the Half Door restaurant was the best place to get a meal in Dingle so I ordered a plate of mussel soup which was okay, but why would you put chunks of half-raw onion in it? From Killarney down, they seem to make their bread slightly sweet, almost like a brack. My fish main was served with a cream-thickened sauce and the same unvarying side dish of spud, turnip, broccoli and carrots that you get everywhere. It was conservative cooking — good but no more.

Dingle (an Daingean) is a great town — a jaunty, live wire of a fishing village blessed with a beautiful harbour and encircled by low-lying hills. I went into a pub called Dick Mac's estab. 1899 on Green Lane to get my shoes repaired. Yes, it was a pub, but there was a leather worker there who sometimes repaired shoes. It was the maddest, littlest place, apparently unchanged since the day it opened, complete with little snug for the women to sit while they waited for their husbands to get sloshed. On the left was indeed a counter with leather-working tools on it and belts, boots, brogues in boxes that looked as old as the pub itself, and gumboots stacked on shelves . . . but no leather worker. On the right was the ancient bar. If you walked through the low doorways you came to other cosy rooms that used to be part of the house but were now part of the pub — the kitchen, parlour etc.

Strolling on down to the harbour I flirted with the idea of a boat cruise then (a) saw line-ups of squalling, snivelling children and (b) remembered my post-traumatic sailing stress syndrome for which I had not yet received counselling so I quickly walked the other way.

Culturally the Dingle Peninsula is uniquely Irish, with the language still being spoken in everyday life, and of course there's a thriving traditional music scene. I went to talk to a uilleann pipe maker by the name of Cillian Ó Briain to see if he had heard of an Irish pipe maker who had lived down the road from me in Auckland but had recently come back to Ireland to live. Without my mentioning his name he immediately said, 'Oh yes, Lorcan Dunne — he lives not far from here, just outside Kenmare.' I looked him up in the booklet Cillian gave me and under Dunne, Lorcan it said:

Practice, half and full sets supplied.
New Zealand black maire and ebony used.
Hand-stitched leather bags.
Restoration, repairs and maintenance of uilleann pipes.
Bags, bellows, chanter and drone reeds supplied.

I decided to pay him a visit the next day and went off in the soft weather to see some Beehive Huts. I found the man who happened to have the spectacular luck of having some ring forts on his land sitting in his non-prehistoric hut creaming it, basically. It's true what they say about Kerrymen — they're mad for money. There are thousands of ring forts all over Ireland and this man charges you a pound to climb up his hill and look at his ancient stone huts. They were enclosed farmsteads of the free farmers of the Early Christian Period, the banks and fosses acting as a fence to prevent livestock from straying and to protect against cattle raiders and wild animals. They were inhabited up till about 1200AD by families who built the houses in a method called corbelling — erecting a circle of successive strata of stone, each layer lying a little closer to the centre than the one beneath and so on upwards till the last little hole was closed with a flagstone. The finished product looked like a big beehive. The stones had a downward and outward tilt so as to shed the water and were interconnected with parts underground. It seemed to me an utterly ghastly, pneumonia-inducing way to live and why fairies liked to inhabit them I couldn't think.

I continued my drive around the stunning Dingle Peninsula with its golden, sandy South Pacific-like Inch beach, hulking mountains and rugged beauty immortalised in the film *Ryan's Daughter*. It was still soft outdoors and I was reminded the Irish are in a permanent state of denial about the weather; they own neither raincoats nor umbrellas, they just ignore it.

Earlier in the day I had met a musician with long hair and a sixties look who told me he would be playing rock and traditional at the Small Bridge bar, one of the two best music pubs in Dingle. I went along and there he was with his electric guitar and a piper, singing Caledonia and An Droichead Beag. It worked really well, actually, which is one of the other great things about traditional music — it lends itself well to rock interpretation and mingling. The two of them up there sort of reminded me of my folk-singing days at the Poles Apart where I sported two long veils of dark hair falling on either side of my face, black eye makeup and an unshakeable belief that I was Joan Baez.

There's something wild and mountain-like about the pipes, especially if the piper is a passionate, intense player like this Eoin Duignan. He looked like a sort of Keith Richards without the hair dye — a wiry, worn, lined, once-handsome face. He also played the low whistle, a beautiful instrument that gives a mellow sound full of character, a bit like the difference between a violin and a cello. The girl next to me told me Eoin was the king of the fairies and I seriously hoped he wasn't lodged in one of those beehives. A guest singer came on and sang some American folk songs, which I am over having done the Poles Apart thing, then the metal rock guitar cut in (acoustic but still out there) with the pipes and the place went wild — like Frank Zappa and the Fairy King consorting in magical harmony.

O'Flaherty's Pub down by the pier was the oldest music pub in Dingle and a completely different kettle of fish — a fantastic old one-room pub covered in photos — Jerry Adams, IRA heroes, family photos, football line-ups, old newspaper cuttings of Michael Collins. 'Without wood we'd have no fiddles and without fiddles we'd have no music and without music we'd be lost.' Another sign I was happy to see was: 'The management wishes to advise patrons that children are not allowed on these premises after 8pm.' Certain sections of Irish society (my mouth is forming into a cat's arse here) are very permissive where children are concerned. Having children in a crowded pub at night is like being the adult who has to sleep with the kids in the tent — the blighters never stop moving and getting in the way of your pint. Which reminds me. Tricia, Mercedes and I went into a sex shop in Dublin for a laugh and lo and behold there were more children in there than adults, ranging from a baby in a pram to little kids waiting for their mother to get her tattoo done. Anyway, Cillian was there in O'Flaherty's strapped into his pipes along with a tin whistle, two fiddles and a French piper from Brittany playing a very flamboyant, super deluxe full set of pipes with tassels, velvet, chrome, shiny keys and all sorts of fandangelry. He was very proud of it and was en route to Kenmare where the French maker lived, to have it repaired.

The next afternoon I finally found Ann and Lorkan Dunne hidden away in the Old School House at Blackwater Bridge near Sneem. Lorcan was a reticent man who loathed talking about himself and his job and getting information out of him was like getting a fairy out of a ring fort — it doesn't usually happen and when it does it's only under cover of darkness. His face only lit up when we went for a walk in their garden where he waxed lyrical about their oak, holly, ash, rowan, maple, fir and fruit trees, ferns, wild roses, rhododendrons of all hues, azaleas, camellias and heather. Waxed lyrical in the way I expected him to about the pipes, but no. Their workshop is out the back and they are inundated with work, such has been the resurgence in pipe playing. Modern uilleann pipes were invented around 1700 and had a much milder and more modified tone than war pipes. From the end of the eighteenth century they were often seen at wakes where people danced around the coffin to their music. I was interested in Lorcan's use of New Zealand black maire. It has proved very popular and he took me to his shed to see 10 years' worth stacked up which he brought with him from New Zealand.

Kinsale is definitely not the gastronomic centre of Ireland but Kenmare and the villages around it on that coast might well be. Kenmare is a small triangle-shaped town, a pretty haven of tranquillity cradled in Kenmare Bay. It is in the enviable position of being right at the meeting point of the Ring of Kerry and the Ring of Beara and lots happens there in terms of both music and food. I scoured the place for culinary ecstasy, X-raying the menus and cross-examining the locals. Going by the law of averages, if enough people mentioned the same restaurant enough times, I might be able to make an educated guess. The trick was not to interrogate just anyone — you had to choose people who looked like you (quite hard in the case of a woman wearing feathers on a stick in her hair, blue platform Italian sandals and a red nylon apron) as they were more likely to know what you meant by good restaurant rather than popular restaurant. In my research I got talking to an artificial inseminator who told me New Zealand semen was of very high quality, a piece of unnecessary information guaranteed to put me off my supper. You and I probably wouldn't use the quality of sperm as a chat-up line but there you go — the charm of country people. When he wasn't tricking bulls into thinking they were doing the wild thing with a comely heifer he played the squeeze box to keep himself sane. I should think you'd need something.

The Lime Tree was the best-known of Kenmare's restaurants and there were at least six other top-notch places, which is amazing when you consider how small it is. When I found out the chef of Mulcahy's on Henry Street. had worked in Australia I knew it would be good. Any Irish chef who has worked in Australia or New Zealand shows it in their cooking, which is much more inventive, exciting and sophisticated than other Irish cooking of the same standard.

Chef Bruce Mulcahy was Irish with an Australian partner/girlfriend, a tall, pretty brunette called Rosalind who looked after the front of house. The decor was modern and cool with burnt orange, slate and aubergine walls and a slightly Japanesy feel. In Ireland they tend to provide you with bread at the beginning of the meal — in this case it was homemade brown and poppyseed with a pesto and sundried tomato dip — and then withdraw it sometime before the main act. They seem to see it as something to keep you from getting dizzy till real food arrives but not something you might wish to eat with your repast. Without exception all the places I ate in took pride in making their own bread. I was given an amuse-gueule of little sushi rolls and morsels of seafood, which exited centre stage down the hatch to allow the lobster bisque to enter stage left. It wasn't memorable but was saved by a little island of salmon-wrapped vegetable sushi roll plopped in the middle like a folly in a pink lake. The Americans at the next table were being pathetic about the sauces. Can't something be done about terminally diet-as-lifestyle Yanks disrespecting a chef's work? As a cook, you would be driven to drink, and as for culinary philistines generally, sure wouldn't you put a horse down for less? as Tricia would say. The black pepper herb-crusted loin of Kerry lamb with wild mushroom, roast garlic and onion stuffing, wrapped in puff pastry with red wine and mint sauce, was very lovely. Meat cooked in pastry can go horribly, soggily wrong but this was fine, crispy and light, not a hint of grease anywhere, the lamb cooked to pink perfection.

The next day was the worst day I spent in Ireland. Because Irish weather is so capricious I had caught a roaring, cascading, head-thumping cold. Taking my condition into account and the fact that the rain was pouring down like impure thoughts or a catastrophe, I decided it would be a really good time to drive on a gastronomic pilgrimage down the peninsula that ends in Mizen Head. I had been informed through various sources of three very good restaurants on this peninsula, had tried calling two of them with no reply or answering machines and was taking a punt on the third. I know what you're thinking — why doesn't she just reserve first to avoid disappointment — but then you see you can't possibly know how a gypsy's mind works. In the traveller's life you have to find a razor's-edge balance between intention and impromptu. I am spiritually disinclined to planning — it makes me sick and uncomfortable and hurts my brain — but it has to be done sometimes, especially if you are paying a fortune for a rental car (which you've already pranged once). Also it was the day in August on which the moon totally eclipsed the sun, which appealed to my poetic side, and Mizen Head was supposed to be the best place in the whole of Ireland to see it.

The guidebook said this area was very rugged and beautiful and I have to take their word for it. Personally I didn't see a thing as I drove through wild mountains on hairy, no-barrier, three-legged-goat roads in the most dangerous conditions possible — rain and fog. Can I say now that fog lights are a joke — have you ever tried to shine a torch through a glass of pea soup? I rest my case.

However, I must say my heart did pulse slightly faster in my breast as I drove through cloud and sleet into the eclipse. The French designer Paco Rabane had of course announced the end of the world on this day to be started off with a massive fire in Paris. My friend Jessica in the Dordogne had organised a huge end-of-the-world ball to celebrate and I was most frustrated not to be able to attend. I had the Gerry Ryan show on the radio to keep me informed and amused. Gerry Ryan is the equivalent of New Zealand's Gary McCormick — hilarious, sardonic and slightly filthy, which accounts for his huge female listener base. Gerry got me through many boring journeys along the highways and byways and one day when he was talking about first sexual experiences I actually had to pull over to the side of the road I was laughing so much. This particular morning he was interviewing a poor mad man about his preparations for the eclipse. This farmer was going on Gavarkis's prediction that the eclipse would be permanent — the world would remain in semi-darkness for at least 250 years. He had borrowed and spent thousands and thousands of pounds on building tunnels for growing vegetables and floodlighting for the farm. He had convinced his wife the twilight would remain and she was working in one of the tunnels, not bothering to come out to see the eclipse.

Suddenly at 11.10am it became quite dark but not pitch, the temperature dropped, the cows lay down in the fields and the birds went into the trees. I literally drove through the eclipse and up an impossible mud track to my first restaurant, Blair's Cove just outside Durrus. Closed for lunch. Lost for words. Slouched out in the steaming deluge on the road to Goleen where I would try restaurant number two — The Sea Urchin, owned by Seamus O'Connell of the Ivory Tower in Cork. By the time I arrived it was light again, the cold had passed and the birds flew out of the trees. When he had invested in it O'Connell had said it would be a seafood restaurant exactly as you would expect in a fishing village — desperately fresh and uncluttered. The menu promised such extravagances as porbeagle shark with lime leaves, confit of John Dory with asparagus and wild mushrooms, coriander and coconut, and fennel-roasted prawns on salsa Romano with white balsamic. Flash stuff for such a hard-to-get-to place. The sign on the door said open, I sniffled a snort of relief and dived in under my umbrella. Except that I didn't because the door was locked because they weren't open for lunch. I bristled but remained calm because I knew that Annie's, further back up the peninsula in Ballydehob, couldn't possibly be closed, besides which I was now seriously hungry as well as wet and sick. Although tragedy comes in threes, as we all know, I bravely strove onwards with hope in my heart and peristalsis in my innards. I am what is called pathologically positive. This was, after all, full-blown tourist season. People have to eat.

Annie's was closed for lunch. Anger added itself to the low blood sugar and the gastric juices that had nothing to do and I feared I might self-combust. I was barely able to be civil to the owner and held on very tightly to my umbrella so I wouldn't take the kitchen knife he had in his hand and plunge it into him. Restaurant rage. I ate some crap somewhere and drank too much wine to drown my sorrows, then dragged myself back to the car again. After that I was supposed to do all sorts of exciting things like visit Castletownbere and the Beara Peninsula but I was so ill and depressed I drove home to Kenmare and spent the afternoon in bed with aspirin, tea and John B. Keane. Mary O'Brien, the wonderful landlady at Hawthorn House, brought me up missionary trays of daecent tae by the gallon and advised me the only true cure for a bad cold was a good stiff Powers whiskey. Failing that, a second one and sure Peta, the secret is in the second one. John B. Keane is a local novelist, playwright and literary man extra-ordinaire who tells hilarious stories. In *The Celebrated Letters* he novelised the letter as a means of communication into a surreal art form. I lay wrapped up in duvets and laughed out loud all afternoon and night at 'Letters of a Matchmaker' in which the hero, farmer Dicky Mick Dicky O'Connor, turned to the trade of matchmaking. A more desperate line of damsels in fair working order, defectives on the trail for 30 years without raising a scent, and mountain mud rats looking to find a mare to sling their saddles over, you would never find. I can tell you, in rural areas things haven't changed all that much. The one tender encounter I had in this neck of the woods resembled not so much a seduction as an attempt at farmyard insemination. I had to get out Harriet's card and tick off 'illusion'.

As I was travelling back up the country the next morning I tuned into Gerry to see what the aftermath of the eclipse had been. What of the man who had spent a fortune and much hard work preparing himself for the never-ending twilight? Gerry had him on again and he was a devastated man, a shadow of his former self. It was heartbreaking. He was a lovely, gentle mad person who genuinely believed what he was doing was right. He had done all his calculations properly had spent 30 years studying Gavarkis and Nostradamus. His wife had just left him that morning, vowing never to return: he had used her inheritance to finance his beliefs. He was now broke and the local pastor was setting up a fund to help save his farm. But Gerry too had been doing some research and had come up with the information that this man had also predicted a great flood some years ago which never came, and all his buildings were on stilts. All this work on his farm had cost him about $250,000. Then as I listened in horror with eyes bulging and mouth dry from hanging open, it was revealed that his parents had buried themselves alive in a bunker some years previously, believing a nuclear holocaust was coming. The ventilation system had malfunctioned and they had died.

'Where are your parents now?' asked the incredulous Gerry.

'They're buried in the back paddock.'

'Now listen to me. What happens now? How are you going to get out of this mess? What are your immediate plans?'

'I've got to put the finishing touches to a sprinkler system I've had installed on the farm.'

'What for?'

'There's a swarm of locusts coming which will destroy everything in their path.'

Chapter six

the north

More happy weeks were spent on my return to the farm in Tipperary, where writing was now done upstairs in my bedroom due to excess of social distractions downstairs. I was reluctant to go up into Northern Ireland; I don't really know why. I suppose it was a combination of a lifelong ill-informed feeling that 'they are the bad guys and the south-erners are the good guys', fear of getting a bullet and a lack of knowledge about the area. Most southerners, which is most of Ireland (Northern Ireland or Ulster is a small bit consisting of six counties at the top right-hand side) don't think about Northern Ireland much and are too busy enjoying their new-found wealth to worry about it. It seems far away somehow. It's not a clear-cut demarcation either — there are areas in the south that are very Anglo-Irish and it's not a problem at all. When Ireland was divided in 1922 the North voted to stay with Britain because a lot of them were of English and Scottish Protestant stock, and they wished also to benefit financially from the association. At the time the majority were Protestant but now the balance has changed and the majority are Catholic and as we all know if we read newspapers there are still problems.

But when I heard that Van Morrison was from Northern Ireland my decision was made. My brother Jonathan is mad for Van the Man so I tried to get an interview with him but when I asked someone well connected they said, 'Forget it . . . you won't get anywhere near him . . . he would never talk to someone like you.' As a matter of interest Seamus Heaney, Kenneth Branagh, Liam Neeson, Barry McGuigan, James Galway and C.S. Lewis are also all from Northern Ireland.

The first things you notice upon entering Northern Ireland are that your cellphone automatically switches from IRE DIGI TO UK VODA, and that you're back to English pounds, black London cabs and red telephone booths. Of course there is a different country code for the phone because you're no longer tech-nically in Ireland, you're in Britain. And they talk funny: they say auch and aye like the Scots; they have a very particular accent which is quite different from the rest of Ireland and defied imitation on my part despite the many lessons I was given.

The setting of Belfast is quite stunning. It sort of just suddenly happens: ringed by high hills, the sea and the river valley. It's an industrial city that has been jazzed up with lots of pedestrian streets and great bars and clubs. The rampantly over-the-top, full-throated Victorian and Edwardian buildings have elaborate sculptures over the doors and windows and stone-carved heads of gods, poets and scientists. Kings and queens stare down from the high ledges of banks and old linen warehouses. The huge City Hall in the centre of the shop-till-you-drop area is very beautiful with its huge statue of Queen Victoria at the front and emerald lawns with benches to sit on all around it. On Friday lunchtimes Ian Paisley can be seen leading open-air evangelical meetings outside it: Paisley, that dark Protestant cloud who has brooded over Ulster since the 1960s, matching the intransigence of the IRA all the way. Inflexible foe of Popery and republicanism, he is a brilliant self-publicist and a brutal but effective orator.

My first evening in Belfast was spent with cousins of my friend Astar, Gary and Avril Kirkpatrick, a splendid, good-looking couple not unfamiliar with the craic as they say. They took me on a little pub crawl then dinner at an Italian rest-aurant, Antica Roma on Botanic Avenue, part of what they call the Golden Mile of restaurants. This place is in some of the best guide books and the food was good but when you're paying the bucks why can't they cook the meat properly? It drives me absolutely bonkers because it's not the hardest trick in the pack for a chef to do medium rare. Much harder to make a proper sauce or whip up a flaky pastry without it getting the soggy droop. Medium rare does not mean cooked through and it never will.

We started off at Sir John Betjeman's beloved, flamboyant

old Crown Liquor Saloon on Great Victoria Street, which was celebrating its 150th anniversary. It was in ruins for ages until the National Trust took it over and restored it to its former Victorian gin-palace splendour. In the old days a lot of pubs were made up of a series of snugs all along one side, and the Crown is one of the few pubs to have retained them. There are 10 wood-panelled, stained-glass cubicles with little doors and buzzers used to press for attention, which used to light up on a panel in the main room. These intimate snugs are the perfect place for a snog, a business meeting or a romantic rendezvous but there were Gary, Avril and I laughing our heads off and telling stories. I was told that serial snugs in a pub is a particularly Northern Irish thing because of the danger inherent in being in the wrong pub at the wrong time. They offer privacy to the criminal as well as the romantic. Over-the-top ornate is how I would describe the Crown, with its scalloped gas lights, gleaming brasswork, opulent marble, delicate stained-glass windows and handsome long bar inlaid with coloured glass. The floor is covered in intricate geometric Italian tile work and there are fine glass engravings every-where. The coolest thing, though, is that they have a live web site where you can log on and actually see what's going on in the pub at that very moment.

Next stop was their friends at the Kitchen Bar on Victoria Square. This long skinny place has been there since 1859 and prides itself on its devotion to real ales and traditional music and, interestingly, holds historical talks. It used to have snugs — the buzzers are still on the wall to prove it — and the accommodation upstairs was originally for country girls working in the city. Down the back is the restaurant where Eileen Catney serves up her simple home cooking every lunchtime. One of their specialities is pizza made on a slice of soda bread rather than with bread dough, which I thought was quite clever. I would like to try making a pissaladière with soda bread dough.

To make soda bread, sift 2 cups of white and 2 cups of wholemeal flour with 1 teaspoon of salt and 2 teaspoons of bicarbonate of soda into a bowl. Make a well in the centre and pour in 2 cups of buttermilk. Incorporate the flour into the buttermilk, turn out onto a floured board and knead for a minute or two. Smooth and shape to a round about 4cm high, cut a deep cross from one edge to the other. Place on a floured baking tray and bake at 200°C for 30 minutes. Eat with lashings of hand-churned butter.

Avril was a pretty, slim woman with soft dark red hair who looked a lot like Astar, even though the blood relative was Gary, who was tall, fair and expansive. Gary was a top-level policeman, an occupation he quietly advised me not to advertise in my big voice. This is the thing that's hard to get your mind around about the 'situation' in Northern Ireland — you have to be what I am not: careful and diplomatic. You never know what company you're keeping or what their views might be in this cultural fluidity, and to an outsider it's confusing. They're all the same colour, they speak the same language, it's the same small island, they're all Christian (yet with a strong residue of paganism beneath the surface), they sing the same songs and eat the same food. Why is it so hard to bury the hatchet? Protestant Northern Irelanders wish to identify themselves as British while southerners now wish to be seen as European.

Gary and Avril were sophisticated, tolerant Protestants, typical Northerners who had friends and colleagues on both sides and just wanted everyone to get along. Most visitors say you would never know anything was amiss in Ulster: the 'ordinary' crime rate — as opposed to terrorist crimes — is one of the lowest in the industrialised world, everyone sips lattes in the chic cafés, goes to the great nightclubs and works calmly together, laughing and talking and living their lives. The higher up the social scale you go and the better your education, Catholic or Protestant, the less of a problem there is. But I always felt an underlying tension, not aided by the overhead helicopters I woke up to in the morning. At first I panicked, then realised it was security for the negotiations that were taking place at the time. Every day on the news there was some incident or other — someone was shot in the leg overnight (knee-capping), troublesome youths were expelled from the province by the IRA because they felt the police weren't doing their job, politicians on both sides accused the others of not coming to the party etc.

I decided to do something I didn't want to do but felt I had to confront. I didn't feel I could eat, drink and sing my way through Northern Ireland and pretend the other thing didn't exist so I took a walk on the wild side, the heart of the beast, the slums of confrontation. In 30 years of sectarian conflict roughly 3500 people have been killed and as many as 50,000 injured. Using the card Lorraine had given me in Dublin I found myself in George's taxi taking a tour through pain. Only accredited taxis were allowed to go into these areas and we started on the Protestant side around Shankill Road. Every second wall was a huge mural with violent slogans and depictions of men in balaclavas with machine guns declaring various gangs and organisations — COMPROMISE OR CONFLICT, 1ST BATTALION WEST BELFAST, PROTESTANT ACTION FORCE etc. British flags flew from most of the houses and rows of them crisscrossed the grim, shabby streets where people lived in a state of determined defiance. Flying the Nationalist southern Irish tricolour flag in Northern Ireland is actually illegal and diehard loyalists still sing 'God Save the Queen' at closing time.

I got out of the taxi and walked around, which George said was safe to do, but it was weird to say the least and I didn't feel safe. I didn't see a big police presence but slate-grey armoured Land Rovers periodically passed by. Crossing the steel 'peace wall' into the Catholic side was another thrill. This ugly high wall topped with barbed wire and spikes separates Catholic from Protestant. Since the ceasefire the checkpoint has been open during the day but is still locked at night so we drove through into the Catholic section. A lot of houses were new because the old ones had been blown up and on Bombay Street, which was burned down when the riots started in August 1969, every single house was new. I saw the old Sinn Féin (Ourselves Alone) headquarters and the new, visited the craft shop that sold such items as the Republican Resistance Calendar full of photos of men in balaclavas, army fatigues, guns and gloves, postcards, pottery, pro-Catholic literature and prison art.

George, you may have gathered by now, was Catholic and had lived in this area with his family all his life. He took me to Milltown Cemetery where rested Fenians, local Catholics and IRA heroes, and a big communal grave of Bobby Sands and the hunger strikers who died in H-block at Long Kesh prison between March and October of 1981. To round off my tour we stopped off at his house to meet his family — the loves of his life: wife, son and daughter. They lived in a better part of this area in a tidy, nicely furnished semi-detached house whose sitting-room walls and mantles were covered with the prizes, medals and trophies of the dancing daughter. She showed me her beautiful traditional dress, put on her crown and told me she hoped to get into Riverdance one day. On parting George gave me a badly written anti-Unionist propaganda book called *In the Name of Carsonia*, outlining in inflammatory prose and dodgy grammar the Belfast troubles of the 1920s.

The only time I came up against the Northern Irish question in the Republic of Ireland was in a pub in Tipperary. It was 3am and we were singing old songs when three drunk young men came in and began singing IRA rebel songs. These were met with stony silence, which hung between us like a blister, to be broken by a woman who quietly said, 'We don't want any more of these songs . . . that's all over now.'

'It's not fucking over. We're still owed six provinces,' they yelled.

'No one wants to know.'

'Well, I want to know and believe me I know what I'm talking about.'

'What about the Omagh bombing?'

This is when the blister almost turned into a fracture, the song into a dirge. People can't forget the Omagh bombing of 15 August 1998 when the IRA killed dozens of civilians in a public place. It was a watershed for most Irish — they admire the old IRA but see the present one as full of thugs and bordering on mafia-like behaviour.

> *Come all ye young rebels and list while I sing*
> *For the love of one's country is a terrible thing*
> *It banishes fear with the speed of a flame*
> *And makes us all part of the Patriot Game*
> — 'The Patriot Game' by Dominic Behan

George advised me to read *The Troubles* by Tim Pat Coogan before he dropped me off at my next appointment — Roscoff restaurant on Shaftesbury Square. They did a three-course lunchtime menu for £17.50 which was a very good price for a Michelin-starred restaurant. My starter was billed as a warm salad of duck with balsamic potatoes, garlic croutons and mixed leaves which presented itself as a plinth of diced potatoes mixed with shredded duck leg meat with a delicate touch of balsamic, surrounded by pink slices of duck breast sitting in cusps of curly sliced croutons and crowned with a light salad. As I slid this balm down my throat I looked around at the bright, modern setting with its cool, dynamic décor, the crisp white shirts and floor-length aprons of the capable staff and permitted myself a few deep thoughts on Belfast, city of contrasts. On the shock of going straight from barbed-wire fences, skinny bleached-out blondes with a couple of kids in the stroller, and clenched-fist murals to the quiet, slick, controlled warmth of the world of Roscoff and luxury food most people on Falls Road would never have even heard of, let alone been able to afford in a month of ice-cream sundaes. How could I wander around a graveyard full of martyrs in a J.P. Gaultier dress and 10 minutes later find myself amid this calm prosperity? It's all pathetically, desperately sad and the hurt is so deep you can almost feel it lifting off the pavements like steam after a summer shower, except there are few summer showers here — they usually come in the shape of shrapnel and shattered knee-caps.

The chefs and owners of Roscoff, Jeanie and Paul Rankin, were sitting at a table near me engrossed in a business meeting. The gorgeous blonde was being very polite and attentive so I assumed they were interested in the proposal as four waitpersons simultaneously swooped down with their meals in a ballet of dramatic co-ordination. Then my stuffed saddle of rabbit with pomme fondant, roasted artichokes and tarragon jus floated down from heaven. I held my hair back, stuck my nose right into it and got tarragon and wafts of broccoli and red cabbage. For once the main equalled the starter. Why is it so many chefs excel in the first course then fall apart thereafter? I love saddle of bunny . . . it's really the only bit worth eating on the beast and is like no other meat for delicate, sweet, gamey tenderness.

The whole place was too good to be true so I asked the maitre d' a technical question about the potato. The place has a Michelin star after all, so a bit of testing couldn't go astray. She didn't blink an eye and without rustle gave me the answer — the potato was cooked, cut into a perfect, thick oval, then fried in melted butter. I like it when that happens and I could hear the adorable Seamus saying in my ear, 'Ah, Jaesus, do you ever stop asking questions? A shpud is a shpud.' The Rankins are Northern Ireland's sexy version of Darina Allen, with successful TV cooking shows and numerous cookbooks behind them. In fact people I spoke to in Northern Ireland had never heard of Darina! A husband-and-wife TV cooking team is unusual and attractive to an audience because they think they're getting love as well as sustenance. I flipped through one of the recipe books and my eye caught on such things as grilled tuna niçoise, Bloody Mary gazpacho, and roast aubergine and coriander soup.

Time to do what I love — jump in the car and zoom: God I love it. If I weren't a writer I would be a travelling sales-person selling . . . who cares? Vacuum cleaners, Bibles, HRT patches . . . First stop was the uninteresting village of Carrick-fergus, where I stopped off for the sole purpose of standing on the castle and singing 'I Wish I Was in Carrickfergus'. If I had been there on 31 July I could have attended Lughnasa Fair, the spectacular revival of a traditional Irish fair, held in the castle. But I was too scared to go in July because of the Protestant marches.

I wish I was in Carrickfergus
Only for nights in Ballygrand.
I would swim over the deepest ocean,
The deepest ocean my love to find.
But the sea is wide and I cannot swim over.
Neither have I the wings to fly.
If I could find me a handsome boatman
To ferry me over my love and die.

In Kilkenny it is reported
They have marble stones there as black as ink.
With gold and silver I would support her,
But I'll sing no more till I get a drink.
I'm drunk today and I'm seldom sober,
A handsome rover from town to town.
Ah but I'm sick now, my days are numbered.
Come all you men and lay me down.

The Troubles have deterred visitors and isolated Northern

Ireland from the outside world. They have retarded social progress and left the province in a time warp from which it is only now emerging. Notwithstanding, London has pumped big money into the province, the British subsidy still exceeding a whopping £3 billion a year excluding security costs, and the EU and International Fund for Ireland contribute tens of millions more. That's a lot of loot for 1. 6 million people. I drove under a bridge with huge graffiti — WELCOME TO LOYALIST LARNE. Painted on the street outside Glynn Village Hall was a huge slogan in red white and blue with GOD SAVE OUR QUEEN and ULSTER at one end and NO SURRENDER at the other. In the middle was a white star with a red hand in the middle — the 'red hand of O'Neill' severed at the wrist, from which no blood should flow, and the kerb stones on either side of the street were painted red, white and blue. I saw the red, white and blue kerb stones in lots of villages, remnants from the 12th of July marches where loyalists parade through Catholic areas commemorating 'in glorious, pious and immortal memory' the victory of Protestant King Billy over Catholic King James in 1690. Funnily enough, this drives the Catholics nuts. Another sign read THANK YOU FOR DRIVING CAREFULLY THROUGH DRAIN BAY. I should think so: with a name like that you would want your wits about you altogether.

The drive along the coast was very beautiful with the harbours, sandy beaches, bays and strange rock formations on one side and the cool forests of the famous Glens of Antrim on the other. Glentaisie, the glen of the Princess Taisie, and Glenshask, the glen of the sedges, run south to north, down to Ballycastle. Glendun, the brown glen, runs north-east into the sea at Cushendun. Glencorp, the glen of the slaughter, runs into Glendun from the south. Glenaan, the steep-sided glen, and Glenballyeamon, Edward's glen and town, meet the sea at Cushendall. Glenariff, the ploughman's glen, runs down to Waterfoot and Red Bay. Glencloy, glen of the hedges, comes out at Carnlough, and Glenarm, glen of the army, at Glenarm village. Sandpipers and dippers, willow-warblers and white throats dipped in and out of the Glens and the slopes were carpeted with bluebells and primrose. Cotton-wool woods of old trees were alive with treecreeper and goldcrest, splashed by freezing, pure waterfalls; I had to leap out of the car every 20 minutes to walk around and luxuriate in the glens. Northern Ireland has a wonderful old-world charm, the pace of life remains slow and the people are kindness itself to visitors. There are little hidden villages nestled in the dales, with shops carrying skinny books by local authors, fishing tackle and dusty notebooks. This is eel, salmon and brown trout territory, the eel fisheries on the Bann and Lough Neagh being the biggest in Europe. Many of the traps (or skeaghs) here are in the same position and are made of the same materials — hazel saplings — as those shown in seventeenth-century records. People still indulge in such traditional pastimes as poaching, smuggling, póitín making and road-bowling or 'bullets'. This latter is played on Sunday after-noons and involves two otherwise sane men hurling 800g iron balls along five or so kilometres of country lane in as few throws as possible.

By chance rather than design I stopped for the night in Ballycastle because that's where I was when I got hungry. I dragged my suitcase upstairs to my room at the lovely Glenluce Guesthouse on Quay Street and went for a stroll along the sea front in the evening sunshine. Unfortunately I had just missed the Oul' Lammas Fair which happens on the last weekend of August. Ireland's oldest traditional fair (1606) lasted a week in the old days and included lots of horse-trading and matchmaking and to this day there are still horse and sheep sales and hundreds of street stalls. I had been advised to dine at Kimark restaurant so I duly presented myself there and settled in with the *Irish Independent*. Just as well — I would have died of boredom otherwise. Dated, old-lady, musty decor and old-fashioned menu sporting such dinosaurs as deep-fried brie, chicken and prawns with mushroom sauce, pork with cider and cream, steak Diane and beef stroganoff. Steak Diane! I ordered my meal and looked darkly at the musty, conservative, older crowd coming in to fill in the seats they had reserved. When foreboding feelings assail you, order the smoked salmon — it's always so good in Ireland and they give you mountains of it, so I ate that and that was okay but I could tell from the customers' plaid cardies that it was going to end in tears. The seafood platter was cooked and hot which came as a shock, and consisted of bits of smoked haddock, salmon, cod, monkfish, three tiny mussels and a prawn — all overcooked. I folded my paper, sighed and hoped the pub would provide more satisfaction.

Up the hill from the port in the village, McCarroll's Bar provided the best night I had the whole time I was in the North. Ox-blood red bar with green trims, two cosy little rooms on the other side of the passage, low lintels, two-foot thick walls and a tiny, tiny snug which at first glance I thought was on fire. It could fit only three people and they were all smoking like a haystack that had gone up in an Irish heatwave. 'Bout yer?' (how are you?) they said when I walked in. I ordered a Guinness and slid quietly into the session going on in one of the little rooms. This session won my award for being the biggest session in the smallest room with a wall line-up of three banjos, two fiddles, a guitar, an accordion, a button accordion, a tin whistle and a bodhrán. Each county in Ireland has a fiddling style of its own and the pubs around the glens are easy places to hear good Antrim fiddling. For the most part the people are the descendants of both the ancient Irish and the Hebridean Scots across the Sea of Moyle, and the glens were one of the last places in Northern Ireland where Gaelic was spoken. In spite of the fairytales that abound in this region, Antrim people are quite staunch and dour (till about two in the morning, when they loosen up). Theodore Roosevelt, whose mother's family came from County Antrim, wrote of them: 'They were a grim, stern people, strong and simple, powerful for good and evil . . . relentless, revengeful, suspicious, knowing neither ruth nor pity . . . they were of all men the best fitted to conquer the wilderness [America] and hold it against all comers.'

This tranquil, serious country session was a relief from the raucous, beer-drenched bars of Belfast's in-your-face electrified music. Also it was now September and mercifully free of tourists which changed everything. The musicians slipped from one tune into another seamlessly as they do . . . 'My Own Dear Galway Bay', 'Moonlight in Mayo', 'My Lovely Irish Rose' . . . old-fashioned songs and hornpipes. Time went by, more people squeezed into the room, more glasses of Powers were ordered and at 1am the sandwiches and chips were passed around. It took a couple of hours for anyone to talk to me and then there was no holding them back as they sang a Dingle song, 'Red-haired Mary', in my honour and paid for my whiskeys. Traditional singing is never done in harmony, there is always one single tune sung and the singing often seems to come late in the proceedings. If you're a bit shy you can always rely on your instrument but not necessarily on your voice because a song is frequently a solo, which means you're the centre of attention, whereas an instrument is played with others. Two men called P.J. Hill and Alex Higgins seemed to be the ringleaders but they were all very good musicians and all men — no women were playing — tirelessly sharing music all night with no question of a break.

Then the Scots arrived and we got treasures like 'The Road and the Miles to Dundee', 'Dunbarton's Drums', 'Flower of Scotland', mouth music which is a fast jiggly sort of singing without accompaniment, and songs in Scottish Gaelic (they pronounce it Gaa-lic). Very late in the proceedings a middle-aged woman from Tipperary opened her mouth and sang in an emotional way I hadn't heard before. Normally they don't show a lot of emotion in their singing but this woman sang in a sobbing, gasping, passionate way that would have seared the hairs off a spider — a bit like the Portuguese fado singing. She sang the slowest, most beautiful version of 'Raglan Road' I have ever heard and when she got on to 'The Fields of Athenry' we were ready to throw ourselves off the pier. More Bushmills flowed ('no I won't have another one' . . . 'auch go on wit ye' . . . 'no really I must be going' . . . 'auch will ye stop talkin' like that, I'll just get you one more wee one').

At some point the musicians went home and the hard core of singers stayed on in full voice till 4.30am. The Scots, possessed of the most Caledonian of names like Farquhr MacKenzie and Ivan Campbell, got on well with the Tipperary folks, waxing maudlin about how they were all Celts and that was all that mattered. Ivan was a tall, dark, handsome man with piercing blue eyes and a bass that would not have been out of place in *The Magic Flute* — a beautiful, rich voice which, like all good singers, he withheld till almost the last.

There was another older man with them whose name I can't remember to my discredit — an intelligent, erudite, healthily cynical soul who every so often would shout: 'Don't sing "Danny Boy" for the love of God!' Devoid of sentimentality as he was, he was almost moved to weeping when Mrs Tipperary sang a very old song that no one else knew. This business of remembering names is a terrible affair — it's miraculous I remember my own, so many times have I had to explain, spell, pronounce, defend and curse it. Once I got the Irish around to Peta, I had to start in all over again with Mathias.

I know we were all shit faced but I really missed these people and thought about them all for days after. Maybe the dawn would have broken the spell of that night but the Celts are not really like that — they'll make friends with a fly but it's not as superficial as it seems because they're basically shy and only become emotionally demonstrative with the drink. They don't forget. Born from a history of poverty and pain, they have long memories and bottomless hearts. A hundred years is yesterday to them; 200 years, the day before. When I left they said, 'Safe home now.'

Later on that warm sunny morning I had to drive to the world's oldest (legal) distillery for an interview with Dave Quinn, master distiller at Bushmills, thus missing the great Glenluce House buffet breakfast. Eily Kilgannon in Dublin had organised it for me, and I couldn't have felt worse if I'd tried, but a girl must honour her appointments and guess what? There's nothing like a midday whiskey tasting to snap those synapses right back into place again. Dave was a very pleasant man with a background in science and biochemistry who, after 13 years of working with the company, moved into production and has never looked back. There was a large tasting room and you could go on a tour of the distillery. Just as I got comfortably settled in front of a selection of five Bushmills whiskeys a voice behind me said, 'Are you from New Zealand? You're on TV, aren't you? What are you doing here?' This time I said yes because I thought it might make me look a bit more credible to the whiskey man, instead of like a carrot with a hangover. Must have worked because when I left, that sterling gentleman gave me a bottle of Bushmills 12-year-old Millennium Reserve and one of 12-year-old single malt.

Whiskey is basically unhopped beer that you just keep distilling. We started with the light and fragrant Original Bushmills, their bread and butter, the one you see in every pub upside-down line-up, then moved on to Bushmills 10-year-old malt, which was fantastic on the nose but too easy on the palate for me. As we moved on to Bushmills 12-year-old and 16-year-old I got more interested because I love the rounded, complex taste of whiskey matured in sherry casks. This is the greatest invention since sliced bread. Bushmills have casks made in Spain from Spanish oak, which they give to Jerez who put their sherry in them for two years, then they get the casks back again and put their whiskey in them. It costs £100 to make a new cask so it's an expensive process. Their American oak casks are seasoned with bourbon in a similar arrangement.

It was now lunchtime and the research department was calling me to Bushmills Inn Restaurant. The day had gone soft on me so out came umbrella number four. Bushmills village has neat narrow streets with shops where you can buy feathers and lures to catch cod and haddock, plaice and mackerel in the Portballintrae River. This was a town where you could buy both the needle and the haystack and enjoy the smell of the turf smoke in the misty air. You could listen to the dark brown rush of the River Bush race under the bridge, around the island and past the old mill. Bushmills Inn was one of those traditionally done-up places with dim alcoves and served food like Port Stewart plaice, burgers made with farl (soda bread), black pudding with apple, and marmalade steamed pudding. It was okay but nothing to write home about. A 'hot Bush', served in local pubs, is made like this: swill some hot water around in a glass, discard it, add brown sugar, cloves, a pinch of cinnamon, a measure of Black Bush whiskey and top up with hot water.

A bit further along this gorgeous coast is the Giant's Causeway, a highway built by the gigantic Finn MacCool to get him across the sea to Scotland. Some versions of the myth say he built it to get at an enemy, some to get at a lady giant he had fallen for on Staffa, an island in the Hebrides. The causeway doesn't go as far as Scotland any more but what a ravingly wonderful idea. MacCool was a great warrior and commander of the King of Ireland's armies, could pick thorns out of his heels while running and was capable of amazing feats of strength. Today the causeway looks like a whole lot of chimneys and columns packed tightly together, the tops of which form giant stepping stones that lead from the cliff foot and disappear mysteriously under the wild, slashing sea.

Altogether there are 40,000 of these stone columns, mostly hexagonal but some with four, five, seven or eight sides, the tallest being about 12 metres high. Some unromantic people maintain this strange place is a remnant of chaos, a geological freak caused by volcanic eruptions and cooling lava. It's quite a dangerous place to climb around because it's almost always softly raining, making the stones slippery, the sea is boiling with big arms that look like they're coming to scoop you up into mythology, and there are sheer cliff drops and strong winds. All in all you feel pretty pathetic and inconsequential with your useless brolly and sensible red shoes.

Driving past the romantic remains of Dunluce Castle or Mermaid's Fort high above the sea, whose kitchen actually fell into the sea while someone was living in it, I decided on a night at Maddybenny Farm in Portrush — well, outside Portrush actually. Portrush is touted as *the* resort place of Northern Ireland but it's been ruined by amusement arcades, ferris wheels and tourism — a bit like Brighton on a bad day. It is full of B&Bs and hotels and this is where you need a good guide book. All through Ireland I used John and Sally McKenna's *Bridgestone Guide* and was rarely led down the garden path — their recommendations proved to be both eccentric and unusual in the nicest possible way.

Maddybenny is a great kettle of brown trout and you can have some for your breakfast if you like. The house is a Plantation Period (when Scottish Protestants were 'planted' in Northern Ireland to populate it with subjects loyal to the Queen) farmhouse built before 1650 and extended and modernised. There are self-catering cottages on the grounds and a riding school run by one of Rosemary White's sons. Rosemary is the matriarch-cum-major-domo of this antique-filled old house and she's very jolly and down to earth and insists you write your breakfast order down on a little piece of paper before you go out in the evening. There's kidneys in orange and mushroom jus, trout poached in lemon and dill, smoked kippers with lemon butter and basil, eggs and soldiers and the full Ulster breakfast to name a few — and that's just the hot stuff. There is no allowance that you might not wish to break your fast, for as everyone knows, people come here from far and wide for Rosemary's famous breakfast.

It was very humid weather and my cosy, comfy bedroom was host to a daddy-long-legs conference, with dozens of the flittery things copulating on the walls, getting in my hair and hanging off the ceiling all night. As I was drying my hair the next morning and scooping the bodies of last night's orgy into the rubbish the power went off and stayed off for an hour. Mmm, I thought, I wonder how Rosemary's going to cook 37 hundred different things for the famous breakfast now? The daughter-in-law knocked on everyone's doors to prevent a riot, instructed us to remain calm: breakfast was not in jeopardy. I flew into the large farm kitchen and asked if there was anything I could do to help but they were all under control thanks to the dear old save-the-day Aga, which was boiling water for coffee, frying fadge (potato bread) and bangers and poaching trout.

'I can't believe this has bloody well happened when you're here. You're going to think this is a backwater and write terrible things in that horrible notebook of yours,' said Rosemary, teatowel over the shoulder, throwing orders left and right.

'God no! Don't be ridiculous,' I said. 'I love it when exciting things happen. It's moments like these we need Minties.'

'I beg your pardon?'

'Nothing. I am now moving into the dining palace.'

The New Zealand daughter-in-law, Karen, had been sequestered to help and calmly moved around the two large dining tables set with silver, linen, flowers, jams, condiments and homemade soda bread. It was a beautiful, beautiful room full of antiques with large windows looking out onto the garden. From the serving table I scooped up a gaggle of strawberries, raspberries, blackberries, grapefruit and prunes and, God forgive me, a cloud of good Antrim cream. Unlike the usual boring inmates of these lodges, my breakfast companions were in fine fettle as we yelled comments to one another across the room. I was full up after the fruit but had ordered the Golfer's fry the night before just to have a look at it because the Great Irish Breakfast Awards said 'her breakfast was magnificent and the presentation faultless'. Someone's porridge sailed past me and my antennae went up.

'I'll bring you a bit so you can taste it, Peta,' said Rosemary.

'I won't fit it in but I love porridge.'

'I serve it with honey and Drambuie.'

'I'll fit it in.'

'Don't worry if you can't eat it — the hound will.'

To enjoy a Maddybenny plate of porridge, pour on honey from the mountains of Mourne that run down to the sea, Drambuie from the Isle of Skye and Antrim cream. Speaking of cream, Rosemary makes her own butter, an ancient art almost lost in Ireland. Although Irish handmade cheeses have been a great success, butter making has ceased to be viable because of Department of Agriculture restrictions. (At least, unlike in New Zealand, they are allowed to use unpasteurised milk for certain cheeses.) If you look closely, however, you do occasionally find hand-wrapped salted or unsalted country butter on some supermarket shelves. The contrasts between hydrogenated margarine, agri-butter and handmade country butter in appearance and taste are exquisitely obvious even to the palate-dead. Rosemary's butter was really sweet and yellow and creamy, a pleasure to pop down in little balls on crunchy toast. It was in the north that I also heard about a product by the tempting name of 'bog butter'. Up until the nineteenth century people preserved fresh butter in the bogs partially for conservation and partly because they actually liked the rancid taste. The butter was wrapped in cloth and packed into wooden boxes or baskets and sometimes flavoured with wild garlic. It was almost always black when it came up again.

The Golfer's fry arrived, resplendent with bacon, sausage, tomato, mushroom, fresh farm egg and the famous fadge or potato cake (except it wasn't the famous one because what with all the drama that morning, Rosemary hadn't made it, but I got the recipe from her). I noticed also that they didn't seem to do black and white puddings in the North but sometimes they did bulls' testicles.

To make Rosemary White's Famous Fadge you need 225g of mashed floury potato, 60g flour, 2 eggs, a lump of butter a bit bigger than a walnut, and salt and pepper. Mix it all together, turn it out and roll to about 6mm thick. You can fry it whole, section it into four while it's in the pan then flip it over, or cut the dough into any shape you like, but the essential is to cook it in bacon fat.

Years ago I had heard about 'hiring fairs' and asked people around the borders if they remembered them but no one could, or if they did they didn't know of anyone still alive who had been the victim of this practice. The words 'hiring fair' sound innocuous and rather jolly, with associations of cattle and matchmaking fairs and girls with ribbons in their hair. But far from it. Hiring fairs seem to have started around the sixteenth century in Northern Ireland and probably ended with the First World War. The Protestant farmers around Strabane used to hold a fair to arrange to hire or rent young, poor, Catholic boys and girls to work on their farms for six-month stints. In his book *Bad Blood* Colm Tóibín says he found it hard to get people to talk about it because there was a stigma attached to having been 'hired' and if you were Irish speaking you kept it quiet because it signalled you had come from Donegal for that purpose. He did eventually meet a woman called Rose McCullough who told him her story. There were many grim stories about children being murdered, raped, abused and beaten and frequently not paid. By the same token there were also stories of a lot who were treated well, some even occasionally inheriting the farms on which they had worked.

At the age of 13 Rose had got out of bed at 2am, walked with her mother in bare feet for six hours to Fintown (Fintona) station, then got the train to Strabane, arriving at about 10am. There they went to the area around the town hall where the farmers would feel the boys for muscles and look at their teeth and the girls would be subjected to a long list of questions regarding their ability to milk, wash, cook, churn and clean. Rose was illiterate and poor and you either got hired or starved. She was duly hired, the farmer jumped up on his horse's back and she had to run after the horse the seven kilometres from Strabane. Upon arrival at his farm she was put to work immediately and housed in a sort of pen at the top of the stairs. Her food was served to her not on a plate but on a bag on the table. After six months she was given her wages of £5 and sent back to Strabane to be picked up by her mother, who sent her straight back to be hired again because money was short at home. This second farm was much worse. It was snowing and she was so hungry she had to steal food, for which she was dragged around the kitchen by the ear. Every six months she was hired till she reached 19 and got married.

Since I was so close I decided to slip into the highlands of Ireland, County Donegal, by way of Londonderry — or Derry to nationalists. This town has suffered appalling urban conflict in the Troubles and been bombed so many times by the IRA they call it 'Tumbledown Derry'. The Bogside lies below the northern walls, where 14 civil rights demonstrators were killed on Bloody Sunday in 1972. However, it is actually the finest walled city left in Europe. The beautifully restored 6m-wide walls form an unbroken circle with bridges spanning the seven old gates.

As you leave Londonderry you go under a huge sign pronouncing you are now entering Free Derry, the cellphone switches back to IRE and you get out your Irish punts again. Donegal is the third-largest county in Ireland and the most northern. It is also one of the most beautiful true wildernesses left in Europe and a lot of Irish people, from both Northern Ireland and the Republic, take their holidays there.

Letterkenny is the first town you hit, a pretty, busy, enlarged fishing village all aquiver over the Women's Open Golf Tournament; a town in which it was impossible to find the tourism office and not one of the many shops had a map of County Donegal. However, it has lots of beautiful pubs and the highest population in the county. I drove up the coastline, past the seventeenth-century heritage town of Ramelton, past the magnificent Lough (lake) Swilly to the pretty fishing village of Rathmullan where the Flight of the Earls took place, and right up to Portsalon almost at the top of the Fanad Drive. This is wild and rocky country with soaring mountains and heather-clad bogs; a place where men are men, women are always smiling and saying 'Well, how are youse?' in their soft lilting accents, and someone driving a car with Northern Ireland plates should watch themselves.

Somewhere along the way I managed to bribe a folklory map from someone. It didn't tell you how to get anywhere and was covered in tacky sentimental songs but had all the good pubs, restaurants and activities handwritten all over it. At the top was a photo of a man called Daniel O'Donnell welcoming you to Donegal. The woman who gave me the map said with shining eyes that it was very special because of Daniel. 'Who's Daniel O'Donnell?' I asked. She almost took a step back, placing her hand over her heart. 'You don't know who Daniel O'Donnell is and you fancy yourself writing a book about Irish music? He's only the best thing in Donegal, a great singer, does a lot of charity work in Rumania and has done so much for this county as well.' She banged on and on about him till it became obvious I was dealing with a local saint and I fully expected to see a statue of him instead of the

Virgin in some windswept grotto on my way up into the mountains. In terms of scenery Donegal certainly rivals Connemara in its harsh, affecting beauty. The memory of it doesn't leave you — it's like the difference between a pretty face and a ruggedly handsome one that has lived and suffered a bit; the difference between picturesque and profound.

My B&B for the night was Croaghross, sitting high on the hill overlooking Portsalon strand, one of the most spellbinding strands in Ireland. They say on a cold day the wind here will almost literally paralyse you with its bone-cutting chill and it's called the 'lazy wind' because it doesn't bother going around you, it just goes straight through. It was a warm, pleasantly windy day so I did the invigorating walk of the almost four-kilometre stretch of pale, cappuccino-coloured sand along the freezing Atlantic water's edge. There is a links course bordering it but why you would play golf (the Irish are obsessed with it) when you could be having an elemental experience on the beach is completely beyond me.

This lodge was purpose built, with all the luxury bedrooms looking out onto at least a garden and at most the thrashing sea. Drinks with the other guests was beyond my powers of social pretence so I hid in my room and read the *Independent* (which has a great weekend section) till dinner time. I was brought a gin and tonic and evil, melting cheesy things warm from the oven, in spite of my strict orders to under no circumstances provoke me with such frippery. The guests were everything I feared but the food was good home cooking — better than home cooking actually with fresh peeled tomato, melon and mint salad followed by mercifully pink roast Donegal lamb with mushroom paté on croutons and of course carrots, broccoli and spuds. Poached local peaches with raspberry sauce went down okay and their only mistake was in serving the cheese after the dessert.

Further on down that coast going south you come across a tiny place called Crolly near the little fishing village of Bunbeg and in the hills is the pub that spawned the famous Irish group Clannad and the ethereal singer Enya, all children of Leo and Baba Brennan. There on a rainy Sunday morning I sat down with Leo and talked music. Both Leo's parents were in showbiz and they had a family dance band for 20 years doing crossroads and dance hall functions which of course no longer exist. Baba is a music teacher and has an award-winning choir which was about to put out a CD. Leo bought the pub 30 years ago to retire and the rest is history because his five girls and four boys had all started off singing and playing on the little stage I saw in front of me. Leo himself hates getting off a stage and although in his seventies, still sings and plays accordion every night in the summer and even encourages whole tour-loads of people to come. It's a medium-sized, well lived-in, one-room pub with ordinary carpet and worn furniture and the walls are covered in the gold, silver and platinum discs of his children, along with photos and other awards. This is one pub where you can really say anyone could turn up for a session and probably have — his own children, U2, Paul Brady, Christy Moore, Joe Elliot . . .

After Leo had arranged for me to stay at his sister-in-law's B&B up the road and informed me of a fundraising concert that evening featuring some well-known local singers, I ducked into a hotel in Bunbeg for Sunday lunch. It seemed like the whole village was there — the large dining room was splitting its sides with country people slurping up vegetable soup and roast dinners and the kids inhaling chicken nuggets and mashed potatoes — with more waiting in the foyer to get in. There is nothing to say about this food I hoped I had seen the last of when I moved into my first flat at 19, except that it was big, plain and circa 1950. Seamus would have killed for it. Busy waitresses flew around wearing teatowels slung over their shoulders, white blouses, straight black skirts and black stockings — you know the look: only Pamela Anderson could make it sexy. The sweets list was disproportionately huge and get this: the crème caramel was smashing; I could have been in any self-respecting routier in Burgundy.

The rainy afternoon was spent trying to read the *Irish Times* in the enclosed sunporch of the B&B. The sills were lined with pots of multicoloured petunias, the women were putting turf on the fire and chatting in Irish and all was well with the world. Because it was summer I hadn't smelt the aroma of turf fires before — a boggy, burning-off, Sunday-afternoon feral smell that gently pervaded the whole village. A lot of people still use turf, which is petrified lake, for their fires as it is slow burning and cost effective.

I say *trying* to read the paper because I was constantly interrupted by an Englishman with a social manner guaranteed to inspire non-culpable homicide. He informed me cheerily and lengthily that he had been chucked out of his ensuite room for a more important guest, namely me. 'Of course someone like you would quite rightly have the ensuite . . . but you're leaving tomorrow anyway aren't you? . . . so I'll go back into it tomorrow . . . I don't mind being pushed around, gosh no . . . unless of course someone even more important turns up again . . . no no, you enjoy the ensuite . . . I don't have much stuff to pack up . . . don't mind being turfed out . . . God, you must be someone special.' I wondered if a simple 'fuck off' would remedy the situation. As it happened the old wild dog solution worked — ignore it and it'll go away.

The charity concert was held in the Ostan Gweedore (Gaoth dobhair), a leisure complex and hotel overlooking the breathtaking Gweedore Bay, carved out by the relentless waves and high winds of the Atlantic over thousands of years. All the road signs are in Irish as this is a gaeltacht region so you spend lots of time going around in circles. And it's hard to guess what the English version might be because often there is no resemblance — the English just changed all the Irish names into something that sounded like the original — they're all phonetic, made-up names. I finally got to the concert in the very flash hotel complex and was put near the front with a little plate of homemade cakes and sandwiches and a daecent cup of tae. All the announcements were bilingual to a huge hall pregnant with women and expectation, waiting for the real point of the day — Daniel O'Donnell.

Leo was just finishing up some croony numbers and some wee fairies leapt onto the stage to do their incredibly complicated jigs, reels and hornpipes, flicking their legs high and rocking on their hard-shoed heels in a way assured to give an orthopaedic surgeon a heart attack. A five-year-old little doll started it off with her ringlets bouncing and her calves already muscly like the grown-up dancers. This lot were mercifully free of the curly wig syndrome but the costumes were the same ravishing, sparkling, embroidered, velveted, laced, satin-lined extravaganzas you see all over Ireland. A lot of the dancers for Riverdance and the Lord of the Dance are recruited from these rugged mountains.

There were a few other acts, then the star turn arrived. A wave of adulation rustled through the room born on wings of polyester, teacups and hairspray. I was so beside myself I didn't know whether to scratch or fart, as my father would say. There in all his glory was a man not unfamiliar with the comb, perfumed, trimmed, slimmed, knife-edge creases to the new grey suit and tie — sort of a younger Donegal Cliff Richard. He sang a mixture of sentimental Irish ballads and country tunes in a very beautiful voice, all the while telling stories and joking with the audience in an exaggerated Donegal accent. He seemed to know everyone there and sang songs specially for them, like 'My Donegal Shore'. A woman shouted out, 'Daniel, if I was 30 years younger, you would not be a single man,' to which he replied, smooth as a whippet, 'Mother of God, If I was 30 years younger that one'd have me exhausted. Sure I'd be fit only to stuff into a dog-food tin.' The entire massed rural womanhood of the north enveloped him in their adoration and love.

A lot of successful singers and musicians come out of Donegal and the folks back home don't like it when they 'elevate themselves to wild heights altogether' so Daniel keeps it grassroots in a very slick sophisticated way. When he talks about his overseas trips he says, 'Ah sure, the singing and language was so bad, I saw Protestants take out rosary beads.' An announcement was made that there was a New Zealand writer in the audience who had never heard of Daniel and would she please stand up and show herself. Huge applause and hilarity that such an unlikely thing could be true. Singers like Daniel may or may not be your thing but there was no doubting the man's charisma and genuineness. He danced with people afterwards and was endlessly available for chatting and photographs, the perfect, charming smile ever at the ready.

After the concert I ran upstairs to try out the upmarket restaurant to see if I could get something other than grey mutton and gravy. I started off with sundried tomato bread and little wholemeal scones slivered with almonds, and ordered a Sancerre and a lobster. Portions all over rural Ireland are for farmers who have worked all day and need a bit of soakage — no allowance is made for average-sized people who work seated. Three large lobster halves, caught in the harbour in front of me, swam toward the table in a lake of garlic and butter. I gasped, knowing I couldn't possibly eat so much of a rich thing and then ate it all, in all its sweetness and tenderness.

In the pouring rain and humidity I navigated my way over to Leo's Tavern in Crolly for one last pint and a singsong. Even in the ghastly weather on a Sunday night people were slowly pouring into the pub and Leo was up there with his accordion that becomes an orchestra with the press of a button, singing the old songs and telling terrible Paddy jokes which the Irish still good-naturedly laugh at — jokes about the Irishman as stupid and whimsical stories that the rest of the world have been told are culturally offensive. He doesn't need to be in a smoky pub singing on a tiny stage at his age with his successful family and business but it's obvious he just doesn't have the words 'exit stage' in his repertoire. There are 32 counties in Ireland and Leo knows all the songs from all of them. Once more the big announcement that there was a woman in the pub who had come all the way from New Zealand and would I sing a song. Then an intoxicated man from Belfast in a filthy T-shirt and Doc Martens got up and played the most stunning, sensitive, virtuoso tin whistle I had heard in any session anywhere.

In the morning I drove all the way to Belfast past some of the most fabulous scenery in the world and didn't see any of it. It precipitated as it can only in Ireland — pelting dam-loads of water. It was like driving for six hours through Niagara Falls with toothpicks for protection. But what the hell. As they say in the North — as you slide down the bannister of life, may the splinters never point the wrong way.

a fast walk
in tipperary

Trisha was most impressed with my dedication to travelling around Ireland, so upon my return to Tipperary this time she decided that some days were to be devoted to tourism. Off we roared in the blue Merc, which by now had a windscreen so streaked with Tipperary mud that I assumed she had it set on automatic pilot. It was raining but as Tricia always said, 'Sure it's sunny somewhere in Ireland today', and that was her general attitude to life. We climbed the Rock of Cashel (meaning stone fort), one of the most beautiful and remarkable examples of religious architecture in Ireland and seat of the legendary Kings of Munster. Corc, King of Munster, descended from Eóghan, the eldest son of Oilioll Olum, built the rock in 370AD and some say it was on this huge rock that in around 450AD St Patrick picked a shamrock to explain the doctrine of the Trinity to the King. The entire royal family were converted and St Patrick lived in Munster for at least seven years. On this ragged outcrop of limestone, the ancient hulk of the powerful-warrior cathedral looms ominously in the middle of a sloped treeless valley, like some monster risen up from the earth in a violent shrug. Since the ninth century this site has been endowed with churches, towers and stone crosses by a succession of religious orders and is the oldest ecclesiastical site in Europe. A completely restored Romanesque church, an intact round tower, the fifteenth-century Hall of Vicars-Choral, stunning carved stone crosses and a buttressed mediaeval cathedral remain to be crawled over by tourists and play host to classical concerts.

My main interest was in the story of one of the inhabitants, the outrageous and notorious Archbishop Miler Macgrath, appointed by Queen Elizabeth in 1571. He held the See, not to mention three others (meaning he was playing with a double deck — both Protestant and Catholic), not to mention a few wives and some 70 livings, through the greater part of his life till his death at 100. His tomb, erected during his lifetime and inscribed with an epitaph of his own flattering composition, still remains at the south side of the chancel of the cathedral.

Tipperary countryside, lying in what is called the Golden Vein, is gloriously beautiful — in the summer covered in orchids and yellow irises with a wealth of twelfth- and thirteenth-century churches and castles. Slievenamon (mountain of the fairy woman) is a conical mountain north of Clonmel much loved by Tipperary residents. The story goes that Fionn and the Fianna warriors had dallied with the fairy women of this mountain, so when Fionn decided to marry, to prevent them getting jealous, he said he would wed the one who reached the summit of Slievenamon first. Meanwhile the fact of the matter was he had fallen in love with Gráinne, the daughter of King Cormac, and had no intention of marrying a fairy woman, so he took Gráinne up to the summit the night before the race. When the strong fairy winner got to her destination 'there sat the delicate, winsome Gráinne and not a feather of her ruffled'. Which goes to show, you have to have even more powers than a fairy to short-circuit a deceiving man.

I was on a quest to find out more about the Longs of Longfield House who may or may not have been related to us so we drove into the posh, horsy Coolmore area near the farm to see if I could get into the house. Suddenly everything turned trimmed and leafy and manicured — no rustic countryside here, baby. Because there were horses worth millions of pounds strolling behind the hedges, security was uppermost everywhere you looked. We quietly crunched through Longfield stud to get to the house of my dreams, walked past the pristine circle of cream and Mediterranean blue stables and found a rather grand, circa-1850, three-storey mansion in pale stone. The gardens were immaculate and a lovely tree-lined walk led down to the River Suir. It was inhabited by five of the stud staff and we talked one of them, Louise, into showing us through. Louise was great on the ghost stories.

'We sometimes hear noises and banging in the maids'

quarters and footsteps going up the stairs,' she said, leading us around the wine cellars and huge Gothic-shaped kitchen complete with live-in fireplace, larders and pantries.

'Really?' we both gasped, leaning imperceptibly forward. 'What else?'

'Oh, you hear muffled voices, tables being dragged and a figure was seen on the servants' stairs. You kind of get used to it after a while.'

'Someting must have happened here,' said Trish, 'because 'tis well known dis house is haunted. Wasn't someone raped and murdered now?'

'Charles Bianconi who bought the house from Long lived here with his wife, his mistress, a maid he slept with regularly plus any other maid he felt like having,' said Louise.

'Ah ha! So the husband killed the maid when he got her pregnant,' I surmised, admiring the pale lemon walls and huge, high windows with the original shutters in the salon.

'No, apparently not. Apparently the mistress killed the maid and she's been dragging her around up here ever since.' Incidentally, Charles Bianconi was a poor Italian peddler who did very well, giving Ireland its first public transport service when he ran his celebrated Bianconi Long Cars from Clonmel to Cahir in 1815. By this time we had climbed up the maids' side stairs and were in the roof, which had almost as many rooms as bats — all dead — thousands of them. The next floor down had four large bedrooms, ruined by the young people living there who cared nothing for the grandeur and fine furnishings. The bedrooms had big, enamel coffin-like baths and copper fittings. We went into one bedroom with a stunning canopied bed which smelled of eau-de-sock and resembled the aftermath of a Brixton nail-bomb attack. Going down the main sweeping staircase, which begged for a Scarlett O'Hara in blood-red ruched silk, we ended up in the large oval entrance hall with its grand rooms on either side. In the sitting room was an ancient rosewood grand piano with column legs, flourishes, embellishments and a long, square-ended body. The fireplace had a club fender with seats on either side and the tall windows were hugged by luxurious quilted curtains. Trish and I both felt that as possible relatives, this house should be ours.

'This place is too big to feel comfortable in — I wouldn't know what to do with a house this size,' said Louise.

Tricia and I looked at each other. 'We would.'

My grandfather James Long was the son of gentleman farmers and although he started life with a large house and lots of land, he lost it all over the years through mismanagement, buying and selling farms and losing on each deal. If he was charming, handsome and popular, he certainly doesn't appear to have been a good businessman. There is a wonderful castle with a round tower near Tricia's farm called Farney Castle that belonged to the Longs, probably my great-great grandfather. Uncle Michael describes his father Jim as almost six foot tall and slim, with an angular face that took on the appearance of severity as he grew older — a determined man with a strong personality, an eye for good clothes and a pretty woman.

He was a very good storyteller, which my mother and I seem to have inherited to some extent. According to Aunty Peg I began telling long involved stories from the age of two, sitting on the kitchen bench, laughing my head off. My brother David and I were put to bed extremely early, which is where I learned to tell even longer stories and sing songs to stop myself going mad with boredom, and where he learned selective hearing and how to keep his mouth shut when a woman is expressing herself. To this day, my friends say David is the only man they have ever met who actually listens to them and he has an enormous tolerance for capricious women.

Jim Long met my grandmother, Margaret Shanahan, she fell for him like a ton of turf, they wed and proceeded forthwith to make nine children for God's glory in a dozen years. She was a good-looking, good-humoured woman who was fairly easy going (just as well) and a great cook, taking the trouble to do things well rather than just all right. Aunty Peg remembers life on the big farm in Tipperary and crossing a river to get to school, carrying two bricks of turf for the school fire. She describes her mother, whom she adored, as being 'straight as a die', with great legs and a figure she maintained till the end. Grandma knew what to do with a pig, making very good black pudding, smoked bacon and hams, and baked a soda bread that was light as a sponge. Being the eldest daughter, Peg devoted her life to caring for her brothers and sisters and parents till they died. Peg never asked for anything for herself in her life, still has a beautiful, tranquil nature at the age of 85 and considers it an honour to have played the role she has in her family's life. I have never heard her speak ill of anyone and she embodies all that is kind and simple and loving in the Irish.

The Longs decided to emigrate to Australia and Jim went ahead to secure a job or a farm, whichever came first. A year later, in 1927, Margaret and the nine children followed, except it wasn't that simple. I had always heard that Grandma had spent the voyage in her bunk and assumed it was sea-sickness but Peg told me a different story. She had recently given birth to triplets, who had lived for a few weeks then died, so she had to make this long sea trip away from the home she never saw again, while recovering from the emotional and physical loss of her babies.

The adults hated the trip and became very familiar with the side of the boat but the children loved it and thought it a huge adventure, with dear Peg looking after them all. They took a horrendously rough ferry from Holywood to London, then boarded the SS *Barabool* for Sydney, via Africa. In the seas off the Australian Bight I nearly didn't get born when the Long family along with everyone else were almost lost in a storm, but 'due to faith and trust in God and much rosary saying' they were saved. One more big wave and it would have been curtains. Peg says the day they arrived in Sydney, 15 August 1927, they thought it was paradise — the sun was shining, their feet were on solid ground and the local press made a fuss of them. There was James to meet them, smartly dressed as usual in a dark suit, white shirt, black tie, shining black shoes and hat. Michael told me that even if he were just going to town to fetch supplies Grandpa always dressed correctly — he would never have dreamt of turning up in an open shirt and trousers.

They went bush fairly quickly and lived on the farm at Bowraville where my mother Ann and her siblings grew up. She met my New Zealand father, Harvey Mathias, in Sydney, married him behind the altar (as punishment from the Catholic Church for marrying a non-Catholic) in a blue crepe dress and brown hat. At five foot one she had the high cheekbones, hazel eyes, soft dark hair and the determined little mouth so typical of the Long women. Being one of the youngest children in such a large family she had been rather spoiled, but was pretty, intelligent, devout and artistic. Harvey came from a well-to-do Church of England family in Rotorua and on the wedding day he was dapper in his brown suit, blond hair and charming, relaxed, humorous smile. Recently someone from my primer one class told me the thing he remembered most about me was my beautiful mother. Between them they brought up six healthy children, none of whom ended up in jail, the home for wayward girls or the National Party. Rather, they all turned out to be bright, fulfilled and mildly opinionated.

To get home we had to drive past Eddie and Mercedes' house, always difficult because (a) they were hospitable and fun and (b) they were on the Internet and I could access my emails there. Mercedes was an attractive, astute young woman with a round face, large dark brown eyes that didn't miss a trick and a sharp, suffer-no-fools sense of humour. Her husband was a ridiculously handsome man with his dark hair and eyes, generous to a fault, funny as you could hope for and hated his computer as much as I hated mine. Together we insulted, threatened and gave the fingers to technology, my incompetent server in particular. Eddie made beautiful furniture and babies and Mercedes had a home decorating shop, also helping Eddie in the construction of their little boy Samuel, an exact replica of both of them. We all kissed this peachy child so much I was amazed he didn't get dislocated joints.

Down the road from Trish, Joe Dwyer grew the best spuds in the area so we drove to his place and ordered two stone of new summer British Queens. There he was in his five hectares of perfect drills, most of which are sewn with Golden Wonders in the winter, digging them up by hand and filling bags for us. He had a large shrine to the Virgin Mary in his garden and handled the potatoes as if they were diamonds. The word spud is derived from the tool used to cultivate it — the spuddle, meaning short knife, and later around the 1860s a digging implement. As a verb, spud has an equally long history, meaning to dig a hole with a tool called a spud.

The question of potatoes evokes great passion among the Irish. Just before I arrived in Ireland there had been a hulla-baloo in New Zealand over an Irishman who had smuggled some potatoes into New Zealand from a visit to Ireland. He had had it up to here (for 55 years in fact) with New Zealand potatoes and was desperate for a decent, floury Irish spud. 'I've put up with a lot of difficult potatoes over the years,' said he, 'and it's high time they did something about all the bad potatoes they have down here.' For his efforts he was fined $750 by MAF who snapped, 'It was a diseased potato intro-duced to Ireland in the 1800s that is believed to have brought with it the dreaded potato blight which resulted in the death of millions of people from starvation.' When I asked people at the Irish consulate in Auckland they all agreed that Irish potatoes were much better than New Zealand ones and I would soon find out for myself.

I love potatoes so it was with beating heart and bated breath that I ate my first spud in Ireland. It was very tasty — delicious in fact — but nothing to risk ruining the potato crop in New Zealand for. As I had the pleasure of eating potatoes almost every day for three months in Ireland I came to realise that the only potato they like is a flour ball — sweet, fluffy and fally-aparty, cooked in the skin, peeled at the table and helped down with a forkful of butter. Historical writing tells us that the peasants used to fling a big pot of boiled potatoes in their skins on the table to be eaten with the hands — no plate or utensils — accompanied by fresh buttermilk. In general we New Zealanders, myself in particular, like a firm waxy potato that doesn't fall apart *unless* we are specifically making mashed potatoes, in which case our Agria is one of the best. The Irish (except in refined restaurants) use floury potatoes for everything — colcannon (fried potatoes and cabbage) scalloped, whiskey potatoes, champ (potatoes mixed with spring onions or nettle tops), fadge (Northern Ireland version of potato cakes) and boxtie (potato bread made of grated, raw potato, mashed potato and milk). Colcannon, the Irish version of bubble and squeak, comes from the Irish cál ceannann, which literally means white-headed cabbage. It is normally served with grilled sausages and rashers. The most delicious traditional thing they do with a spud is coddle, a great Dublin speciality in which sliced potatoes and fried rashers and sausages are layered in a baking dish, covered with chicken stock and baked for an hour till they all stick together. In a food magazine I found an article on the different potatoes you could buy in Ireland — Home Guard New, Golden Wonder, Rooster, Record, Kerrs Pink — and they were all described as floury, dry and earthy.

You can't talk about potatoes without talking about the famine. The lifestyle of the Irish peasant in the nineteenth century was simple and poor. They grew grain which was sold abroad to pay the rent, and grew potatoes to feed themselves.

The population was huge — eight million in 1845 in a country the size of New Zealand, and only the north-east had heavy industry; the rest of Ireland was completely dependent on the potato crop and it was a very viable one when it worked. You could get a high yield from a small plot, they were hard to destroy and could be stored easily. The peasants also grew some oats, turnips and cabbages but not in enough quantity. As Ireland is surrounded by sea teeming with fish, one might ask why they didn't turn to eating fish but they weren't big fish eaters, the sea was wild and there were few proper fishing vessels available.

Famine was not new to Ireland, in fact part of the crop failed every year, which led to many warnings that the country was on the verge of starvation. Then the big one hit and there was absolutely nothing to fall back on — green Ireland became black with the blight giving off an appalling stench, it was the coldest winter in years, disease was rife, the English landlords were by and large merciless and the people starved in front of their eyes. In their despair they ate pigs, horses, dogs, took blood from cattle and mixed it with cabbage or mushrooms and ate nuts, roots and leaves. Help was given in the form of soup kitchens, the importation of Indian corn (described as the most odious mass ever designed for human consumption), relief committees and food and clothing distribution by the Quakers, but the tragedy went remorselessly on devouring the land. It was finally over in 1848, a blood-letting from which the whole island has never recovered.

I used to have conversations with my French friends about potatoes.

'One of the main reasons I like roasts is there are always lots of potatoes,' I would say.

'There's no viable reason for your potato obsession, Peta. You're in a European culture now and it's not necessary to retain your immigrant tastes. What was appropriate for your grandfather in Ireland is no longer appropriate for you. Get a life and try some salad or lentils.'

'Get a life? No, no, no, you don't understand. The potato is genetically programmed into me. The Irish had their land ripped off them by those English bastards who then turned around and made them pay exorbitant rent. And where did they get the money from?'

'Where?'

'Why, from their only crop — potatoes, and when they rotted [the potatoes, not the English] 1.5 million people died of starvation. Personally my genes haven't really recovered and I feel I can never eat enough potatoes to make up for it.'

'But what is the connection between potatoes and your sense of self, Peta, and why do you take it so personally?'

'The connection is that with the potato famine the English finally brought my ancestors to their knees, wiping out their very Irishness — their souls, their culture, their spirit. Don't you see? My only memory of my mother's culture lies in this potato in front of me,' I would say passionately.

'So the famine eradicated your memory of what you were before it happened.'

'Exactly. All I have left is an inappropriate predilection for potatoes, a short fuse and an Irish passport.'

One of the most entertaining and hilarious things you can do in County Tipperary is attend an agricultural fair. Tricia dressed in jeans, boots and a jumper; I dressed in Zambesi top, leather skirt and gumboots and we set off for the Tipp Fair, driving through such magically named places as Slievna-muck, Ballynamrossagh, Baurnagurrahy, Knockaterrif, Carrig-eenina and Knockastakeen. First we met cousin Richard Long and his wife Kathleen, who had the farm next to Tricia's, for lunch in Tipperary (Tiobraid Árann — the Well of Ara) Town. God knows, this must be the most famous town in Ireland on account of it being such a long, long way and all but it is in fact a rather unremarkable farming town. Cashel and Thurles are much prettier. The song 'It's A Long Way to Tipperary' was composed in 1912 by an Englishman from Birmingham who had never even been to Ireland. Jack Judge's wartime song sold a million copies the year it was released but if you sing it in Tipperary they will shoot you.

I had heard a lot about Irish funerals from my mother and hoped an occasion would arise to attend one. As we ploughed through our huge roast dinners and pints of burnt barley in the pub, Richard scanned the deaths column in the local paper for a funeral for me, and Tricia scanned the property column to find me a house to buy, so convinced was she that I should stay 'home' for ever.

The show was a wonderworld of beautifully scrubbed Charolais cattle, plaited sleek showhorses prancing to judges attired in jodhpurs, tweed jackets and bowler hats, Clonakilty saddle stalls, delirious dog shows, grass seed and animal feed stalls, high-stepping horse and traps driven by top-hatted men in navy felt aprons, formal jackets with a flower in the lapel and discreetly spotted tie and leather gloves, accompanied by plump female dumplings in straw hats. Being a horsewoman (she belonged to the Tipp Hunt Hounds) Tricia was always very happy at these shows, her love of all animals making it a carnival of equine overdose for her. She spoke to them very positively, full of charming compliments about their beauty and personality, reassuring them regarding their personal problems and relationships with other animals. She passed comment on both animals and humans along the lines of 'Look at your man over dere . . . his legs are so tin you could clean the barrel of a rifle with them' and 'Isn't she standin' lovely now . . . fine majestic way of holding herself' and 'Mudder but yer desperate in yer outfit wit yer gumboots . . . get over dere by dat heiffer and I'll take a photo of ye' and 'I'll tell you something about her — she's all fur coat and nae knickers'.

I lost interest in the 'creathurs' in about five minutes and dived into the competition traditional dancing tent where I found things had changed a little since my day. Well, the setting was exactly the same — with the lone fiddler, makeshift stage, families crowded everywhere and judge sitting at a table in front of the stage — but the costumes were outrageous compared with the relatively simple green dresses I had worn. Little girls were decked out in heavy, extravagant costumes, ghastly curly hair-pieces with crowns and, God preserve us all, gold lurex knickers. I told Father Brenhan to cover his eyes and avoid an occasion of sin, then asked a mother how much these costumes cost and she said £1000 for a new one, £300–450 for a second-hand one.

The refreshments tent was full of fine country women in shirts and pants madly slathering butter onto cakes and sand-wiches with their thick arms and no-nonsense faces, pouring huge scalding cups of tea and quietly finding out who was your one with the accent. To the tune of mobiles ringing in the mud and people talking loudly about form and carriage, I perused the Show Book I found in front of me. Equine dentistry said the ad — nervous and difficult animals a speciality; reasonable rates with reductions for large yards. I was too terrified of this statement to even contemplate the connection between a large yard and a root canal.

Renewed by my slice of apple pie, ham sandwich and tea I walked outside onto grass so green it was psychedelic. At that very moment the sun came up out of the rain like an orchestra from a pit, giving me a clear view of the high Galtee Mountains. By the end of the afternoon the sun had settled into the cups of the multi-hued hills, a mixture of red sand-stone and Silurian rocks, now topped with meringues of cloud. I tramped over to the food tent where prizewinning fruit cakes, sponges, scones, breads, flowers, turnips, spuds, grass (yes, grass) and eggs were on display behind chicken wire. They were numbered and one could purchase them to take home at the end of the day. Next to that was a tent selling such delicacies as potato farls, spotted dog, porter cake, apple pies and crumbles and homemade lemon curd, all reeking of the generosity and purity of the countryside.

The best food shop I found in the area was in the Anglo-Irish town of Nenagh at a little place called Country Choice. Tricia liked this unspectacular town for its good antique shops but also for the exotic and high-quality produce we discovered together at this delicatessen overflowing with heart and ambiance. The front counter was resplendent with Irish farmhouse cheeses including the famous Cashel Blue, the hard-to-get Mine Gabhar goat cheese and Ardrahan, patés, salads, smoked salmon, marinated olives, fresh pasta, Nenagh butter, bacon, breads, organic vegetables and cured hams. Proprietors Peter and Mary Ward had the best ham on the bone I tasted in Ireland. Just thinking of it makes me weak — Nenagh piggie cooked to perfection, melting, sweet and succulent. No matter how hard we tried not to, Trish and I always ate this ham on the way home in the car.

You had to get past the Italian estate olive oils, balsamic vinegars, homemade dressings, sundried tomatoes, jams, 70 per cent cocoa chocolate, dried fruits, Italian and French wines, dried pasta and preserves to get to the eating department out the back. Their vintage marmalade was delicious — lots of caramelised peel cooked on their Aga overnight, leaving your gums tingling and salivating for more. The café had very good cooked tongue, brawn, smoked fish, soups and rhubarb crumble with summer berries and cream. Peter spoke fluent Irish and was unconditionally fascinated by food, his customers' reactions and the high quality of Irish primary produce.

Because of its farming wealth, Tipperary has for a long time been forward thinking, well educated, middle class and progressive. In the eighteenth century it was a county of landlords and relatively prosperous peasants. To this day many priests have their own farms as well as tending to their human flock. Also, because Tipperary county is not on the glamorous coast and is farming country, it is of a lot less interest to tourists so the natives are less into the bullshit and blarney and are more 'real' Irish.

The earliest written language of Irish was confined to monasteries, which were the seats of learning, but over many centuries the writings and manuscripts were destroyed. However, the oral tradition continued in secret and in metaphor like an underground river. By the end of the nineteenth century English was replacing the Irish language and things were being written down in English, education improved and people could now read and write. They had almost lost the Irish language except in certain areas such as the Aran Islands and parts of Kerry, and the oral tradition was being eroded too, just like that of the Maori — the wonderful tradition of storytelling for hours and hours into the night and scaring the shit out of each other. My grandfather was an accomplished seanachaí (old-style storyteller), seamlessly and calmly frightening everyone half to death with his banshee tales.

Another thing the Irish used to specialise in was spells and curses. There were charms against disease in cattle, bleeding, bed-wetting and illness in general, and curses were often sent out with the help of heated stones which were then hidden. They used the phrase 'until these stones go on fire' and the curse could affect descendants for many generations. The best one I ever heard of was 'May the seven terriers of hell sit on the spool of your breast and bark in at your soul-case'. The Catholic clergy tried to put a stop to other-worldly stories a hundred years ago, as did they any talk about fairies, spirits, changelings, spells and curses. Conversely, as recently as my mother's lifetime, the priests still performed 'churching', the purifying by blessing and prayers of postnatal women — welcoming them back to the church after the 'unclean' act of giving birth.

People rarely talk about leprechauns or banshees any more, although I did meet an educated, intelligent man who told me his grandfather had caught two leprechauns who eventually escaped. He remembers his father going into the bedroom upstairs to look at them but the children weren't allowed in. This man was genuinely offended when I allowed a cloud of scepticism to pass my brow. The expression 'he's away with the fairies' now refers to someone who is absent minded or a dreamer but once it had the much more sinister meaning that you had been taken away or your body had been supplanted by a fairy, leaving a changeling in its place. Also you could be 'gone astray', a term for someone who had wandered off temporarily or got inexplicably lost. This would happen in a 'gentle place' under the influence of 'the gentry' and some fields were also known to have 'a stray' or a lost soul in them.

The Irish are a people with deeply rooted spirituality and this is linked to their extraordinary imagination and poetic but fatalistic way of looking at things. Yeats said that the Irishman's mind escapes out of daily circumstance 'like a bough held down by a weak hand'. They fly from the surface of life when and if they have to through song, religion and the cult of fairies, now branded as superstition. The 'west room' in a house is the path by which fairies pass and food used to be left out to keep them happy and prevent bad luck; no outhouse or shed was ever built on this side of the house. Primroses were tied to the cows' tails at May eve to prevent the fairies from stealing the milk. Tricia still throws holy water over her fields, would be very upset if she found a rotten egg in a drill of vegetables because that would mean crop failure, and would gasp if she found butter smeared on the gate of a field of calves for they would all die of the scour (diarrhoea). I said, 'Tricia, you don't really believe that.'

'Well, I'd rather not take the chance that way, ye know like. A farmer would never disturb a fairy fort on his property. I tink forts were originally made by shepherds to guard their

sheep in and in the old days before the liberation of Catholicism the priests used to say Mass hidden in them. And I'll tell
ye what else. I would never fail to salute [wave] to magpies.

Salute one magpie for sorrow
Two for joy
Three for a girl
Four for a boy
Five for silver
Six for gold
Seven is a secret
Eight never to be told.

I thought the fairies must have been gnashing their teeth over
Mass being said in their beautiful but dangerous forts, considering how anti-Christian they were, but I loved the vision of a
people so constant, so strong that they secretly huddled
around altars of rock, hidden from land and sea, visible only
to their God. Mythology says fairy forts were ancient Celtic
fortifications that the fairies took over when they fell to earth,
and that fairies were in fact fallen angels, expelled from heaven
as followers of the rebellious Lucifer. They didn't get to hell
but instead landed on the water or land and stayed hovering
there, which explains their capriciousness. They were not
entirely evil because they still hoped to get back to heaven one
day but they were greatly feared and respected by humans.
They had various names: a phooka was dark and stormy and
performed feats of reckless daring; elves played in the rings
and woods, a banshee was famous for its eery wail at the scene
of death, and a cluricaune, leprechaun, leprachaun or
lewricaun (names for the same being) was less fun loving and
more business-like.

Leprechauns are the ones I like best because they resemble
many Irish humans I know. They were very fond of good
wine, good food, the good life and had a personality I admire

— mischievous, insolent, cutting and sarcastic like Puck. They hid their treasure in caves in the earth and had enormous respect for an ancient family, especially if they had a good cellar. Most mysterious of all were the sidhe — the shape-changers or shadows from the Country of the Young or Tír na nóg. They were invisible and could take any form they wished — human, bird, beast, wool, dust, grass. They were every-where: in forts, thorn bushes, under the ground, in the sea or maybe even in a house resembling a human's one. Sidhe, like leprechauns, were gourmets, robbing the goodness and taste out of food, leaving worthless muck in its place, wouldn't touch salt and robbed cellars of their good wine. Their music was more beautiful than anything of this world, they loved a good fight and, interestingly enough, were great hurlers, stealing young men's strong bodies for this purpose. Each of their households had a queen who had more power than the rest but the real head honcho was Amadan-na-Briona, the Fool of the Forth — strong, wicked and deadly. When he struck, no one lived to tell the tale. They were forces of both bad and good because their numbers were partially made up of our dead. They often helped humans with knowledge, curing illness, giving back people they had taken or saving someone from death. When the sidhe passed by in a blast of wind you had to say words of blessing, for there may be among them some of your own dead.

While I was there the book *The Burning of Brigid Cleary* was published. This is an extraordinary account of a dreadful crime committed in Tipperary near Clonmel (the honeyed meadows) in 1895. A good-looking, bright, normal young woman was burned to death on the kitchen floor of her own home by her equally apparently normal husband because he believed she was a changeling. It was extraordinary not only because of the gruesomeness of incinerating someone alive but because they were educated, reasonably well-off people, supposedly way beyond believing in such things as fairies.

Brigid was in fact suffering from severe bronchitis and obviously had a fever that went untreated. A combination of tiredness, sexual jealousy and resentment of her strong character and independence combined to seduce Michael Cleary into believing his real wife had been stolen away by the fairies.

When a fairy took over a human body the only way to get the real person back was believed to be to burn the changeling out. He said he believed she would subsequently reappear at the nearby ring fort of Kylenagranagh riding a white horse. She would be tied to the saddle and he would have to cut the ties and drag her off to save her, otherwise he would never see her again. Needless to say she never turned up. He and her family, who had been party to the whole thing, buried her grotesquely charred body in the bog and he got 20 years for manslaughter. Ireland was deeply shocked by this mysterious event in one of the least backward counties in the country and Brigid Cleary was the only adult victim among documented cases of changeling burnings in the nineteenth century.

When in residence at the farm I went for a fast walk every morning I could, weather and inclination permitting. My fast walks around the muddy country roads of Clogher quickly became known by the locals, who all tooted loudly as they roared past, my eccentricity by now being almost beyond comment. First people just stared uncomprehendingly, then saluted, then slowed down, then stopped to talk, crawling beside me as I marched along, head in the air.

'Hello there, Pip. Ah sure, 'tis a lovely day for a walk, surely it is. Will ye not stop and say hello to a friend?'

'Hello, hello.' (Walk walk)

'Why are ye walking so fast? Where are ye going?'

'I can't stop — that's why it's called a fast walk. The point is to raise my heartbeat, thereby giving myself a cardiac workout.'

'A cardiac workout? Jaesus, Mary and Joseph but why are ye getting yerself so excited at this hour of the day? Come around to my house — I'll raise yer heartbeat for ye.'

I had to promise to visit everyone on the way back for a cup of tea, so a 40-minute walk in Tipperary took two or three hours, smelling the almond fragrance of gorse blossom and picking elderberries all the way home. Kathleen and Richard's was the best stop because I always got her homemade soda bread and marmalade. Richard belonged to every club you could invent and when I asked Kathleen if she belonged to any she replied, 'Yes, the feckin' housework club.' We loved being invited over to their place for lunch because Richard was a great storyteller and knew lots about the family history and Kathleen was a generous country cook, serving up groaning boards of thick soup, boiled bacon and steaming cabbage with turnips, and apple and rhubarb pie with bowls of outstanding Tipperary cream.

They cook lots of roasts in Ireland, something I never got in all the years I lived in France. In French cuisine a roast as I know and understand it from my childhood cannot exist. A potato can never be soft in the middle and crispy on the outside, having absorbed the juices and fat from meat over a period of at least an hour, because a lump of French meat is never permitted to stay in the oven that long. A proper roast takes time — precious time the French don't have but the Irish do. I believe it is for this reason the French had a revolution. It wasn't over bread at all, it was over meat. Someone in a brocade coat and pointy shoes said, 'All meat has to be half cooked, otherwise you will end up overweight and ugly like the English and have a royal family that dresses like the village banker.'

At home we ate the Sunday roast on Saturday night because my mother refused to cook or work on Sunday. In point of fact cooking a roast for only a couple of hours, as did she, is really borderline nouveau riche. A real roast should be cooked for at least two to three hours with absolutely no allowance for size, budget or personal taste. It doesn't matter what animal it is, everything gets cooked for the same length of time. Normally a roast is a rather egalitarian meal — you can put it all on the table and people eat as much as they wish but the law in the 1950s was that you had to eat everything on your plate (probably a hangover from the privations of the war). This is a rule that doesn't exist in France, for example. Because of the revolution French children are allowed to eat what they wish, which has resulted in moral decline and all the children eat nothing but chocolate sandwiches which give them coalmines instead of teeth and a high sex drive. In my day children remained seated at the table till they had eaten every single thing no matter how repulsive — gloopy floury white sauce with onions, turnips, pumpkin, mayonnaise made from condensed milk. No amount of silver-tongued negot-iation worked. You remained at the table till death if necessary. It didn't matter if you cried, vomited, laughed or fainted. No mercy was shown, no quarter given, the result of which is a nation of control freaks and emotional cripples who have an aversion to turnips and sex.

But back to Tipperary. On Friday mornings Trisha and I would try our best to get to the farmers' market in Thurles. To get Tricia anywhere at any specific time was beyond the powers of an obsessive-compulsive punctuality freak even such as myself. I was usually still recovering from 'a wee pint and a song' till the small hours and she from trying to 'do her chores', talk nonstop on the phone and cook Seamus's dinner (lunch) if he was lucky. We would burn the road to Thurles in the blue Merc with the dogs running after us, saluting and tooting everyone we passed. If it was an old man Tricia with her heart of gold just couldn't drive past. I would give her the old-fashioned look and she would say, 'Ah sure, I'll only talk for a minute, Pip, I swear.'

'If we're late, Trish, I'll miss Marie Ryan's butterfly buns again.' Screeching to a stop in front of the hall, we'd fly in straight to the back where the flowers were, grab what were left and work our way up to the front, picking up vegetables, jams, breads, cakes and hopefully a dozen of Marie Ryan's melt-in-your-mouth butterfly buns.

These little farmers' markets are in halls all over Ireland but no visitor would ever find them because if you blink you miss them. They start at 11am sharp and there is a queue outside long before, with people jealously guarding their place and squaring their shoulders. Within 15 minutes all the best produce was gone, borne away by the good women of Thurles.

We passed many hours in the pub: if we went Ballagh way it was Gleesons; Clonoulty way, cousin Mulhall's. One night in particular in August I was trying not to watch the parish-hall-yo-yo pointlessness of the Rose of Tralee competition on the bar television. It's like trashy magazines in the gym — your eyes light on them out of boredom, then you became fascinated by the superficiality and ghastliness of it. The winner standing there trembling and in shock as if she's just saved the world from extinction or something. The little-known fact that I was entered into the Auckland Rose of Tralee at the age of 16 and got nowhere has nothing to do with my bitter attitude. Even then I realised I had nothing in common with the practised girlie faces around me.

A less vulgar but equally mind-numbing version of it graces Tipperary in the guise of the Miss Macra contest to find the finest specimen of farming womanhood in the country. Tricia and Mercedes were heavily into this contest, hosting finalists at their homes and attending such exciting events as water balloon fights with the escorts and dances where wild, love-hungry bachelor farmers came down from the mountains to see if they could find a filly to throw their saddles over. Oh, keen they are in Tipperary to savour the life-enhancing twang of a double bed spring, but as cousin Jim so eloquently says to engaged men: 'Get all the sex you can before marriage because you'll get feck-all after, lads. Love may be blind but marriage is an eye opener.'

The Miss Macra contest was one issue on which Seamus

and I were united. He put his foot down quietly, Eddie didn't but wished he had, and I went to the final night complaining loudly all the way. Mercedes' claim to fame was that she only billeted winners — Misses Cork, Wexford and Down were the favourites. Only a fool with no sense of occasion would miss out on the Miss Macra contest.

We settled into our table on the big night at the Anner Hotel in Thurles and watched strong-boned country girls being escorted down the hall in their beautiful gowns with hulking handbags slung over their shoulders in case a bit of saddling might need to be done. We rose for grace and people sent messages down the tables asking who was your one with the red hair and was it real? Eddie doesn't drink so he didn't even have alcohol to save him from the tedious, interminable speeches. Trish had taken a new Italian handbag from a recess of one of her three dressing rooms and had never even opened it except to stuff her fags in as she ran out of the house in a summer dress and high heels. When she opened it at the table she discovered the newspaper stuffing was still inside so Mercedes and I smoothed it out and recited the news aloud in Italian. Dinner was plenty and nasty — even Tricia wouldn't eat it — and when they still hadn't announced the winner by 1.30am I grabbed Peter Brenhan and said, 'We're out of here.' Tricia was nowhere to be found so he said, 'You can stay in my spare room if you can't find the key to Tricia's house.' I could imagine the tongues of Clonoulty on that one — 'Oh, we saw your one wit the mad hair wandering out of Fadder Brenhan's house, bold as brass at 10 in the mornin' and him out the back feeding his horses calm as ye like.'

I did find the key unfortunately and on the way home we had a good old talk about Catholicism and how nice it was that we were now encouraged to follow our consciences rather than man-made rules. Tricia got home at five, Mercedes had picked another winner in Miss County Down, Eddie said, 'Never again and that's a bloody promise.'

The Irish sense of drama is very evident in their attitude to death, ceremony comes as easily as breathing, and they welcome emotion. You don't really get any good, old-style wakes any more, except maybe in Galway or in outposts like the Aran Islands where they keen and sit around the coffin telling stories, smoking pipes, drinking and singing nonstop for days. I have never heard keening but J.M. Synge in his inimitable writings on the Aran Islanders described the oldest women bending their foreheads to the flat gravestones while calling out to the dead with a perpetually recurring chant of sobs, their faces stiff with grief and emotion.

'This grief of the keen is no personal complaint for the death of one woman over eighty years, but seems to contain the whole passionate rage that lurks somewhere in every native on the island. In this cry of pain, the inner consciousness of the people seems to lay itself bare for an instant, and to reveal the mood of beings who feel their isolation in the face of a universe that wars on them with winds and seas. They are usually silent, but in the presence of death all outward show of indifference or patience is forgotten, and they shriek with pitiable despair before the horror of the fate to which they are all doomed.'

In *The Year of the French* Thomas Flanagan talked about ancient wakes that involved excessive drinking and unbridled conduct of young and old where they even used to lift the corpse up and dance with it. There were 'wake games' of quite a pagan sexual nature, giving rise to the common saying that more marriages were made at wakes than at fairs or dances.

I did, however, attend the funeral of one Jimmy O'Gorman. Everyone loves a good funeral because you get to combine melancholy with a social occasion and Tipperary mountain funerals are particularly well attended, lasting two days. No one ever reads the death notices — barely has the breath left the deceased than the news whips around by bush telegraph and the community close in to pay respect, support the family, bake the cakes and say the prayers. This same method was used to monitor my every move in Tipperary.

Expense is never spared for a funeral, a dinner or a wedding — you do what has to be done and pay the bills later. At 7.30pm we arrived at the long, low, whitewashed family home to find hundreds of people standing outside in their Sunday best, chatting in the clear evening. We joined the queue to enter the house, signed the book and filed into the parlour. The old gentleman was laid out in the open coffin in the middle of the room, neatly groomed, wrinkles fallen away, rosary beads entwined in his folded hands. All around the walls the family were seated on upright chairs and people filed past shaking their hands and offering condolences. As I tried to mutter something appropriate in my shuffle, at least three of them drew me closer, squeezing my hand, saying, 'I heard you singing in the pub on Saturday . . . fine voice you have on you.' Sheila turned up looking stunning in a brown suit, gold nailpolish and high heels, said, 'Mudder of God but I'm wrecked,' paid her respects and left. The coffin was then closed and borne by the pallbearers to the church, followed by all the people.

It was a beautiful kilometre-long walk along the tree-lined country road in the twilight, the lone church bell knelling slowly in the distance. A late summer chill filled the air, the moon was at half mast and everyone softly chatted arm in arm and caught up on events. At the church prayers were said by Father Brenhan and the body then remained there all night. The two most important things in Irish life are still the church and the pub so all we had to do was file across the road to the pub to finish the night off. Some people went back to the house for tea and food. The funeral Mass was held the next day and everyone went with the body to be buried, then to a hotel where a meal was put on by the family. This sometimes continues on into drinking all night, getting completely sloshed and reminiscing about what a fine man the deceased was altogether.

The church and the pub are also common locations for the one thing the Irish still get into fights about — land. Intrigue is never far from the fore in their lives; to them it is like oxygen and they relish a good entanglement whether it be in the realm of relationships, horse-trading or funerals. I heard a story of a punch-up between two families outside the church after Mass one Sunday. 'God, it was desperate,' they said, 'and as they all left in their cars, they rolled down their windows and said, "Excuse me, Father" to the parish priest.' That night the two families turned up in the local pub as usual as if nothing had happened but it was hard to keep a straight face with the bruises and bandages and all. Within hours the whole area knew about it and for the best part of a week it was the only topic of conversation, not in a gossipy way but in a quietly-sliding-it-into-the-conversation-in-between-two-draws-on-a-cigarette kind of a way. 'Were you at Mass on Sunday at all?' Nobody really knew the true story but many possibilities of where the rot lay were passed around like ham sandwiches at a wake.

This fascination with intrigue has of course been of great benefit to Irish literature, giving it its density and complexity. At the same time I received a letter from the mother telling me of a conversation she had had with my six-year-old nephew Harrison. He had asked her what an undertaker was and she had replied he was a person who made coffins to bury people in.

'You don't bury people in a coffin, Grandma, you put them in a grave.'

'You put them in a coffin, nail the lid on, then put them in the grave.'

'You *nail* them in?' he recoiled in horror. 'What about their thoughts and stuff?'

'They all go out when they die.'

'Where do they go?'

'Up to heaven with your soul.'

'So if I shot you could I see your thoughts come out and could I catch them.'

These are the kind of circular philosophical exchanges they have all the time.

Meanwhile Tricia's lamb, Bubba, had been getting bigger and bigger and more and more testosterone ridden, which exhibited itself in serious charging and head butting. The whole neighbourhood was terrified of him, children refused to get out of the car if he was around, and many times I had to leap up onto a wall or throw myself into a hedge to escape his advances. On top of that he was still relentlessly trying to mount the dogs and hanging around the kitchen door listening to the radio. Something had to be done. Bubba had never known another sheep, in either the biblical or the social sense, but Tricia was his mother and she couldn't let go. Even when her cattle went to the factory to be killed she hated it because every heifer had a name.

'Give him back to Father Brenhan and he can be out in the field where he belongs and sire some lambs,' said Seamus, who by this point had had it right up to here with Bubba.

'Oh, no-o-o,' Tricia wailed, 'who will talk to him and cuddle him? He'll be lonely so he will.'

'Tricia, he is a ram. He will be living the life he was born to.'

'Sure I'll tink about it next week.'

Finally Jim and Eileen Shanahan suggested 'the squeeze', which is a sort of semi-castration, resulting in a much quieter animal. The following day I arrived home from my fast walk to find the squeezer there and no Trish to hold Bubba down.

'Well, you can do it,' he said.

'Are you out of your mind?' I shrieked. 'Have you seen the size of that thing?'

An hour later he returned and, with the help of a visiting male, Bubba was thrown on his back on the front lawn and the instrument for doing the job was got out. I took one look at the squeezers, couldn't bear to watch or listen to the screams I was sure would ensue, so grabbed Tricia and closed her in the kitchen. But brave Bubba didn't make a sound, got up afterwards, stood shaking for a while, then for the rest of the day stood very quietly at the kitchen door, looking mournful and in need of TLC.

One summer's evening I cooked a dinner party for friends and family, giving myself the responsibility for the food, Tricia the location and Seamus just to turn up. For him it would surely be a trial an evening with all sorts of fancy get-up food instead of plain daecent shpuds. Their house is now known as the house of red wine and rotting cheese, sitting out on the press for all to see, instead of in the fridge where it belongs, and would you believe she's on the TV with all her strange ideas.

'Don't talk to me about that fridge,' Seamus would say to his friends, 'there's not a ting in it to eat. It's full of incredible tings like cured ham, strong sauces, taboulé, steaks she eats half raw, mustard all over everyting, anchovies, olives, patés. I tell you . . . if ever a man suffered.' He loved Tricia's stews. She would run into the kitchen in the morning, throw lamb chunks, bones, vegetables and a stock cube into a big pot of water, put it on the Aga, bring in the eggs, check the cows up in the fields, help the farrier do the horses' legs and hooves, clean out the bird house, come back four hours later and the stew would be perfect: tender, creamy and aromatic. Seamus ate carefully and slowly, while Tricia and I grabbed the bones and sucked every last capillary off them.

For my dinner party Tricia chose the courtyard between the house and the farm buildings. The chooks and new chick, which I named Lulu because it kept losing its balance and falling over, followed her around blinking in amazement as she scrubbed that courtyard to within an egg-shell of perfection. While I toiled and boiled in the kitchen under the bleeding heart of Jesus, I could see her out there in her bikini, washing the iron chairs and putting them in the sun to dry, watering the flower bowls, moving the tractor out of the way. The local scouts hall was relieved of its long tables, which she set up in a T. A separate serving table was laid with flowers and silver spoons, and out came Grandmammie's bone china, gravy jugs, good wine glasses, tablecloths and silver. Tricia, who was capable of inviting another dozen people to a dinner as she went about her day, was warned several times not to extend the guest list without my permission. 'Jaesus, Pip, but you're a tyrant,' said she, flashing the green eyes and flinging the mane back. We got into clean clothes and out came the avocados with salsa, roast pork with anchovy sauce, grilled tomatoes, aubergines and courgettes, risotto and salad. Finally we were all seated — Richard and Kathleen, Majella and daughter Deirdre, Geraldine and Gary, Theresa and husband P who had to be dragged along. Sheila, around whom the entire dinner had been arranged, was nowhere to be seen.

When called up she muttered, 'Mudder of God but I'm wrecked — I'm almost in me bed.'

'Get out of it so!' we all yelled. 'Or the pig will take off altogether and there'll be no supper for ye.'

They ate it all because the Irish are very polite people — even Seamus and P ate it but they couldn't be talked into wine. Then something happened that never happens in my household — at a telepathically transmitted signal, the women stood up as one and cleared the table, did the dishes, put everything away, made coffee and tea, brought out the chocolate and almond tart with summer berries and whipped cream. The men sat out in the darkening evening talking the cloudless talk of people who are used to women doing all the work in the hospitality department. When the night chill crept over us like a cool caress, we moved into the kitchen and the everlasting Aga, sitting in a circle on stools to continue the talking till 2.30am.

My strictness in not wanting the whole neighbourhood to turn up at my dinner party was, upon reflection, really going against the grain of a Celtic woman such as Tricia. The Irish person's deeply ingrained sense of hospitality goes right back to ancient times. As in all heroic societies, Celtic feasting was the way you rewarded faithful warriors and sealed deals. They were riotous affairs, awash with alcohol, fights and unbelievable amounts of food. The feasts went on non-stop for days, with visitors coming and going and being served by attendants. Right up until the early modern period, they were still sitting on straw on the floor, wolfing down the contents of huge cauldrons and roasting pits full of beef, boar, veal, lamb, pork, the heads and feet of aforementioned beasts, wheat cakes cooked in honey and choice fruit.

We know all this from the unrivalled screeds of writings from Irish monks, who provided a priceless insight into the range of Irish food and produce in a rather romantic and dramatic way. The Irish ate a large variety of foodstuffs based on cereals and dairy produce with a predeliction for salted butter, salted pork and bacon served with lots of fat, which has remained with them to this day. Unpressed curds were eaten with hazelnuts, wild garlic, wood sorrel and honey, and there is frequent mention of soft and hard cheeses. They also enjoyed freshwater fish and salmon (often pickled) with watercress and berries.

One of the last things I saw Tricia making before I left Ireland was her crabapple jelly. To make it you throw lots of the little apples into a pot of water, put it on the Aga, then go away and see to the horses for a few hours. When it is all smooched and mushed up together, you tie your long hair up into a big knot so as not to dip it in and pour the mixture into an old cotton pillowcase. (Tricia's mother also had very long hair which she wore swept up with one dramatic movement and attached on top of her head. To trim it she brought it over her shoulder, attached a big steel clamp to the ends and burnt them with a match.) Tie the top of the pillowcase in a knot around a broomstick and balance it between two stools, letting the jelly drip through into a pot overnight. The next morning there will be a pink-coloured, bitter apple liquid in the pot. Give the pillowcase a good squeeze and feed the animals the contents (that's why Tipperary pork is so sweet). The only thing left to do is add sugar to taste and then bottle it.

I finally got invited to Mary and Sheila's for dinner. A big week-long novena (praying, Masses and sermons day and night) was in progress at Holycross Abbey with thousands of pilgrims and I supposed Mary's knees would be ruined from it — I almost expected her to open the door wrapped in bandages.

'Ah, there you are, Pip,' said she, eyes sparkling mischievously. 'We got a sermon today entitled "Yes, There is Such a Thing as Sin". Would ye like to know about it?'

'Mary dear,' I smiled, putting my arm around her shoulder, 'I could have told you that without your getting your knees in such a state. All you have to do is read my books.'

She screamed with delight. 'Come in, come in now wit yer divilment. I can see how the night's going to go. Come and meet me husband.'

I was quite interested to meet the man who had provided Mary with such a wonderful daughter as Sheila, a high standard of living and negative insights into the sacrament of marriage. The men — Sheila's fiancé Sean, her brother Seamus, Peter Brenhan and Mary's famous husband, Thomas — were all lined up on couches and chairs on one side of the large parlour, sipping whiskey. Thomas was a very nice, rather quiet man with a cute sense of humour, weathered farmer's face and gentle voice. He told lots of stories till the roast was ready, when we filed into the dining room and nobody could remember the last time there had been a dinner party in there. Farmers always eat in the kitchen. There in the most gorgeous room of inlaid and engraved dressers, chandeliers and gilt mirrors, Sheila had set the oval mahogany table with antique candelabra, silver utensils and crystal glasses. With dogs everywhere underfoot we dived into the roast leg of lamb with vegetables and mint sauce that Sheila had cooked, accompanying it with hours of talk and plenty of wine, an unusual drink in that household.

The next day I called Sheila at her post office in the village of Golden. 'I'm dyin',' she said.

'Go to bed,' I said.

'Sure I can't — I've a funeral tonight. Me mudder says I'm not to be makin' a fool of meself.'

I called Mary. 'I'm dyin'.'

'What's wrong with you all?' I asked.

'Tell Tricia to keep an eye on the death notices. I don't know if I'll come out of this one. 'Tis your fault, Pip, wit yer fancy wine ideas. If I'd stuck to the whiskey I'd have no problem, as if I don't suffer enough altogether. In the name of God I have it every way. 'Tis dyin' I am.' This lament was followed by a long groan.

'Mary, listen to me. Take two aspirins and go to bed.'

'Sure I'm in bed,' she whimpered. 'Where else do ye tink I'd be, the condition I'm in?'

On a Saturday night in September we were all in Mary Gleeson's pub — Tricia, Seamus, Sheila, Theresa and other acquaintances (in other words the rest of the pub). The session room was around a corner in a little nook so you couldn't see who was playing unless you went right in. Presently I realised there was a session going on that was quite different from normal and I wandered in to have a look. What I found was a middle-aged man with wild hair, a face that might have seen a few non-prescription substances and some burnt barley, snakeskin cowboy boots and a Hawaiian shirt playing unbelievable country/rock acoustic guitar and singing. Seamus's cousin Noel was on the mandolin, there was another guitar, an Irish bazooki and a double bass. A huge double bass in a tiny low-ceilinged pub was a very unusual sight. The other distinctive thing about this session was the atmosphere among the musicians. In a traditional session there is no leader but here the musicians were quite obviously deferring to the snakeskin boots and there was a discernible air of reverence.

I sat down near them with my mouth open at the brilliance of the guitar playing and high standard of musicianship in the others. Gradually the rest of the pub realised what was going on and the whispering began. 'Mudder of God, do yes know who that is? It's Philip Donnelly . . . what's he doin' in here?' Several versions of Philip's life went past my ears involving castles, America, money, highs and lows of fame and being in the bath with his boots on. The one talent everyone agreed on was his guitar picking. It turned out he had agreed to play with his friends to celebrate the birth of a baby to the bass player, Paul.

At about one in the morning Mary started her litany of 'Come on now, lads . . . this is the last song . . . it's time to go home now', of which no one took the slightest notice except to say, 'Don't be talkin' like that now, Mary.' At two she said, 'It's two in the mornin', lads . . . I'll let you do one more song . . . I'm not as young as I used to be . . . Tricia, you don't always have to be the last to leave now.' She passed the three o'clock hurdle, gave up and shouted the house a round of drinks and at four-thirty no one was actually capable of continuing, thanks to the burnt barley. Philip sang 'Living in These Troubled Times', 'From Here to Clare' and lots of Dylan, Donovan and Nancy Griffiths songs, in fact he was playing Nancy Griffiths' guitar. One of the many songs he sang to which everyone knew the words was 'The Speed of the Sound of Loneliness', a beautiful song first done by John

Prine and covered by Philip in 1990. More than 11,000 copies of Philip's single were sold in Ireland and it stayed in the Irish charts for many weeks.

You come home late and you come home early
You come on big when you're feeling small
You come home straight and you come home curly
Sometimes you don't come home at all.
What in the world has come over you
What in heaven's name have you done?
You've broken the speed of the sound of loneliness
You're out there running just to be on the run.

In the wee hours I was asked to sing a few Piaf songs, which Noel accompanied with a natural understanding of the emotion and unusual keys. Mary said, 'Well, this'll go down in the books . . . they're all aquiver that they're hearing Piaf songs here in Ballagh . . . look at your one with the red lipstick keepin' her mouth shut till we're halfway down the road. And Philip Donnelly . . . everyone else has to pay £1500 for him and I get him for free in my own pub!' Philip and I were naturally drawn to each other like two colours in a black and white photograph. A man who starts a conversation off with 'You have the most beautiful hair I've ever seen' can't be all bad so I set to picking his brains about music, his in particular. The entire pub recorded our transaction, whispering and nudging.

'He's trouble,' someone opined.

'And you tink yer one with the mad hair isn't? Two bits of trouble gettin' together — isn't it grand?'

As we said our goodbyes we all agreed that there would be another session the following Sunday for my going-away party.

'Goodbye, God bless and watch out for yourself,' said Philip. 'I'll call you.'

'You won't.'

'I'm not like the others.' A few days later he turned up at the farmhouse in a violet shirt, black jeans, leather coat and dark glasses to take me to lunch. The ostensible purpose was for an interview but as we talked for 10 hours straight, the pretence of an interview sort of faded. Philip was a compulsive communicator and we spent an entire day and night going from restaurant to bar to restaurant, borne along on a bacchanalia of loud in-your-face effusive words, extravagant gestures and bad food. For two people who adore good eating, we didn't get one good meal all day but it didn't matter — I could have devoured his words and been satisfied. He checked the wine glasses then started cleaning them, told endless stories that included physical demonstrations and sound effects, complained good-naturedly about my steak, jumped up with arms spread to explain a point, sat down, cleaned the table, kept talking fast and loud as if his life depended on it, asked me if I was ever going to put the bloody notebook away, slammed his hands down on the table, threw his head back and laughed.

'Can you lower your voice?' I asked.

'I can't.'

'Why not?'

'Because I get excited.'

'About everything?'

'Everything.'

We went to his friend John's auction house to buy a dresser for his kitchen and I found out about reshodding. In the old days dressers were often built inside the house, the dirt floors would make the feet rot and the carpenter would have to come in and reshoe the dresser. When one was bought, the house frequently had to be partially dismantled to get it out. In the bar at Cashel Palace I drank Irish coffee, which Philip told me was invented at Shannon airport for the pilots after a long flight, and he drank rum and tonics one after another in the same glass. When I asked him why he wanted them in the same glass he replied that when all the lemon slices got to the top, it was time to go home. Cashel Palace, built in the Queen Anne style in 1730, used to be the residence of the Church of Ireland bishops and is resplendent with wood panelling and carving.

Philip was a man who had music in his DNA — it was the great passion of his life — a man of whom Proust might have been thinking when he said, 'People can have many different kinds of pleasure, but the real one is that for which they will forsake the others.' We covered mythology, Catholicism, superstition, how turf is made, ancient and modern Irish music, life in Nashville, the renovations to his farmhouse in Tipperary and how Donovan taught the Beatles to do the claw-hammer finger-picking guitar style. In passing he mentioned that he was going through the worst year in his life but was feeling better every day.

An Irishman born in Clontarf, Dublin, Philip has played with John Prine, Lyall Lovett, Gram Parsons, Donovan, Emmylou Harris, the Everley Brothers and many more, and made nine albums with Nancy Griffiths. He was one of the key people who brought Nashville to Ireland, has played guitar on some 2500 recordings and was a founder member of the sixties Irish band Elmer Fudd. He was musical director and technical adviser for The Session, a highly successful television series of live concerts of Irish and American music.

In spite of a huge, almost overwhelming personality in terms of both ego and intelligence, he had a tender, childlike, kind side that I found very touching. It's not every day you get a man in snakeskin cowboy boots opening car doors, standing up every time you move and bringing down God's blessing on your head. The only time he was quiet was in Holycross Abbey where he took me to see the faded wall painting and relic of the True Cross presented by Pope Paschal II in 1110 to Murtagh O'Brien, King of Munster. Here he lit a candle and touched my forehead with holy water.

I enjoyed a few maniacal dinners at Philip's house. The first one was the inaugural have-a-guest-for-dinner in the newly decorated house, which threw him into such a state that he drove the car into a bridge on the way home. The farmhouse was beautiful, painted in Santa Fe colours with sumptuous leather couches, an inlaid, mirrored antique drinks cabinet, a collection of unusual percussion instruments and a dynamite sound system. The kitchen was still rudimentary but functioning and in the dining room was an adorable little pale blue Wellstood oil-burning stove. He lit the candles, put on Townes Van Zandt's 'No Deeper Blues' and then the farmers down the road arrived for a spontaneous visit. We sat together by the fire talking about their 14 children, God, triple bypasses, night life in the country (a euphemism for sex) and interior decorating. They left after a while and as everyone knows, when God made time he made plenty of it so Philip started cooking the roast leg of lamb at 11pm, by which point I was still charmed by his eccentric behaviour but almost in a diabetic coma. It was worth it — young Tipperary lamb rubbed in a mixture of paprika, garlic, oreganum, salt, pepper and olive oil with potatoes sautéed in chilli and garlic washed down with a Château Margeaux '94 and lots of fine Spanish wine. And I finally got to dance with a real Irishman.

Philip's 'last supper' on my last night in Ireland was a fiasco worthy of an Almodovar film — in the morning he had driven into a field of mud for a shortcut and ploughed straight through two wires. I arrived at his isolated farmhouse in the dark to find no one home so forced the window, climbed in and lit the fire while he hooned around the countryside trying to find his son's nanny. Friends of his, Tony and Victoria, were the other guests and Victoria was going to cook except that they got held up and when they finally arrived had forgotten the pork. Philip came flying in with his darling little boy, having not found Nanny, asked me to do the dishes, said, 'This is a fucking nightmare' and flew out again. Victoria set to cooking with what she had for the nightmare dinner party, Philip came back having safely deposited his son, the Wellstood went out and no one knew how to relight it, so we ate salad and drank to drown our sorrows. Philip was agitated, Tony and Victoria were talking happily and cheerfully and I was slowly sinking.

Then a combination of tiredness, sadness at leaving Ireland and stress at Philip's nutty behaviour combined in a huge rush to overwhelm me. I decided it was the worst last night in Ireland I could imagine and burst into uncontrollable sobbing. Philip looked as if there was only so much more a man who was, after all, only trying to do his gobshite best, could be asked to suffer. The evening was supposed to have gone perfectly. He had cleaned the house, bought new candles, put fresh linen on the beds, introduced me to his son (the most fabulous child in the universe) and got a stunning beautiful woman to cook something special for me and the best I could do to express my gratitude was to stand in the courtyard and nourish the flowers with my tears. His friends laughed their heads off, opened another bottle and said, 'Why can't you find yourself an uncomplicated woman?' which I thought was only partially fair, considering that my single crime had been to walk into a house of madmen. We had a huge fight and a good talk which made us feel much better but didn't convince Philip to rearrange his priorities in the slightest. In spite of my desperation to sleep, emotional exhaustion and impending flight out of Ireland the next day they stayed up till 4am singing and talking. You cannot fight the Irish — the best you can do (and you would be doing yourself a huge favour) is to join them.

There was a farewell session at Gleeson's, reuniting the original group, and another one at Mulhall's shebeen next door, at which Philip also played and sang. My last day in Ireland passed pleasantly in an insomniac, tranquillised state (have you ever noticed how stoned you get if you take two sleeping pills *and they don't work?* You walk around all day being uncommonly nice and tolerant). Philip was back to his whimsical, warm-hearted, attentive self and I girded myself for my fifth attempt to leave Ireland. I had come for a month, stayed for three and my heart was breaking with the unreconciled pain of leaving. I was about to appreciate the old songs of departure on a personal level.

The woman in the post shop said, 'Well, Pip, are ye lonely to be leavin'?' Flood.

The butcher said, 'Hope you've enjoyed our Tipperary beef so.' Flood.

The florist said, 'When are ye coming back and did ye like us?' Flood.

Philip's mobile rang and I heard him saying, 'Well, lads, we're on for a session in Golden on Sunday.' Flood.

How could I ever live without sessions, without circular conversations, without fluffy shpuds? How would I deal with the boredom of succinct road directions? What would I do when people answered my questions with a simple answer rather than a long yarn? How would I live without people who love you no matter how dreadful you are? I got out Harriet's card and ticked off 'love' — love of a man, love of Tricia and, by extension, their compatriots.

I thought it best that Trish not take me to the airport in Cork so Philip had the gruesome task, which he performed with his characteristic desire to make everything okay, being entertaining and jolly. He seemed to me a man who wanted everyone to feel loved but perhaps had trouble believing how much other people loved him. A flawed hero in snakeskin boots.

Tricia and I said goodbye to each other outside the house beneath the roses to the silent staring of the now quiet Bubba and the gently fragrant, falling rain. She wept, strands of her long hair sticking to her face. Seamus enveloped her in his protective arms as they became smaller and smaller in the distance. The card they gave me said: 'Words cannot say as much as the memories that we have,' then 'Nil áon thiatán mar do thiatán féin' (There's no place like home).

The weeping, which had started two days before I left Ireland, became a wall of saline through which I navigated my path to the plane, wrapped in the silk velvet shawl Geraldine had given me. Placing my hand on the painful area in my chest I assumed to be my heart, I said goodbye to the rain-smelling air and green fields of home. Philip put his arms around me, swore that his life was not as mad as it looked and said,'Goodbye, God bless and watch out for yourself.'

*When Friday night comes around and he's only in the
    fighting.
My Ma would like a letter home but I'm too tired for
    writing.
And the only time I feel all right is when I'm into drinking.
It eases off the pain a bit and levels out my thinking.
Well, it almost breaks my heart when I think of Josephine.
I promised I'd be coming back with pockets full of green.
I dream I hear a piper play, maybe it's a notion.
I dream I see white horses dance upon that other ocean.
Oh, there's four who share the room as we work hard for the
    craic.
And getting up late on Sunday I never get to Mass.
It's a long long way from Clare to here,
It's a long long way from Clare to here.
Oh, it's a long long way, it gets further day by day.
It's a long long way from Clare to here.*

— 'From Clare to Here'

list of illustrations

PAGE

3		Seamus and Peta
6	top	uilleann pipe player
	bottom	typical Irish street
7		Moore Street market, Dublin
44	top	my mother Ann Mathias
	middle	my grandparents Margaret and Jim Long
	bottom	me
45	top	the Long family, just arrived in Australia
	bottom	Farney Castle, Tipperary
68	top	the entrance to Tricia's farmhouse
	bottom	Tricia feeding Bubba
69	top	Cashel Blue cheese
	bottom	Jim o' the Mills
106	top	Fisherman's Cottage, Inisheer
	bottom	curraghs, Inisheer
107	top	Robbie, Galway
	bottom	Galway
146	top	Dingle
	bottom	Cillian ó Briain playing uilleann pipes
147	top	typical Irish cottage
	bottom	Ballycotton
188	top	Belfast
	bottom	Donegal
189	top	Belfast
	bottom	Giant's Causeway
218	top	a music session
	bottom	Wellstood Stove
219	top	Tipperary Fair
	bottom	thatched cottage
260		Charles guarding Tricia's fireplace